Fundamental Skills for Modern Lawyers

EDITED BY ALEX DAVIES

Commissioning editor
Alex Davies

Managing director
Sian O'Neill

Fundamental Skills for Modern Lawyers
is published by

Globe Law and Business Ltd
3 Mylor Close
Horsell
Woking
Surrey GU21 4DD
United Kingdom
Tel: +44 20 3745 4770
www.globelawandbusiness.com

Fundamental Skills for Modern Lawyers

ISBN 978-1-83723-188-1
EPUB ISBN 978-1-83723-189-8
Adobe PDF ISBN 978-1-83723-190-4

GPSR Compliance: EU Authorised Representative: Easy Access System Europe – Mustamäe tee 50, 10621 Tallinn, Estonia, gpsr.requests@easproject.com

Contents

Executive summary

The modern lawyer is expected to be technically excellent, emotionally intelligent, adaptable and commercially aware – often all at once. But legal workplaces are not one-size-fits-all, and neither are the people who work in them. To thrive in today's legal profession, lawyers must master the human skills that underpin trust, influence, and effective leadership. From handling difficult conversations and giving feedback, to building resilience, negotiating effectively and developing a strong professional profile, lawyers need tools to perform in an increasingly complex world.

Emotional intelligence, decision-making and delegation, networking and adapting to change are fundamental to success, and it is these human strengths that will succeed in a technological future.

The book is introduced by Sara Fowler, president of CILEX, who explains why so-called "soft" skills are now core legal skills, taking into account the changing expectations of clients, firms, and regulators. From technical excellence to trusted adviser, Sara outlines how the fundamental skills outlined in the chapters that follow will drive career progression, wellbeing, and commercial success.

Part one of the book looks at mastering yourself.

Chapter one, by Kim Tasso, explores emotional intelligence in legal practice, and how this is a superpower for lawyers. Cognitive and intellectual abilities have always been highly prized in lawyers. Yet our fast-paced, AI-driven world will further increase the importance of those human (personal and interpersonal) skills, wrapped up in the envelope of emotional intelligence (EI or EQ). Research shows that EQ accounts for 58 percent of performance in all types of jobs and is the single biggest predictor in the workplace. In the chapter, Kim considers what emotional intelligence means, how it is measured and developed, and why it is important for lawyers and their leaders. She explores how empathy underpins effective communication and relationship building and demonstrates that improving the superpower of emotional intelligence enhances both performance and wellbeing.

Simply put, resilience is an individual's and team's capacity for stress-related growth. Decades of research show that resilience is not a fixed trait that you either have or don't have, but rather, a set of skills that individuals and teams can build. Paula Davis has been studying, teaching, writing, talking, and thinking about resilience since she first discovered the science of it for her master's studies at the University of Pennsylvania. She has seen countless lives and teams transformed by the power of resilience, including her own. Yet, for all its ubiquity, resilience is one of the most misunderstood concepts at work. It's also one of the most important, given the level of uncertainty and change that is and will continue to be present in the legal profession into the foreseeable future. The research literature can be confusing because there are many definitions of resilience and most of them have a clinical or trauma-related focus, rather than a work focus. In chapter two, Paula talks about the ways in which lawyers and legal teams can enhance their ability to develop this important set of skills.

Law is a loss-saturated profession, and the cumulative impact of repeated exposure to conflict, harm, failure, and high-stakes pressure quietly erodes judgment, decision-making, leadership capacity, and organizational cohesion. Traditional legal culture equates professionalism with composure, reinforcing a norm of suppression that is often mistaken for resilience, but carries measurable risk. In chapter three, Tom Spence explores the often-unacknowledged realities of grief and trauma in legal practice, framing them as operational and leadership issues rather than personal vulnerabilities.

The chapter introduces the concept of a grief-literate firm – one that recognizes cumulative exposure, supports regulation rather than suppression, and integrates structured support, leadership modelling, and clear pathways for addressing strain. It distinguishes between individual and collective resilience, emphasizing that sustainable high performance depends on systemic buffers, distributed regulation, and culturally embedded practices that enable teams to function effectively under pressure.

Practical strategies for implementing these ideas include deliberate resets before key decisions, structural transitions between matters, language shifts, leadership modelling, and accessible, destigmatized support pathways. Tom argues that grief literacy and collective resilience are not softening the profession – they strengthen judgment, ethical clarity, and long-term performance. Ultimately, the chapter reframes legal practice culture – exposure to loss is inevitable, but by acknowledging it and designing systems capable of metabolizing it, firms can create steadier, more resilient organizations, enhancing both human and institutional capacity.

In chapter four, Danielle Gleicher-Bates and Emma Llanwarne explore neurodiversity in legal practice – practicing as a neurodivergent lawyer, working with and enabling neurodivergent colleagues, and serving neurodivergent clients' best interests and needs. Neurodivergent neurotypes are distilled into primary areas of divergence before examining the importance of strengths-based framing, personal identity, and language, alongside the unique tension between neurodivergence, disability identity, and disability in law. The chapter turns to the overlap between common neurodivergent strengths and the soft skills required as a lawyer, in addition to the potential challenges and barriers, not least the interplay between masking, imposter syndrome, and burnout, which legal environments are prone to fostering. Core issues are addressed through practical considerations and frameworks for disclosure, managing your working style, requesting and making reasonable adjustments, and effective allyship, with the significance of reasonable adjustments in empowerment and working well embedded throughout. Whether you are neurodivergent or not, the key takeaways and insights are relevant to everyone.

In chapter five, Nikki Alderson looks at why lawyers struggle with time, analyzing the importance of personal responsibility, the cultural pressures that exist in law, the impact of remote and hybrid working on boundaries, and how unmanaged time pressure contributes to stress and burnout. The chapter explores how to distinguish urgency from importance, managing competing stakeholders and deadlines, focus, energy, and burnout, and practical systems for busy legal professionals. Nikki outlines how technology boundaries and improvements, as well as clear communication protocols, can create systems that support long-term wellbeing and professional effectiveness.

Chapter six explores how lawyers can make effective decisions in high-pressure situations, where time is limited and information is often incomplete. It highlights common decision-making traps and examines the balance between risk and professional judgement. Alice Boullier de Branche and Jean-Baptiste Lebelle address how perfectionism, while valued in legal work, can become a liability when swift action is required. Emphasis is placed on the importance of collaborative decision making, drawing on the insights of others to strengthen outcomes. Finally, the chapter underscores the need for confidence in decisions, while remaining open to revisiting and adapting them as circumstances evolve.

Part two then looks at how to work effectively with others.
Chapter seven brings a practical, performance-based communication lens to one of the most challenging and career-defining aspects of legal practice. Drawing on her work helping professionals communicate with clarity and confidence under pressure, alongside her background as a prize-winning opera singer, Susan Heaton-Wright offers a distinctive approach that blends preparation frameworks, emotional regulation, voice, and presence. The chapter provides lawyers with clear, usable tools to prepare for high-stakes conversations, manage emotion and defensiveness (their own and others'), navigate power dynamics, and turn conflict into clarity.

Susan's focus is on helping lawyers show up powerfully when it matters most – structuring difficult conversations around purpose and outcomes, using non-verbal communication intentionally, listening with impact, and maintaining authority without aggression. A highly practical chapter, it includes real-world examples, short exercises, and simple models that readers can apply immediately in client and colleague conversations.

Chapter eight examines the role of feedback in building and sustaining a truly client-centered culture. Drawing on practical experience, Wayne Hassay explores how effective feedback must flow across all levels of an organization and align with clearly defined values and expectations. The ability to give and receive feedback is a fundamental skill, and the chapter considers how client-driven frameworks – such as structured feedback tools and resolution processes – can strengthen relationships and accountability, particularly when supporting large, demanding clients. Central to the discussion is the challenge of making feedback genuinely constructive – not just shared, but translated into clear, actionable steps. It also reflects on a common disconnect in many organizations, where feedback systems exist in principle but fall short in practice, offering insight into how this gap can be addressed.

In a legal world where the modern lawyer is expected to be technically excellent, emotionally intelligent, adaptable, and commercially aware, delegation and supervision are no longer administrative tasks – they are core leadership capabilities. Chapter nine explores how supervision and delegation can be used not only to deliver high-quality legal work, but to develop resilient, capable teams in modern workplaces that are more diverse, flexible, and complex than ever before. Pam Loch offers practical and human-centered observation and advice that recognizes the shift in how newer entrants to the profession approach work, communication, and accountability, and the impact of digital fluency of technologies such as AI. She discusses the increasing importance of managing teams in ways that do not rely on disclosure, conformity, or outdated supervisory models, delegation as a strategic leadership tool rather than a source of risk, and how to maintain commercial viability in the face of increased management responsibilities. She also outlines how management can impact retention through effective engagement and development of people, opening up career opportunities, creating psychological safety, and setting good working habits from the early stages.

Negotiation is not a separate skill from communication – it is a form of communication and every interaction a lawyer has is potentially a negotiation. In chapter ten, Jonathan Middleburgh suggests that lawyers often default to adversarial (or positional) communication, whereas communication focusing on the achievement of each side's interests is preferable. Jonathan unpacks a range of practical skills that should be part of the communication toolkit and encourages readers to reflect on their level on each of these skills. The chapter also focuses on where and how the negotiation happens and encourages readers to think about how most effectively to communicate, dependent on mode of communication. Ethical and professional conduct issues are also considered, as is the impact of AI on negotiation and communication.

Chapter 11 explores how agile and lean principles are reshaping collaboration in modern legal practice. In a rapidly evolving, tech-driven landscape, Maria Govis highlights the growing importance of lawyers developing a practical understanding of digital tools to enhance teamwork and efficiency. She emphasizes the value of aligning with clients' terminology and ways of working, enabling effective collaboration. The chapter introduces agile and lean methodologies as flexible, alternative approaches to organizing knowledge work, and considers how these principles can be applied within legal teams to improve communication, adaptability, and outcomes. Ultimately, Maria argues that even a basic proficiency in technology, combined with these collaborative frameworks, can offer a meaningful competitive advantage.

Part three explores influence, visibility and career development.
The section begins with chapter 12 reframing relationship-building as a critical skill for modern lawyers. As legal markets become more commercial and trust-driven, purposeful networking rooted in curiosity, authenticity, and strategic intent supports both career progression and firm growth. Rebecca

Overend challenges misconceptions about networking, emphasizing value-led, ethical relationship-building across internal teams, clients, peers, and wider professional communities. She offers practical guidance on starting conversations, maintaining connections and selecting opportunities wisely. With tailored advice for different career stages, she reinforces that consistent, long-term engagement, rather than transactional interactions, creates meaningful networks. Purposeful networking is not selling, rather it is sustained professional development.

Business development is no longer optional in modern legal practice. As lawyers become more senior, their ability to generate, retain, and expand client relationships directly impacts their career trajectory, influence, and earning potential. Still, many lawyers approach business development with uncertainty, unsure where to start, what to prioritize, or how to do it authentically. In chapter 13, Yuliya LaRoe reframes business development as a learnable, practical skill rather than a personality trait or sales tactic. She introduces a clear, structured framework that integrates networking, visibility, relationship management, and follow-through into a manageable system. Readers will learn how to move from reactive outreach to strategic relationship management, increase visibility without compromising authenticity, and build BD systems that support consistent client engagement. By the end of the chapter, readers will see business development not as an uncomfortable add-on, but as a skill that reinforces – rather than distracts from – great lawyering.

Chapter 14 by Rebecca Harding examines what it truly means to build a professional profile in a legal context, moving beyond superficial notions of self-promotion to focus on credibility, reputation, and value. Rebecca encourages lawyers to reflect on their individual strengths and interests in order to define a clear and authentic niche. The chapter addresses common discomfort around visibility, offering practical ways to build a presence and reputation without feeling overly self-promotional. Rebecca emphasizes that consistent, value-driven engagement is key to being recognized in the profession. The chapter highlights the role of thought leadership through activities such as writing, speaking, and sharing insights. These avenues are presented as effective ways to demonstrate expertise, build trust, and enhance professional standing over time.

Part four then looks at leading through change, and the fundamental skills necessary for future leaders.

When change initiatives fail to take root in legal organizations, the explanation is rarely the one that gets cited first. The strategy was not the problem. The technology was not the problem. The rollout plan was not the problem. The problem, consistently and across change types, is human. According to research, 38 percent of all implementation difficulties trace back to human and proficiency factors – the learning curve, the gap between training and practice, the absence of sustained support. Technical implementation issues account for only 16 percent of the same failures. This pattern holds whether the change in question is a new operating model, a process redesign, or – as is the defining challenge of this moment in legal – the adoption of artificial intelligence.

The implication is uncomfortable but important – most change programs in legal are not failing because the wrong approach was chosen. They are failing because the human architecture of change was not designed. The roles that every successful change requires were left unfilled, undefined, or misunderstood. AI adoption makes this visible more starkly than most changes because the gap between access and genuine use is so measurable – but the underlying dynamic is not new, and it is not unique to technology. Chapter 15, by Andrea Miskolczi, maps those roles. It describes what each one demands in practice – not as titles to be assigned on an organizational chart, but as functions that must be actively performed. Some individuals will hold more than one. Others will hold none, even when they might be expected to. Understanding the difference between what a role is called and what it actually requires is often the starting point for making change work.

The chapter covers seven roles – the sponsor, managers and partners, the change leader, the project manager, the power user, the change champion, and the sponsor alliance. Together, they form the cast of characters that every successful legal change story needs.

Chapter 16, by Daan Potjer, explores how legal practice is evolving in response to rapid technological change, particularly the rise of artificial intelligence. It begins by outlining the shifting landscape of the profession and redefining what it means to be a modern lawyer in a digital-first world. The focus then turns to the essential skills and mindset that lawyers need to remain relevant and adaptable, emphasizing continuous learning and openness to innovation. A key theme is the transformative impact of AI on legal workloads, highlighting how routine tasks are being automated and how this reshapes the lawyer's role. The chapter also stresses the importance of leveraging technology effectively, encouraging lawyers to work smarter rather than harder. It underlines the need for law firms to cultivate a culture of innovation to stay competitive. Finally, it examines how the value proposition of lawyers is changing in the AI era, and concludes by encouraging legal professionals to actively embrace and adopt AI as a core component of modern practice.

Ever since David Maister's book, *The Trusted Advisor*, was written in 2001, this has been the declared ambition of most law firms in relation to their client relationship. But what does this actually mean in practice? And is this the right target? In chapter 17, Stuart Maister (David's cousin) sets out an updated version of this approach, starting with a focus on trust as the critical foundation for all client engagement. By defining trust, he sets out how lawyers can consciously and intentionally design high trust relationships and use this as the basis for winning, retaining, and growing major accounts. He then looks at the second part of the formula, analyzing the difference between being a trusted supplier and an advisor. One is transactional, the other is based on a relationship. He suggests there is an even higher level to aim for – being a trusted partner, which puts you on the team with the client. This chapter maps out the mindset and skillset required to develop this status with a client, and includes exercises to help the reader apply this in their own context.

AI is the single biggest disruptor to lawyering – arguably ever. Basic lawyering skills – as traditionally understood – will increasingly be outsourced to the machine. The need for a rounded skill set will be taken to the next level as AI will increasingly do the core technical lawyering work. The consequence will be a fundamental shift in essential lawyering skills. The differentiated law firm will the one where client service and the meeting of client expectations is as close to optimal as possible, and where lawyers add maximum value – with the best / most innovative solutions, and commercial value add. In this final chapter, Jonathan Middleburgh argues that the Profoundly Human Law Firm (PHLF) will be the winners in these disruptions, and the building blocks of the PHLF are profoundly human lawyers (PHL). As a fitting end to this book on fundamental skills, the chapter endeavors to unpack the core skills of the PHL.

About the authors

Nikki Alderson is an international talent retention and women's leadership specialist, TEDx and keynote speaker, coach, bestselling author, and former criminal barrister with 19 years' experience. She supports law firms, barristers' chambers and other legal organizations to retain female talent and empowers female lawyers to achieve their career ambitions. Nikki specializes in three areas – women's leadership, enhanced career break returns and new working parent support, and workplace resilience, mental toughness, confidence and wellbeing.

Alice Boullier de Branche is senior HR manager in the Paris HR team at A&O Shearman. She graduated from business school (ESSEC Global BBA) and has a Master's degree in Sociology (Paris VII). Alice has been working on HR matters at A&O Shearman for over ten years. She joined A&O to work on training and development, then later specialized in providing human resources support to the fee earner population. She is especially engaged in areas such as performance evaluation, compensation strategies, recruitment, retention, and talent development, as well as wellbeing, and diversity and inclusion initiatives.

Paula Davis JD is a global speaker, strategic advisor, and award-winning author who helps leaders reduce burnout and build team resilience by improving how work is designed, led, and sustained. Paula left her law practice after seven years and earned a master's degree in applied positive psychology from the University of Pennsylvania. As part of her post-graduate training, Paula was selected to be part of the University of Pennsylvania faculty, teaching and training resilience skills to senior leaders in the military as part of the Army's Comprehensive Soldier and Family Fitness program. The Penn team trained resilience skills to more than 40,000 soldiers and their family members.

Paula is the author of *Beating Burnout at Work: Why Teams Hold the Secret to Well-Being & Resilience* (2021) and *Lead Well: 5 Mindsets to Engage, Retain,*

& *Inspire Your Team* (2025). Both books have been selected as "must reads" by the Next Big Idea Club, which is curated by Adam Grant, Susan Cain, Malcom Gladwell, and Daniel Pink. The Next Big Idea Club selected *Lead Well* as one of its top 11 leadership books for 2025. She recently collaborated with ALM to learn more about burnout and psychological safety in the legal profession. They collected data via a national survey of lawyers and legal professionals, and she is the author of the resulting report titled *Lawyer Strong®→Law Strong*.

Paula has shared her expertise at educational institutions such as Harvard Law School, Stanford, Wharton School Executive Education, and Princeton. She is a two-time recipient of the distinguished teaching award from the Medical College of Wisconsin. Her expertise has been featured in and on The *New York Times, O, The Oprah Magazine, Inc., Fast Company* and many other media outlets. Paula is also a contributor to *Forbes* and *Psychology Today.*

Sara Fowler is an NHS leader whose career spans law, patient safety, and public service. In July 2025, she became the 62nd President of CILEX, placing access to justice, social mobility, and diversity at the heart of her presidency. Sara holds a Law Degree from City, University of London, a Master's qualification in Strategic Leadership and Management, and is a member of the Chartered Management Institute. She is a passionate advocate for access to justice and social mobility, championing greater diversity within the legal profession and promoting flexible pathways into legal careers. In addition to her professional roles, Sara is a Trustee of the Access to Justice Foundation and serves on the Judicial and Legal Diversity Board, where she contributes to advancing fairness, representation, and equal opportunities across the justice system.

Maria Govis is a legal technology expert within global legal business services at KPMG. She has over five years' experience driving large-scale digital transformation projects for legal and compliance functions of global corporations, with a proven track record of delivering high-impact AI and automation initiatives. She played a key role in a life sciences corporation's transformation program that was recognized by *Financial Times* Innovative Lawyers 2021 and 2022 Awards. Throughout her legal tech and consulting career, she has delivered projects using agile methodology and facilitated legal process improvement workshops for 70+ legal professionals. Maria holds a law degree from the University of Düsseldorf, Germany and a prior degree in translation and interpreting from Moscow State University, which included an academic stay at the University of Basque Country in Spain. She is fluent in English, German, Spanish, Brazilian Portuguese and Russian, and currently works out of the UK. Maria's research and writing focus on organizational management in the age of AI, non-linear career paths, and the future of work.

Danielle Gleicher-Bates is an award-winning neurodiversity advocate passionate about diversity, equity, and inclusion, recognized in the Women and Diversity in Law Awards 2024 and Shaw Trust Disability Power 100 2024. As a late-diagnosed, multiple-neurodivergent and disabled woman, she uses her lived experience to challenge perceptions of neurodivergence and disability. Danielle is co-chair of neurodiversikey® which she co-founded in 2023 to improve neuroinclusivity in the legal sector and justice system. A proponent of knowledge as a tool to enable and empower, Danielle has created educational resources including co-authoring *ADHD in Custody: A Guide to Police Custody for ADHDers*. As an aspiring barrister, Danielle was awarded scholarships by the Honourable Society of the Inner Temple and City Law School to pursue the Bar Vocational Studies course.

Rebecca Harding is an international professional services consultant, with specialisms in marketing, public relations, and business development. She was, until September 2022, the worldwide chairman of the Society of Women Writers and Journalists, as well as retired vice chair of the UK's Chartered Institute of Marketing. She founded Saltwhistle in 2000 and has developed an impressive portfolio of clients within business and professional services. Clients have ranged from multi-national firms, such as accountants Deloitte, PWC, and EY, to law firms like Stephenson Harwood, Norton Rose Fulbright, and Weightmans, as well as international businesses such as J Walter Thompson (now Wunderman Thompson), Mediacom, and Mindshare (all part of WPP). Saltwhistle now specializes in supporting SMEs worldwide and international marketing. Prior to establishing Saltwhistle, Rebecca was head of communications at Andersens. She worked across Europe, the Middle East, India, and Africa. Rebecca also worked in marketing within the oil industry, with corporations such as BNFL, BP, ESSO, and Shell. She was awarded Highly Commended Finalist in the UK's Institute of Directors' Non Executive Director of the Year award in the UK. She is a professional member of the Chartered Institute of Public Relations. She speaks regularly at conferences on matters ranging from innovation to winning business. Rebecca is an author and has written three publications for Globe Law and Business. She has been quoted and published widely in trade journals, as well as national newspapers, such as the *Sunday Times*.

Wayne Hassay is managing partner of Maguire Schneider Hassay, LLP in Columbus, Ohio. He leads a consumer-facing practice and focuses on building systems that translate legal judgment into a consistent client experience – clear scope, timely communication, dependable follow-through, and measurable service standards that lawyers can actually execute. His work centers on feedback loops, delivery mechanics, and technology-enabled workflows that improve client outcomes and reduce friction without diluting independent professional judgment. Wayne's broader mission is access to justice – using modern delivery models and operational discipline to make competent legal help more affordable and more predictable for ordinary people. He earned his J.D. from the University of Akron School of Law and is admitted to practice in Ohio.

Susan Heaton-Wright is an award-winning communication specialist, professional speaker, TEDx speaker, author, and podcaster, and the founder of Superstar Communicator™, a CPD-accredited training company. She works internationally with companies, professional services firms, and membership organizations to develop the essential communication and interpersonal skills required for success in today's business environment.

A former professional opera singer, Susan brings a distinctive performance-based approach to communication, combining artistic excellence with commercial insight. Her methodology translates complex communication challenges into practical, actionable strategies, enabling professionals to communicate with clarity, confidence and credibility in high-stakes situations. Susan delivers keynote speeches, masterclasses, and facilitated workshops, and provides one-to-one coaching across all areas of impact, presence, and credibility. She supports individuals and teams at all levels, from emerging talent to senior leaders, helping them enhance their effectiveness in meetings, presentations, pitches, and business development activities. She is known for her engaging, high-energy delivery and her ability to create immediate, lasting change in how people communicate. She is a Fellow of the Royal Geographical Society, the Independent Society of Musicians, and the Professional Speaking Association.

Yuliya LaRoe is an award-winning consultant, coach, and speaker who helps lawyers build the leadership, management, and business development skills that modern legal careers demand. She works with lawyers who want to do more than excel technically – they want to lead with confidence, strengthen client relationships, expand their influence, and create greater impact over the course of their careers. She is widely known across the legal industry as the Income-to-Equity Coach who helps non-equity partners get promoted to equity status at their firms. With over 20 years in the legal industry, Yuliya has coached and trained over 5,000 lawyers and professionals. As a former practicing BigLaw attorney with an MBA from Boston University's Questrom School of Business, she brings a rare combination of legal credibility, business strategy, and real-world practicality to her work. Her insights have been featured by the ABA, NALP, PDC, ALM, Law Practice Today, Attorney at Work, and other respected industry platforms. She is passionate about personal growth and cultural intelligence.

Emma Llanwarne is a consultant criminal defense paralegal and chartered legal executive. She is an unregistered barrister, called to the Bar of England and Wales in 2022, having been awarded the Rosina Hare scholarship by the Honourable Society of the Middle Temple. As a neurodivergent legal professional, diagnosed after a successful career in midwifery, Emma combines personal and professional experience to bring distinctive insight to her work. Her commitment to neurodiversity was recognized at the Women and Diversity in Law Awards 2025 in which she was highly commended for DE&I Champion of the Year (Legal Services Professional). Emma co-founded and is co-chair of neurodiversikey®, a non-profit organization dedicated to advancing neuroinclusion across the legal and justice sectors. Informed by her professional experience of the criminal justice system, Emma focuses on accessibility, support, and challenging systemic barriers, demonstrated by her co-authorship of *ADHD in Custody: A Guide to Police Custody for ADHDers*.

Jean-Baptiste Lebelle is the HR director of A&O Shearman's Paris office. He holds a law degree from Paris II Assas and graduated from Sciences Po Paris. Jean-Baptiste taught at the Sorbonne and HEC on recruitment, retention and career management in law firms. He has over 25 years of HR experience in the consulting sector and is especially engaged in topics related to compensation policies, recruitment, talent retention, inclusion, and wellbeing applied to law firms. He switched from headhunting for law firms to HR, becoming PWC Legal's HR director for Paris before A&O.

Pam Loch set up Loch in 2007 to respond to the need for commercial and bespoke legal and people solutions for clients. She has continued to evolve the business to respond to client needs and is now proud to have services offering solutions in all elements of HR, employment, and business law. As well as being the managing director of Loch, Pam has also been a specialist, award-winning employment law solicitor for over 20 years. Her passion for finding solutions to help businesses manage and look after their people is reflected in the development and success of the businesses across the group. Unusually, Pam is a dual qualified solicitor, having qualified as a solicitor in 2000 in Scotland and England & Wales. Clients like her pragmatic, commercially focused approach and solutions. Pam is a seasoned commentator on the TV and radio on employment law and HR issues and is often involved in providing training. Pam is a member of the Employment Lawyers Association and is also qualified as an accredited mediator.

Stuart Maister gives keynotes, trains, and consults firms in the areas of strategic storytelling and building trust. He helps clients gain clarity – in their strategy and the way they communicate it, in the strategic narrative that makes them stand out in the marketplace and win business, and in the way they intentionally build trust with clients and colleagues. His background as a TV and radio reporter with the BBC, ITN, and Sky News led him to work with the world's biggest companies on their storytelling. One of his businesses was sold to a NASDAQ-listed US company and Stuart became SVP for international markets. He now runs his own company, Strategic Narrative, based in the UK. Stuart is the co-author of *Choose Trust: Building Relationships For Business Success*, published in 2025. He is an experienced offsite and conference facilitator, leading workshops around the world using his experience as a journalist and business leader.

Lauren McLaughlin has a wealth of employment law experience, having specialized in this area for over ten years, and leads the team at Loch's London office. Having trained at a boutique employment firm, Lauren qualified in 2014 and continued to build her reputation at a larger City firm. Lauren practices the full spectrum of employment law – both contentious and non-contentious. In particular, she has extensive experience of the day-to-day running and strategic aspects of Employment Tribunal litigation. Dealing in complex, multi-faceted claims of discrimination, victimization, harassment, and whistleblowing, Lauren has been involved in thorny legal matters right up to the Court of Appeal and is noted in the Legal 500 for her expertise in sex and pregnancy discrimination. Lauren has experience in a range of HR matters and is well equipped to advise businesses on managing senior executive exits, conducting internal processes, redundancies, and reorganizations, as well as routinely drafting employment contracts and policies.

Jonathan Middleburgh is a specialized and highly experienced consultant to law firms, in-house legal departments, and senior leaders in the legal sector. He advises and consults primarily on issues relating to people, management, and leadership within the legal services sector. He is a principal of Edge International, a leading global consultancy to law firms. Since around 2003, Jonathan has consulted to law firms and in-house legal departments in the UK, Europe, and internationally, with a focus on developing senior legal leadership, helping senior leaders to interact more effectively, guiding and coaching senior leaders through behavioral change, and steering senior leaders towards the adoption of more effective managerial and leadership behaviors. He has also helped law firms with the development, refinement, and practical implementation of succession strategies and in particular the working through of complex succession transitions, including in founder firms. He has collaborated with colleagues in helping law firms to refine their strategies and to reevaluate and, where appropriate, overhaul their remuneration structures.

Having studied Law as an undergraduate at Oxford University (where he graduated in the top five of his cohort), Jonathan taught for a year at the University of Chicago and for short stints at Oxford and King's College, London. He then practiced as a barrister for around 12 years. Prior to leaving the Bar, Jonathan obtained undergraduate equivalence in psychology and subsequently Masters' equivalence in occupational psychology. A deep understanding of psychological processes and dynamics underpins the work he does with senior legal leaders. In recent years, Jonathan has consulted to, and advised, senior lawyers on every continent save for Antarctica. He continues to relish having a broad international practice and advising across a wide range of cultures, as well as spending time with his family in London.

Andrea Miskolczi helps legal leaders turn innovation ambition into operational reality. As managing director of InterAlia Consulting, she works with law firms and in-house legal teams facing stalled AI and LegalTech projects, low adoption rates, and fragmented innovation efforts. Her clients typically struggle to formulate their strategy for Board approval, align it with day-to-day execution, build internal buy-in, and deliver measurable outcomes. A Prosci-certified change practitioner, Andrea brings structured change management methodology to the challenges that innovation initiatives in legal most commonly stall on – the human side of transformation. Andrea began her career as a practicing lawyer at Clifford Chance and Linklaters, before moving into leadership roles in innovation, business development, and marketing at Wolf Theiss and Dentons. She has led cross-border, award-winning initiatives recognized by the *Financial Times* Innovative Lawyers Program for their impact on collaboration, client experience, data literacy, and workflow automation.

With experience spanning the UK, Germany, Austria, Hungary and leadership roles throughout Continental Europe and CEE, Andrea brings a pragmatic, pan-European lens to what actually works – and what doesn't – when modernizing legal functions.

Rebecca Overend is a business development and marketing professional with over 20 years' experience building relationships, driving growth, and shaping strategy across professional services. She currently holds a business development role at leading law firm Irwin Mitchell, where she leads business development strategy across multiple practice areas, working closely with partners, firm leadership and key stakeholders.

Operating as an autonomous, trusted adviser, Rebecca sits at the intersection of strategy and human connection – helping lawyers turn technical expertise into trusted, long-term client relationships. Her work spans referred business generation, cross-practice collaboration, strategic networking frameworks, and long-term client development planning. She has led firmwide initiatives including the development of referrer networks, networking structures for junior lawyers, and sector positioning campaigns. Alongside this, she co-chairs the IMpowered Diversity & Inclusion network in London. She is known for her pragmatic, ethical, and people-centered approach to networking, viewing it as a professional skill rooted in curiosity, consistency, and reciprocity. Rebecca is passionate about demystifying business development and empowering lawyers at all career stages to build meaningful, credible networks that support both personal progression and firmwide success.

Daan Potjer is director of commercial and legal excellence at Loyens & Loeff, a European law firm based in the Netherlands, Belgium, Luxembourg, and Switzerland. He is responsible for business development, marketing, innovation, data and analytics, and knowledge management. Daan is driving AI-strategy and delivery of AI solutions at the firm. Before joining Loyens & Loeff, Daan worked for over 25 years in leadership roles in the financial sector and the real estate sector, most recently as COO for Colliers Netherlands. Daan is vice-chairman of the Supervisory Board of Dynamic Credit Group. He studied economics at Erasmus University Rotterdam and the London School of Economics and is currently a PhD-candidate in History at the University of Antwerp.

Kate Rigby is an HR director with over 20 years of experience, helping businesses across a wide range of industries maximize the potential of their people. Combining strategic HR management with hands on expertise, she partners with businesses to align their people strategy with their vision, values, and commercial objectives, ensuring that talent and culture become key drivers of their long-term success. Alongside her strategic focus, Kate has extensive experience across all aspects of the employee lifecycle and provides practical HR support, from talent attraction and onboarding to performance management, employee relations, and day-to-day people operations. She has a proven track record of building high-performing teams, developing leaders, and driving employee engagement and performance. Passionate about building high-performing cultures where employees feel valued, Kate helps clients strengthen engagement, develop capability, and drive sustainable business performance through their people. Kate is CIPD qualified and holds a BSc in Banking and Finance, giving her a strong understanding of both business and people challenges.

Tom Spence is a chartered management consultant and co-founder of Donoma Advisors, a London-based legal search and advisory firm. He has nearly 20 years' experience in the legal sector, where his advisory work includes supporting law firms and legal teams on growth, leadership, and strategic direction. He is also, with his wife, the creator of Beyond Us, a human-centered initiative through which he draws on personal experience of grief and trauma to support individuals and organizations navigating loss, building resilience, and sustaining wellbeing. Beyond Us bridges professional insight with lived experience, creating space for reflection, connection, and shared learning. Tom brings a rare perspective at the intersection of professional performance and the human experience of loss. He works with professionals and communities to sustain clarity, ethical judgement, and effectiveness under pressure, while remaining grounded in the human realities of loss and care.

Kim Tasso BA (Hons) DipM FCIM MCIJ MNCPS (Acc.) MBA is managing director of RedStarKim Ltd (a management consultancy specializing in professional services) and Tasso Talking Therapy Ltd (a private psychotherapy practice). After graduating in psychology and working for several years in the technology sector, she worked for leading professional service firms Deloitte and Nabarro. She started her own business in 1994. For over 30 years she has worked for over 300 clients, including solicitors, barristers, patent attorneys, accountants, insolvency practitioners, actuaries, and surveyors. She advises on and provides training and coaching in the strategic and operational aspects of management, change, and relationship management. She has published seven books (on selling and business development, media relations and social media, soft skills for lawyers, growth strategies, and business relationships). As an accredited therapist, she started her private psychotherapy practice at the start of 2024 and has held non-executive director positions in the property sector. She was also a trustee of a mental health charity.

About CILEX

CILEX offers a flexible and open route into the legal profession, creating specialist CILEX lawyers, paralegals, and other legal professionals with the practical skills employers are looking for. We take pride in helping thousands of individuals each year advance their legal careers through our qualifications and professional membership, alongside collaborating with organisations on their talent development strategies – all while advocating for diversity and accessibility within the profession.

CILEX lawyers are fully qualified legal professionals authorised to practise as specialist lawyers alongside solicitors. CILEX lawyers can explore various career paths beyond traditional legal roles – individuals with CILEX qualifications have become partners in law firms, coroners, judges, and advocates in open court.

A suite of interactive e-learning modules developed by CILEX Education from the content contained in this book has been designed to help lawyers and legal teams thrive in the realities of modern practice. Grounded in the insights from *Fundamental Skills for Modern Lawyers*, these modules translate proven concepts into practical, real-world skills that can be applied immediately.

Accredited by CILEX and ideal for meeting CPD requirements or for personal and professional development, this suite of e-learning modules offers more than just training – it's an investment in how you practice and present yourself as a lawyer.

Become not just a skilled practitioner, but a trusted, modern professional equipped for the evolving demands of legal practice. Visit www.cilex.org.uk for more information.

Introduction
Why soft skills are now core legal skills

By Sara Fowler, president, CILEX

The legal profession has long been built upon historical legal milestones, strong academics, and technical expertise. The ability to understand, interpret and apply the law, analyze complex legal matters whilst identifying risk to provide clear practical advice remains key in professional practice, and in the delivery of justice. These skills are the backbone of the legal profession and will continue to be the base of professional legal competence for generations to come. But is this foundation alone enough to succeed and excel in the modern legal world?

The legal landscape is evolving rapidly. The environment and expectations within which lawyers practice has shifted significantly. While a good lawyer may possess a strong technical foundation, a truly great lawyer is distinguished by their ability to communicate well, deliver measured and commercially astute advice, remain responsive, and think strategically under pressure. These skills have historically been described as "soft skills", but in modern times the distinguishment between core legal skills and soft skills is less distinct and simply what is essential to succeed.

Throughout my career, it has become increasingly clear that the difference between a competent lawyer and an exceptional one lie within their ability to build trust, inspire confidence, and steer a steady ship through choppy waters. Clients (be that an individual or a corporate client) rarely seek advice in isolation. They present with a commercial challenge, a regulatory issue, or a personal private matter and expect their lawyer to navigate uncertainty and do so in a composed matter. In circumstances such as this, strong academics and technical legal expertise can never be enough. Clients require a trusted advisor who balances legal expertise with practical guidance as to the wider implications of any decisions and strategy to be taken.

The law has always been, and always will be, a people profession. Regardless of the area of legal specialism, each matter centers around people and relationships to some extent. Clients rely on their lawyer during some of the most significant milestones of their lives and careers and true success in the law is born from trust, credibility, and the ability to form meaningful connections with clients, colleagues, and stakeholders. Clients retain lawyers who listen, communicate clearly, and genuinely understand their dilemmas. They recommend lawyers who are responsive, reliable, and able to translate complex legal matters into tangible actions and advice. These qualities are what transitions the lawyer into a trusted advisor.

Trust is therefore fundamental in the client–lawyer relationship. Most clients are not in a position to interpret the quality of the technical legal advice itself and will judge their experience and quality of lawyer based on a combination of what would have historically been referred to as soft skills, and a successful outcome. The soft skills are what set a great lawyer apart and often determine whether a long-term professional relationship is established.

These qualities are increasingly important in a rapidly evolving legal profession. The regulatory landscape is shifting public expectations, ethical considerations, and expected outcomes, whilst simultaneously operating in developing professional environments with regards to culture, wellbeing, and inclusion. Technology is unprecedentedly impacting legal services, with the introduction of artificial intelligence being one of the most significant developments the profession has experienced in recent years. Whilst there is much academic consideration as to the extent to which artificial intelligence will impact on the legal profession, it will transform the ways in which lawyers operate. AI is a useful tool that creates significant opportunities for the profession in assisting with routine legal tasks such as research and data analysis, but what it cannot do is create the soft skills required to be a truly great lawyer – and so the human aspects of the legal profession become all the more important. It seems likely that, as technology evolves and is able to replicate to some extent historic core legal skills, strategic thinking, relationship management, and leadership in the law will be the distinguishing factors between a good and a truly great lawyer. This is increasingly important for the generations of lawyers to come.

The chapters that follow explore themes from a variety of perspectives and consider how modern lawyers can build resilience, strengthen communication, build influence and professional networks whilst leading through change. Together, they reflect the modern reality of legal practice in that success can no longer be achieved based on technical expertise alone.

So, is the traditional foundation of technical legal expertise alone enough to succeed and excel in the modern legal world? The answer is clear – no. Success in the law belongs to those who can do more than understand the law. It will belong to those who provide steady leadership, deliver clear, non-jargon guidance, and build trusted relationships. The modern lawyer's success is not just based on what they know – it's also how they think, how they communicate, and how they make their clients feel.

Chapter 1:
Emotional intelligence in legal practice – developing a superpower for lawyers

By Kim Tasso, managing director, RedStarKim

Emotional Intelligence (EI or EQ) refers to the ability to perceive, recognize, understand, integrate, and reflectively manage our own emotions, as well as influence the emotions of others.

The immediate reaction of many lawyers to this is that emotions are not as relevant to legal practice as intellectual capability and technical expertise. So please bear with me while I explain why emotions are more important than you might, at first, think.

Having worked with hundreds of legal practices since 1989 on business development (which fundamentally relies on relationship skills) and as a practicing psychotherapist, I have long been an advocate for developing lawyers' emotional intelligence. Emotional intelligence is critical for the functioning and growth of law firms and also the wellbeing of lawyers and the staff that support them.

I remember conducting research into leadership development two years ago and speaking to senior leaders in professional services firms. I asked the managing partner of a medium-sized and fast-growing legal firm what he felt was the most important leadership attribute required by law firm leaders. He said "self-awareness". This is one of the four core attributes of emotional intelligence.

When researching my book, *Essential Soft Skills for Lawyers*,[1] the topic of emotional intelligence arose regularly amongst the 20 case studies from firms, including Cleary Gottlieb, Davitt Jones Bould, Hempsons, Keating Chambers, Law South, Mundays (later acquired by Knights), Norton Rose Fulbright, Osbornes Law, Ropes & Gray, and Thomson Snell & Passmore.

Today's legal market is focused on the great debate on automation – AI vs EI (Artificial Intelligence vs Emotional Intelligence). As technology and digitization disrupt the law firm model beyond recognition, and lawyers fear their skills and revenue models are under attack, it is those uniquely human skills within EI that will serve as our salvation.

What does emotional intelligence really mean? Why is it important?

Psychologists Peter Salovey (now President of Yale University) and John Mayer (University of New Hampshire) formally published the concept in their 1990 article, "Emotional Intelligence".[2] Daniel Goleman, in his book, *Emotional Intelligence: Why it Can Matter More Than IQ*[3] popularized the concept.

Early research published in *Emotional Intelligence 2.0*[4] by Jean Greaves and Travis Bradberry indicated that:

- Only 35 percent of people are able to accurately identify their emotions as they happen.
- Tested alongside 33 other important skills, EI subsumes the majority of them, including time management, decision making, and communication.
- EI accounts for 58 percent of performance in all types of jobs.
- EI is the single biggest predictor and strongest driver of leadership and personal excellence.
- 90 percent of high performers are also high in EI.
- EQ skills are more important to job performance than any other leadership skill.

Why is emotional intelligence important for lawyers?

In May 2019, the International Bar Association argued that lawyers need to be taught more about emotional intelligence,[5] whilst in June 2024, law firm CMS reported an impressive array of research statistics about the importance of emotional intelligence for lawyers.[6] These included the following.

Client service and loyalty

- The UK's Solicitors Regulation Authority reports that 78 percent of clients currently consider the emotional intelligence of legal professionals just as crucial as their legal expertise.
- The Chartered Institute of Legal Executives indicates that legal professionals with high EQ are 12 percent more likely to have successful client engagements. Emotionally intelligent legal professionals are also 15 percent more likely to rise to leadership positions within an organization.

Communication and client satisfaction

- The Institute of Leadership & Management found that emotionally intelligent legal professionals are 18 percent more effective at adapting their communication style to the needs of each client, ensuring a clear understanding, and minimizing the risk of costly misunderstandings.
- The UK Project Management Association discovered that legal professionals with strong EQ are 24 percent more successful at understanding and managing stakeholder needs and perspectives, fostering a sense of partnership and exceeding client expectations.

Team dynamics and leadership

- The Chartered Institute of Personnel and Development revealed that legal professionals with high EQ are 22 percent more effective at fostering inclusive and respectful team environments, unlocking the full potential of their colleagues.
- The Chartered Management Institute found that legal professionals with high EQ are 15 percent more likely to be promoted to leadership roles thanks to their ability to inspire, motivate, and bring out the best in their teams.

Conflict resolution and resilience:

- The Chartered Institute of Arbitrators discovered that emotionally intelligent legal professionals are 22 percent more effective at addressing underlying emotions, facilitating open discussions, and guiding parties towards resolutions that preserve relationships and move projects forward.
- The Chartered Institute of Management Accountants found that legal professionals with strong EQ are 19 percent more likely to demonstrate resilience and adaptability in the face of unexpected challenges and deliver exceptional results regardless of the circumstances.

Influencing and trust-building

- The Chartered Institute of Marketing revealed that legal professionals with high EQ are 27 percent more effective at tailoring their approach to the emotions and motivations of those they interact with, giving them a significant edge in high-stakes negotiations.
- The Solicitors Regulation Authority emphasized the importance of trust-building, with 78 percent of clients believing that their legal professionals'

emotional intelligence is just as important as their legal expertise in fostering an environment of authenticity, collaboration, and trust.

Law firms appear to be wising up, with, for example, DLA Piper organizing a webinar for July 2026 on how legal teams can collaborate more effectively by understanding the values, motivators and perspectives that shape people's behavior at work.[7]

The four key components of emotional intelligence

Let's start with a simple model of Emotional Intelligence. As Figure 1 shows, there are four key components of emotional intelligence:

	What I see *Awareness/recognition*	What I do *Actions/regulation*
Personal competence *Self*	Self-awareness	Self-management
Social competence *Others*	Social awareness *(empathy)*	Relationship management

Figure 1: Emotional intelligence. Adapted from Emotional Intelligence 2.0 *by Travis Bradberry and Jean Greaves.*

There are two personal competences – self-awareness and self-management – and two social competences – social awareness (empathy) and relationship management.

1. Self-awareness

Emotions are how we interpret physical and chemical reactions in our bodies. They are complex, temporary physiological and psychological states – such as joy, anger, or fear. They occur in response to internal or external events. For example, before presenting to an audience we may feel butterflies in our stomach and interpret this positively as excitement or negatively as nervousness.

Research suggests that although 95 percent of people think they're self-aware, only 10-15 percent actually are.[8]

Emotions vary by type (joy, anger, fear) and intensity (mild, moderate, intense), influencing how they are experienced and regulated. Think about anger. In its mild form it may feel like discomfort or irritation. As it grows in intensity it becomes annoyance, exasperation, and even rage.

So, the first EI competence is being aware of and recognizing our emotions – in tune with our bodies, alert to chemical and psychological changes, and labelling them accurately.

2. Self-management

Having identified an emotion, how good are you at controlling it?

Emotional regulation is something we learn as children – the ability to identify, name, and manage an emotion appropriately. We learn from our parents and caregivers, the prevailing social and cultural context, and early situations at home and at school.

Self-management skills appear to increase steadily with age. Unlike IQ (Intellectual Quotient) – a measure of intellectual capability – which is relatively fixed, our brains are neuroplastic, which means we can develop our EI skills throughout our lives.

While women and men are roughly equal in their ability to recognize their own emotions, men have recently caught up in their ability to manage their emotions and in other skills – so the gender gap is closing.

Being consistent in your behavior – not prone to unpredictable outbursts – means it is easier for people to trust you. But self-control is limited – we get decision fatigue as the day goes on. That's why we can be grumpy with our loved ones in the evenings after a tough day at the office.

Therefore, the second EI competence relates to how well we regulate or manage our emotions when we experience them. There's an excellent 2025 book called Shift by Ethan Kross,[9] which explains how to manage your emotions so they don't manage you.

3. Social awareness (empathy)

Empathy is "The power of identifying oneself mentally with (and so fully comprehending) a person or object of contemplation".

One of my favorite quotes about empathy is from the Cherokee Native Americans: *"O Great Spirit, Grant that I may not find fault with my neighbour until I have walked the trail of life in his moccasins".*

There are different types of empathy:

- *Cognitive empathy* – the intellectual ability to identify and understand another's perspective, without feeling them yourself.
- *Emotional or affective empathy* – the ability to actually feel what another person is experiencing.
- *Compassionate empathy* – going beyond feeling to being moved to help and reduce another's distress.

Part of our empathy skills come from an ability to read people's non-verbal communication (NVC) and to assess the extent to which the words they say are congruent with their body language – their expressions, their gestures, their posture, and tone of voice.

Empathy is one of the three components (along with logic and authenticity) of trust. All lawyers need to build trust with their partners, colleagues, and clients. It's fundamental to relationships and enshrined in the concept of the trusted advisor.

4. Relationship management

Having recognized how other people are feeling, how good are you at managing their emotions?

Key aspects of relationship management include:

- *Effective communication.* Use assertive, non-defensive communication while listening actively.
- *Build bonds and trust.* Establish rapport and foster long-term, trust-filled relationships through consistency.
- *Give and receive feedback.* Being able to both give and receive feedback is vital to growth.
- *Influence and leadership.* Guide, inspire, and motivate others. Act as a change catalyst and develop others.
- *Conflict management.* Approach and resolve emotionally-charged disputes constructively rather than avoiding them.

In her 2015 book,[10] Lindsay C Gibson PsyD gives helpful advice on how to recognize an emotionally-mature person – someone with well-developed emotional intelligence. She identifies traits such as being realistic and reliable, consistent and responsive.

There are various psychometric tools available to measure our EI and thus our ability to manage relationships. This ability is vital to managers whether considering leadership, change management, conflict resolution, sales, negotiation and business development, supplier arrangements, or business growth. There are also various commercial assessments for emotional intelligence that are both valid and reliable. These enable us to obtain the starting scores for people's EI. The baseline then provides a tool to help those people develop their abilities in the required areas.

Self-awareness and emotional intelligence under pressure

Most EI assessments are typically conducted when people are in a rational and calm state. However, law firm environments are usually far from calm. Most lawyers work under a lot of pressure – demanding clients, high stakes deals, a lack of time, the constant need to perform, billing targets, low capacity to complete the volume of work, competition from peers, and fears about their future, to name but a few.

Emotional intelligence does not disappear under pressure, but access to it often changes. When conditions become demanding, people tend to operate with reduced emotional range, narrower attention, and greater reliance on habit.

Many will be familiar with the work of psychiatrist Professor Steve Peters,[11] who suggests that human mental function comprises three components:

1. The rational side of the brain or ego (the human);
2. The more emotional id, which is the set of impulses that need to be managed to achieve high performance (the chimp); and
3. The super-ego, which governs automatic behavior and memory and can greatly influence both (the computer).

When we are under pressure, the chimp part of our brain can take over. In those situations, it prompts our threat response (driven by the amygdala in the brain). There then follows a flood of chemicals evoking the stress response. Most people are familiar with the ensuing fight, flight, fear, and freeze reactions. This is why individuals who are thoughtful, empathic, and self-aware in calm situations may appear less so when pressure increases. Capability is still present, but it is harder to reach. The emotional chimp and/or computer has taken over the rational human.

If pressure and stress are prolonged and chronic it can lead to burnout – a state of emotional, physical, and mental exhaustion. It manifests as overwhelming exhaustion, deep cynicism, detachment from work, and reduced professional efficacy. Burnout is a real risk in law firms, and it is a growing concern. In 2025, the legal sector mental health charity LawCare reported supporting 753 people – more than any previous year, including during the pandemic.[12]

Lawyers therefore need to develop resilience. Resilience is our ability to bounce back from difficulties, adapt to stress, and recover from adversity. There are different types of resilience:

- *Emotional resilience* – how we manage our emotional responses to challenges and deal with our feelings and strong emotions such as anger, fear, vulnerability, or sadness. It is part of us accepting the reality of our situation while also having the emotional capacity to get through it. It is our ability to manage and regulate feelings like anger or fear. It is part of emotional intelligence.
- *Psychological resilience* – the mental capacity to deal with or adapt to uncertainty, difficulties, and adversity. Sometimes this is referred to as "mental fortitude". Psychologically resilient people develop coping strategies and skills that enable them to stay calm and focused during a crisis and move on without long-term negative consequences such as distress and anxiety.
- *Physical resilience* – the body's ability to recover from illness, injury, and stress. This is built through sleep, nutrition, and exercise.
- *Social resilience* – being able to draw strength from supportive relationships, community, and a sense of belonging.

Leading EI consultancy EQ Works argues that the six pillars of resilience for stress management[13] (based on neuro-linguistic-programming (NLP), EI (emotional intelligence) and positive psychology frameworks) are:

1. Satisfaction with lifestyle.
2. Supportive relationships.
3. Physical wellbeing.
4. Solution-focused coping.
5. Emotion-focused coping.
6. Positive beliefs.

Managing emotional triggers in adversarial environments

Managing your emotions is key to emotional intelligence. As mentioned above, it's called emotional regulation.

> *"Emotional regulation refers to the process by which individuals influence which emotions they have, when they have them, and how they experience*

and express their feelings. Emotional regulation can be automatic or controlled, conscious or unconscious, and may have effects at one or more points in the emotion producing process."[14]

There are three components of emotional regulation:

1. Initiating actions triggered by emotions.
2. Inhibiting actions triggered by emotions.
3. Modulating responses triggered by emotions.

We are not our emotions. We may experience sadness without being depressed, we may experience anger without acting out. We can choose how we react to our emotions.

Emotions are thought by some to be adaptive responses from evolutionary biology. Emotional regulation helps us to filter out the most important pieces of information and allows us to attend to it in a way that doesn't provoke stress or fear.

As well as the obvious benefits, such as feeling better in the present moment, strong emotional regulation skills can also enhance long-term well-being, improve performance at work, enrich personal relationships, and lead to better overall health.

Because we develop most of our emotional regulation abilities when we are young, we are often unaware of what it is that is triggering an emotion – it is a subconscious process. In 2018, Harvard Business School's Gerard Zaltman[15] showed that 95 percent of our decision making takes place in the subconscious mind – for example, a comment that is largely ignored by most people may have a dramatic impact on one person, because it triggers a memory of a strong emotional response from their past.

When we experience a strong emotional reaction to something or someone, we should spend some time trying to understand what it was that caused the reaction. Was it something in that particular moment or was it evoking a memory of something in the past? Uncertainty – a daily occurrence in legal practice – triggers a "threat response" in the brain. This can cause anxiety, fear, and stress. Ambiguity impairs decision-making and often leads to maladaptive behaviors such as rumination, avoidance, or excessive risk-avoidance.

There are healthy approaches to emotional regulation, including:

- Talking with friends;
- Exercise;

- Writing in a journal;
- Meditating;
- Engaging in therapy;
- Taking care of oneself when physically ill;
- Getting adequate sleep;
- Paying attention to negative thoughts that occur before or after strong emotions; and
- Noticing when you need a break – and taking it.

There are also unhealthy approaches to emotional regulation, including:

- Abusing alcohol or other substances;
- Self-injury;
- Avoiding or withdrawing from difficult situations;
- Physical or verbal aggression; and
- Excessive social media use.

Some research indicates that emotions only last for 90 seconds. A good first step in emotional regulation is to pause for 90 seconds before responding. You shift your approach from reacting (to the emotion) to responding to the point raised by whoever spoke the triggering words. The "respond, don't react" technique is why some people may speak more slowly – with more pauses.

There are many techniques to help manage emotional states, such as the SIMPLY method by Owen O'Kane:

- Space – step out to look in.
- Identify – consider "what's going on?"
- Meet, greet, and enquire – tell your anxiety "I'm here".
- Pacify – quieten the body.
- Letting go – release the symptoms.
- You – remember you are always the solution.[16]

Be aware too of emotional contagion. Your emotions, feelings, and mood may be affected by those around you. It's a particular challenge in adversarial situations. I encourage people to consider whether those around you generate warmth and positivity (the radiators) or leech out your joy with negative dialogue (the drains).

Similarly, how you feel will be picked up and "infect" those around you. This is particularly so when you are in a senior or leadership position. People will subconsciously tune in and mirror your emotions.

The way you communicate will also have an impact on the emotions of those around you. Neuroscience offers the SCARF framework,[17] which captures the common factors that can activate a reward or threat response.

The SCARF model involves five domains of human social experience:

- Status is about where you are in relation to others around you – your sense of personal worth.
- Certainty concerns being able to predict the future.
- Autonomy provides a sense of control over events.
- Relatedness is a sense of safety with others, of friend rather than foe.
- Fairness is a perception of impartial and just exchanges between people.

You can use this model to manage interactions to minimize threats and maximize rewards in each of these five domains. You can activate reward responses to motivate people more effectively using internal rewards. When the brain and body register a social threat in these dimensions, they light up the networks of the brain that register the threat of physical pain – a finding that has substantial implications for leadership practices. The model is especially relevant for leaders or anyone looking to build trust and influence others.

We become psychologically exhausted as the day progresses. Psychologist Roy Baumeister[18] has demonstrated that there is a finite store of mental energy for exerting self-control and making quality decisions – so decision fatigue can set in. When we are tired at the end of the day, we have less energy to regulate our emotions. Try to schedule situations that are likely to evoke strong emotions for early in the day.

Empathy without losing objectivity

Some may fear that by being empathic they may lose their objectivity. But just because you feel empathy with someone doesn't mean this is so. Dialectical Behavior Therapy (DBT) has a model that helps you balance the two extremes of thinking: Rational mind and Emotional mind into Wise mind:

- *Rational mind* focuses on facts, logic, and problem-solving. It's where we analyze situations without emotional influence.
- *Emotional mind* is driven by feelings, urges, and reactions. It's where our passions, fears and impulses come from.
- *Wise mind* is the intersection of both, where we make decisions with a

balance of logic and emotion. It helps us respond thoughtfully rather than react impulsively.[19]

Think of it this way – if Rational mind is a scientist and Emotional mind is an artist, Wise mind is the skilled mediator who listens to both and finds a balanced, effective solution.[20]

If you still need convincing, consider the FBI model used in hostage negotiations – the Behavioral Change Stairway Model (BCSM).[21] This is a five-step framework developed by the Crisis Negotiation Unit that moves from active listening to empathy, rapport, influence, and finally behavioral change. It focuses on understanding the subject's perspective to achieve a solution. Whilst trained to be highly empathic, no one would suggest that FBI hostage negotiators lose their objectivity.

EI as a risk management and leadership tool

Let's summarize the different aspects of emotional intelligence by considering a more complex model of EI – building on those four main components considered above. This one was developed by Daniel Goleman and Richard E Boyatzis and looks at EI domains and competencies. They are structured as follows:

1. **Self-awareness**
    - Emotional self-awareness

2. **Self-management**
    - Emotional self-control (emotional regulation)
    - Adaptability (learnability, curiosity and the ability to unlearn)
    - Achievement orientation
    - Positive outlook

3. **Social awareness**
    - Empathy
    - Organizational awareness

4. **Relationship management**
    - Influence
    - Coach and mentor
    - Conflict management

- Teamwork
- Inspirational leadership

Self-awareness	**Self-management**	**Empathy**	**Relationship management**
Emotional self-awareness	Emotional self-control	Empathy	Influence
	Adaptability		Coach and mentor
	Achievement orientation	Organizational awareness	Conflict management
	Positive outlook		Teamwork
			Inspirational leadership

Figure 2: Emotional intelligence domains and competencies. Adapted from Daniel Goleman and Richard E. Boyatzis, Emotional Intelligence Has 12 Elements. Which Do You Need to Work On?[22]

These 12 domains encapsulate the vast majority of the subjects covered in this book. Let's take a closer look at EI in leadership and risk management.

Research reported in a 2020 article[23] by the Center for Creative Leadership identified ten essential leadership traits or characteristics:

1. Integrity
2. Ability to delegate
3. Communication
4. Self-awareness (a core component of emotional intelligence)
5. Gratitude
6. Learning agility
7. Influence
8. Empathy (another core component of emotional intelligence)
9. Courage
10. Respect

In a recent article, a leading EI consultancy suggested that effective leaders should:

1. Stop confusing effort with impact (don't confuse the effort of a conversation – how difficult it might be – but think instead about what people will remember – the impact);
2. Let feedback set the agenda (listen to others and develop empathy with them); and
3. Pause long enough to read what the moment actually needs (relating to the ability to tune into what others need and emotional regulation suggestions above).[24]

I was struck by a March 2026 LinkedIn post by Dan Kayne, founder of O-Shaped lawyer (Open-minded, Optimistic, Opportunity-oriented, Originality and Ownership), who was soliciting views on future skills for lawyers.[25] Human-centric skills (i.e. EI) dominated the many responses including:

- Intersection of law, business and people;
- Self-awareness;
- Human communication;
- Asking the right questions;
- Relationship building;
- Influencing;
- Collaboration;
- Resilience;
- Compassion;
- Managing people;
- Commercial pragmatism;
- Financial acumen; and
- Using LegalTech.

Also on LinkedIn, Placida Uzoamaka Ojinnaka posted that "before anything else, we are human". She went on to say:

- Our identity as lawyers is important, but it's secondary to the qualities we bring as people – courage, emotional intelligence, and the ability to truly read a room.
- AI may have its place, but it still lacks the compassionate, relational experiences that we possess.
- Chronic stress and anxiety are all too common in our profession. When stress takes over, it can cloud our judgement and lead to poor decisions.

- It's vital to take moments to pause and reflect, as unresolved stress can accumulate and lead to burnout.
- Psychological safety should be a priority in leadership – creating an environment where people can challenge ideas without fear leads to better information flow and addresses systemic pressures.
- It's important to remember that being a good lawyer doesn't automatically mean being a good leader.
- Senior management and leadership must model healthy boundaries to promote sustainability. Creating a safe workplace isn't about following dominant norms; it's about nurturing genuine wellbeing.[26]

In risk management, emotional intelligence is crucial because it enables better decision making, enhances communication, and fosters a collaborative environment, ultimately leading to more effective risk mitigation strategies.

The neuroscience of risk decisions shows the dual-process theory in action. Our brains operate two distinct system when processing risk – System 1 (fast/emotional) and System 2 (Slow/analytical). Professional risk management requires training System 2 to override System 1's natural responses. A little like the "respond, don't react" technique above.

In an article about traders, Kit Dimic states that those who maintain their composure and systematic approach significantly outperform those who let emotions drive their decisions.[27]

Dimic explored the emotional cycle of risk perception:

1. Complacency – overconfidence.
2. Awakening – decline triggers uncomfortable feelings. Skilled people recognize these feelings as information, not instruction. They use discomfort as a signal to review risk parameters rather than panic.
3. Fear response – fear-driven decisions typically involve abandoning a systemic approach in favor of emotional reactions.

So we see the importance of emotional intelligence when we consider day-to-day decision making and risk management.

Emotional intelligence and wellbeing

Law firm leaders have a duty of care for the wellbeing of their employees. It is a key risk in legal practice – to manage performance and to avoid prosecution. Wellbeing includes both physical and emotional safety. Former practicing lawyer, PhD clinical psychologist and former leader at the

American Psychological Association (ASA), Traci Cipriano has formulated a model that enshrines a significant amount of emotional intelligence.

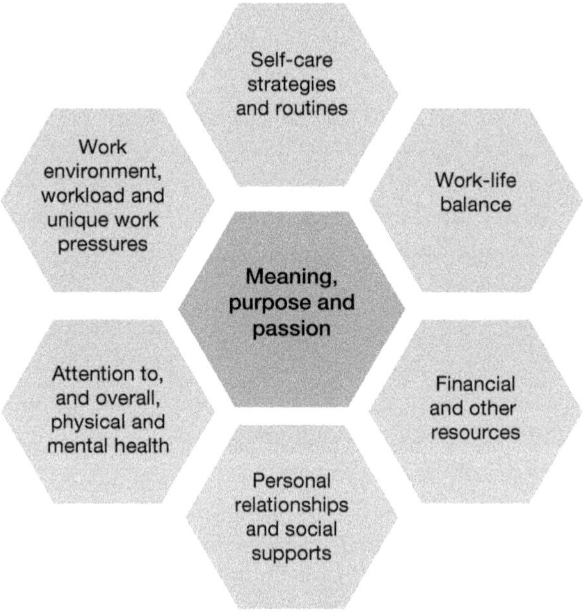

Figure 3: A multi-dimensional model of lawyer wellbeing. Adapted from Cipriano, The Thriving Lawyer.[28]

Emotional intelligence is important for risk management in terms of:

- *Reduced professional liability claims.* Emotionally intelligent lawyers are more adept at managing client expectations and navigating difficult conversations.
- *Conflict mitigation.* EI allows lawyers to address underlying emotions in negotiations and disputes, supporting resolution and preventing escalation.
- *Improved decision making.* By managing emotions, lawyers avoid decisions driven by ego or stress that can lead to poor legal advice.
- *Enhanced team stability.* Higher EI lowers rates of burnout and turnover, reducing the risks associated with poor wellbeing and instability within legal teams.

In a June 2025 article,[29] Rich Bracken argued that what separates good attorneys from the greats is emotional intelligence. He maintains that EI is a strategic advantage that increases success with client retention, courtroom performance, teamwork, and leadership. He also asserts that we should stop calling it a "soft skill" and recognize it as a critical skill. It enables lawyers to build stronger, trust-based client relationships, navigate high-stakes emotions without losing control, differentiate in a crowded market, lead and influence more effectively and make better decisions under pressure.

References

1 Kim Tasso, *Essential Soft Skills for Lawyers: What They Are and How to Develop Them*, Globe Law and Business, 2020: www.globelawandbusiness.com/special-reports/essential-soft-skills-for-lawyers-what-they-are-and-how-to-develop-them

2 Peter Salovey and John D. Mayer, "Emotional Intelligence", *Imagination, Cognition, and Personality*, 1990. https://scholars.unh.edu/psych_facpub/450/

3 Daniel Goleman, *Emotional Intelligence: Why It Can Matter More Than IQ*. Bloomsbury Publishing, 2009.

4 *Emotional Intelligence 2.0*, Jean Greaves and Travis Bradberry, 2009: https://kimtasso.com/book-review-emotional-intelligence-2-0-travis-bradberry-jean-greaves/

5 International Bar Association, "Why lawyers need to be taught more about emotional intelligence". www.ibanet.org/article/bc769d24-a76e-447a-aff1-fd92903bbd60

6 CMS, "Navigating Legal Excellence: Insights in Legal Operations & Project Management": https://cms.law/en/gbr/publication/emotional-intelligence-a-secret-weapon-for-elevating-legal-professionals

7 DLA Piper, "Empathy meets impact: Emotional intelligence for high-performing legal teams". www.dlapiper.com/en-gb/events/bespoke-webinar-programme-for-in-house-lawyers-2026/empathy-meets-impact-emotional-intelligence-for-high-perfor ming-
legal-teams

8 Forbes, "Only 15% Of People Are Self-Aware – Here's How To Change". www.forbes.com/sites/jeffkauflin/2017/05/10/only-15-of-people-are-self-aware-heres-how-to-change/

9 Kross, Ethan, *Shift: Managing Your Emotions – So They Don't Manage You*. Penguin Random House (2026).

10 Lindsay C. Gibson PsyD, *Adult children of emotionally immature parents – how to heal from distant, rejecting or self-involved parents*. 2015.

11 Professor Steve Peters, *The Chimp Paradox – The Mind Management Programme for Confidence, Success, and Happiness*. 2012.

12 https://todaysfamilylawyer.co.uk/lawcare-supported-record-numbers-in-2025/

13 www.eqworks.co.uk/6-pillars-resilience-model/

14 Gross, J. J. (1998). "The emerging field of emotion regulation: An integrative review". *Review of General Psychology*, 2(3), 271–299. https://doi.org/10.1037/1089-2680.2.3.271

15 www.library.hbs.edu/working-knowledge/the-subconscious-mind-of-the-consumer-and-how-to-reach-it
16 Owen O'Kane, *Addicted to Anxiety*, 2026.
17 www.youtube.com/watch?v=5Wu33SdjeCs
18 https://thedecisionlab.com/biases/decision-fatigue
19 https://dialecticalbehaviortherapy.com/mindfulness/wise-mind/
20 www.insightscc.com/blog/finding-your-wise-mind-balancing-rational-and-emotional-thinking
21 https://brain.mikecordell.com/behavioral-change-stairway-model-(bcsm)
22 https://hbr.org/2017/02/emotional-intelligence-has-12-elements-which-do-you-need-to-work-on
23 www.ccl.org/articles/leading-effectively-articles/characteristics-good-leader/
24 www.talentsmarteq.com/from-intent-to-impact-3-things-effective-leaders-do-differently/
25 www.linkedin.com/posts/dan-kayne-b784b435_closethegap-activity-7435035308242575361-UF_8/
26 www.linkedin.com/posts/activity-7439203821353992192-61SO/
27 https://medium.com/@KitDimic/emotional-intelligence-in-risk-management-the-psychology-of-protection-17b5f665e0cd
28 Cipriano, T. *The Thriving Lawyer – A multidimensional model of well-being for a sustainable legal profession.*
29 www.jdsupra.com/legalnews/the-underleveraged-advantage-of-6696668/

Chapter 2: Building resilient lawyers and legal teams

By Paula Davis, JD, MAPP, founder and CEO of the Stress & Resilience Institute

"Ugh, Paula, do we really need more resilience?" That was the question posed to me by a chief legal officer at a roundtable presentation, ironically focused on building resilient teams.

I have been studying, teaching, writing, talking, and thinking about resilience since I first discovered the science of it during my master's studies at the University of Pennsylvania. I found the masters of applied positive psychology (MAPP) program at Penn when I was contemplating a career change due to burnout toward what became the end of my law practice. Because of my experience, I wanted to learn whatever I could to help lawyers, legal teams, and legal organizations improve how work is designed, led, and sustained. As soon as we started talking about the science of resilience, I knew I had discovered a big piece of that puzzle. I have seen countless lives and teams transformed by the power of resilience, including my own. Yet, for all its ubiquity, resilience is one of the most misunderstood concepts at work. It's also one of the most important, given the level of uncertainty and change that is and will continue to be present into the foreseeable future. In fact, the World Economic Forum recently identified "resilience, flexibility, and agility" as a top cluster of skills people will need today and within the next five years at work.[1]

Let's start by defining resilience. The research literature can be confusing because there are many definitions of resilience and most of them have a clinical or trauma-related focus, rather than a work focus. Most definitions of resilience include these two components:

1. *Capacity.* Resilience is the capacity to manage small and large challenges, pressures, and stressors.
2. *Growth.* A hallmark of resilience goes beyond bouncing back and into bouncing forward. Resilient individuals, teams, and organizations learn valuable lessons from setbacks, obstacles, and stress and apply those lessons to future challenges going forward to enhance agility.

Simply put, resilience is an individual's, team's, and organization's capacity for stress-related growth.[2] So, when a leader asks me very skeptically, "Paula, do we *really* need more resilience," I ask in response, "Does your team need more skills and tools to better manage stress and uncertainty, to make the best business decisions possible, and then learn and grow from those challenges so that future challenges sting less?" Almost every leader says, "yes!" That's resilience.

Unfortunately, resilience has become embedded in many organizations' wellness efforts such that the concept is often viewed with an eye roll and not taken as seriously as it should be. As a result, legal organizations fail to take full advantage of the way resilience can help support other important business objectives and leadership and team development. Research shows that individuals and organizations with higher levels of resilience are happier, healthier, and more successful in uncertain and changing environments, and companies with higher workforce resilience see 320 percent more year-on-year growth than those with lower levels.[3]

Research also shows that employees who are adaptable tend to have an edge when it comes to managing change and adversity – adaptability acts as a buffer to the impact of workplace stress.[4] However, research also shows that it is misguided to see building individual resilience skills as the sole solution to workplace challenges because individual skills alone cannot fix an unsupportive or toxic work environment, and, while resilient lawyers are better able to work in difficult work environments, they are less likely to tolerate them.[5] In fact, one survey showed that employees with high resilience and adaptability were 60 percent more likely to say they planned to leave their company if they experienced unfavorable work environments compared to those with lower levels of resilience and adaptability.[6] Importantly, the World Economic Forum cites "resilience, agility, and adaptability" among the top skills needed to navigate the future of AI-driven work.[7]

Many of the qualities that support organizational resilience, like strong leadership and having good networks and relationships, also offer tangible benefits to the way an organization generally operates.[8] When people see resilience embedded and talked about as critical to good teamwork, as a leadership skillset, and as a skillset to help the organization itself, it takes on new meaning. Legal organizations shouldn't ask people to "be more resilient" if they are not first willing to address the very work environments that often make work more challenging than it needs to be.

What the legal profession can learn from the US Army

When I left my law practice, I never in a million years thought I would work with drill sergeants and soldiers in any capacity. I hate war movies and drill sergeants seemed particularly intense. The Comprehensive Soldier and Family Fitness Program (CSF2), a program designed by United States Army senior leadership and researchers at the University of Pennsylvania, was created while I was still practicing law and piloted during my MAPP studies. When I graduated, I became part of the Penn-CSF2 training team.

The Army created an integrated, proactive approach to developing resilience and wellbeing in soldiers, their family members, and the Army's civilian workforce.[9] During my time working in this program, CSF2 consisted of four components:[10]

1. An online assessment tool called the Global Assessment Tool (GAT) taken by all soldiers and used to identify resilience strengths;
2. Online self-help modules tailored to the results of the GAT;
3. Master resilience training using a train-the-trainer method to teach senior officers and non-commissioned officers the resilience tools so that these leaders could conduct resilience training down to the unit level; and
4. Mandatory resilience training at every Army leader development school.

The resilience training components of the CSF2 program were based on the Penn Resilience Program. The Penn Resilience Program is one of the most studied resilience programs that exists, is one of the only resilience training programs implementing a train-the-trainer model that has also been scientifically reviewed, and has been adapted and applied to professionals in the military, healthcare, first responders, athletes (collegiate and professional), educators, and via my own work in some of these industries and within the legal profession.[11]

The train-the-trainer aspect of the master resilience training program was critical because Army senior leadership didn't want to just train soldiers – they wanted those soldiers to turn around and go back to their units to teach other soldiers the same skills. During the early stages of the program, the Penn-Army team trained more than 40,000 master resilience trainers.[12] CSF2 evolved over the years, and the program officially ended in 2025.[13]

Lawyers and soldiers – there are similarities

The approach the Army took to scaling resilience is something that the legal profession could replicate, in whole or in part. Teaching methodologies, examples, and overall scope may need to change, but there are more similarities between the challenges that soldiers and lawyers face than you may first think.

Both groups undertake tasks for society that are very important, but that can impose huge personal costs. While some tasks soldiers are asked to undertake involve armed conflict with external forces, soldiers spend most of their time leading troops and dealing with everyday work/life pressure. Lawyers frequently wade into the toughest interpersonal conflicts our society produces, with the charge that they resolve them, or at least mitigate their consequences. The outcomes lawyers seek (or seek to avoid) may involve substantial amounts of money, a person's livelihood, or the very future of a family. These disputes often involve conflicts in the fundamental values that lawyers and their clients hold dear, and such disputes frequently cannot be resolved by simply "doing the right thing".

Disputes and negotiations often involve zero-sum components with "winners" and "losers", "win-win" outcomes may be few and far between and that only increases the pressure to succeed. Much like soldiers, lawyers do their work in an adversarial context with a trained opponent on the other side. Doctors, for example, don't have to worry about another doctor interrupting a surgical procedure in an effort to see that the patient dies.

Often, lawyers have to do things that cause others emotional or even physical pain (e.g., cross-examining a witness, facilitating corporate layoffs), and they do all of this in cultures focused on rules and authority, verbal facility, and, for private practitioners, extrinsic rewards, most notably money and status. The damage these challenges inflict – both in law school and for practicing lawyers – is now well documented.

Interestingly, there is evidence to suggest that, as with the Army, training in resilience skills can help within the legal profession. My friend and colleague, Dave Shearon, the former executive director of the Tennessee Commission on CLE and Specialization, studied the CLE Commission's records and realized he had spoken to and/or taught resilience skills to over 900 attorneys in a two-year period. With the Commission's permission, he surveyed those attorneys to see if the resilience work had any effect. What he learned matched the experience of the Army MRTs – those lawyers who reported using the skills found that they made a difference; in fact, those lawyers who used the skills were three times more likely to report that their commitment, energy, and engagement in their law practice was somewhat or much improved.[14]

Building resilience in law

Resilience is not a fixed trait that you either have or don't have; rather, it's a set of skills that individuals and teams can build.[15] It's also not blind perseverance – it's perseverance with a purpose. When a challenge happens, big or small, you must evaluate whether you, your team, or your legal organization are pursuing the right course of action to manage it. If you are, stay the course. If you are not, the resilient response may be to pivot or to stop something altogether.

The table below highlights the qualities that most strongly contribute to increased resilience for individuals,[16] teams,[17] and organizations[18] (all of which can be taught, practiced, and improved).

Table 1: Qualities that contribute to increased resilience.

Individuals	Teams	Organizations
Emotional regulation	Team-efficacy (the shared belief among team members that they can be effective together)	Strong internal and external partnerships
Mental agility	Clear roles, responsibilities, ways of communicating, and familiarity with each other's knowledge and skill set	Strong leadership practices
Optimism (how you explain difficult situations and setbacks)	Improvisation (deliberately adjusting to demands on the fly)	Sufficient resources
Self-compassion	Psychological safety	Preparedness and planning – you practice and test plans at regular intervals to identify weaknesses and vulnerabilities
Self-efficacy (the belief in your ability to cope with a broad range of challenging demands and to succeed)	Motivated workers who are fully committed to organizational goals (and where wellbeing is prioritized)	Situational awareness – proactively monitoring the legal industry to have early warning of emerging issues.

While the focus of this chapter will be on individual and team resilience, I have included information about organizational resilience in the table to highlight some of the key pathways for building it.

Strategies for building individual resilience

Resilience in the legal profession is often misunderstood as endurance, when in reality it is a set of skills that allows lawyers to manage pressure without sacrificing performance or wellbeing. Too often, the profession rewards consistently pushing through exhaustion over work sustainability, but resilience is not about simply tolerating difficult conditions. It is about developing the capacity to think clearly under pressure, regulating your energy, and responding to challenges in ways that preserve both effectiveness and longevity. The good news is that these capabilities can be intentionally developed through a set of practical, evidence-based skills. I label all the skills, frameworks, and strategies I teach as TNTs, or tiny noticeable things. I do this to reinforce the message that creating healthy legal practices and strong team cultures are built on the foundation of small shifts in mindset and practice. Here are three such strategies that I have taught to many lawyers.

TNT: Limit catastrophizing

Catastrophizing is also called worst-case scenario thinking. It's those moments when you experience a stress-producing event and, in what feels like seconds, your brain spins a story that ends with you living in a van down by the river. Importantly, the stress-producing event that kicks off this cascade of worst-case-scenario thoughts doesn't have to be major. When I ask lawyers to practice this skill, I see a lot of their stress-producing events. One first year associate catastrophized because he called a partner the wrong name. Other lawyers worry about negative feedback, while some have a hard time with uncertainty – a partner or a client sends an email that says, "come see me now" or "call me back" with no other details.

While not everyone catastrophizes, lawyers are professional issue spotters who, by training, are good at finding the downside of things easily. If this counterproductive thinking style happens to you, follow these steps:[19]

- Step 1: Write down your Horror Movie. Capture all the worst-case scenario thoughts you have, preferably on paper.
- Step 2: Capture your Disney Movie. Make up an equally unlikely, positive, story to get a boost of positive emotion. Don't worry if your Disney Movie is illogical – it's supposed to be.

- Step 3: Create your Documentary. List the most likely outcome using just the facts. Your Documentary might include negative consequences – but the point is that you're seeing the full picture in an even-handed way.

TNT: Increase self-efficacy

Self-efficacy is the belief in your ability to cope with a broad range of stressful events and challenging demands and to succeed. As I pointed out above, high efficacy is also an important resilience-building pathway for teams. Luckily, the process to build self- and team-efficacy is the same.

First, you need to select a skill or an ability you want to improve or develop. Let's assume you want to improve your public speaking skills. The pathways to build your public speaking efficacy are as follows, and they are presented in order of effectiveness, from strongest to weakest:[20]

- *Pathway 1:* Learn by doing (most effective). You (or your team) need to do the thing you seek to improve. If you want to increase your public speaking efficacy, then you need to start speaking in public. You may decide to join a local speaking association chapter, offer to speak at a legal conference, or volunteer to lead a future practice group meeting.
- *Pathway 2:* Learn by watching and observing others. You may decide to watch TED Talks of your favorite speakers to see how they hook an audience or to determine which speaking style feels most authentic. You may also observe a colleague who is a great orator and then ask him or her about some of the strategies they use to speak effectively.
- *Pathway 3:* Learn by being coached by a credible and respected source about your efforts. You might record yourself delivering your opening argument and then show that to a trusted colleague for some feedback. You may also decide to hire a professional coach to give you more 1:1 support.

This is the classic pathway to increasing efficacy – accept a goal, make an effort, get feedback on that effort, improve, keep trying, and eventually succeed. And the good news is that, as your efficacy about a particular problem increases, it tends to persist. It's a lasting mindset shift that permanently changes what you believe you are capable of. As a result, you're more likely to persevere, commit to challenging goals, and to take good risks.[21]

TNT: Use the 4/4/4 way to end your week

Positive emotions, reflecting, and savoring are all great resilience boosters, and this skill combines them all.[22] Set a reminder in your calendar to try this skill at the end of your week. I know for most lawyers, it feels as though your week never actually ends, but for the purposes of this strategy, let's use Friday afternoon. Each "4" represents an activity you can do in four minutes of time, for a total of 12 minutes. I picked 12 minutes because I thought it was a doable amount of time for busy professionals.

Part 1: Spend four minutes reflecting on and capturing the positive experiences you had during your work week. How did you make progress on important tasks, even if that progress was small? What were some of your small wins and successes?

Part 2: Spend four minutes thinking about what you want to focus on next week. This provides some clarity and direction. What tasks do you need to start or complete? What relationships do you want to strengthen? What are some personal strengths or values that you want to bring more fully into alignment?

Part 3: Spend four minutes sending a note of appreciation, recognition, or gratitude to someone (or more than one person).

There are many other pathways to increase your resilience, some of which include building hope, recharging and managing stress, and maintaining strong relationships. While building your own resilience is a good start, it's also important for teams to create a good environment that facilitates resilience.

Strategies for building team resilience

The ability to make decisions, act with increased responsibility, and the capacity to bounce back (and forward) after adversity are critical given the pace of change, uncertainty, and the elevated speed at which law firms and legal teams and organizations must change to thrive in the world today. Team resilience has been shown to enhance team and project performance, team creativity, and organizational effectiveness.[23]

Highly effective teams are ones that demonstrate:[24]

- Sustained performance (generating positive results over time);
- Team resilience (working through challenges and bouncing back from adversity); and

- Ongoing vitality (maintaining energy and resources needed for future success).

There are four areas in which leaders need to focus to help a team increase its resilience:[25]

1. Creating a shared belief in the team's capacity to succeed across various tasks and situations. To do this, team goals and processes must be clear.
2. Creating a shared understanding among team members about goals, tasks, and team roles.
3. Enhancing the team's ability to improvise. Team members need to know who knows what on the team and each other's strengths.
4. Strengthening psychological safety. Leaders can do this by being accessible, encouraging the discussion of mistakes, and showing appreciation for team members' input and ideas.

Psychological safety has long been recognized as a foundational element of resilient teams, and we now know a little more about it in the legal profession. I recently partnered with ALM (now Centellic) to survey lawyers and legal professionals about psychological safety and burnout, and almost 900 lawyers and legal professionals responded.

We used the seven-item questionnaire for measuring psychological safety created by Dr Amy Edmondson[26] and asked respondents, "Which of the following statements describe how you feel at work? Please select all that apply." The responses that you see below are people who marked "yes" to the statements. For example, 515 respondents (59 percent) marked yes to the statement, "My work efforts are not deliberately undermined".

My work efforts are not deliberately undermined	515 (59%)
My unique skills and talents are valued at utilize at work	458 (53%)
I am able to bring up problems and tough issues at work	408 (47%)
It is difficult to ask others for help	**372 (43%)**
If I make a mistake, it is often held against me	**282 (32%)**
It is safe to take a risk as part of my work	239 (27%)
I am sometimes rejected for being different	**158 (18%)**

We then further categorized the responses in bold as the "psychologically unsafe" group. We discovered that this group is almost 70 percent associates and female, and more than one-third are 25-34 years old. There is a clear opportunity for legal leaders to improve this skill set.

The TNTs below will help provide you with some ideas to not only build psychological safety on your legal teams, but to also address some of the other resilient team pathways.

TNT roadmap: Actions to consider before, during, and after a challenge
It's important for teams to act intentionally before, during, and after a challenge. This roadmap will help your team increase its stress resilience by preparing in advance, reacting appropriately during the adversity, and then growing from it after.[27]

Before	During	After
Anticipate challenges and plan contingencies	Make real-time adjustments quickly if something isn't working	Debrief – what went well; what do you need to improve?
Know team members' capacity levels (is someone operating beyond capacity such that it will impact his/her ability to help or to respond effectively?)	Re-clarify roles and goals for teams that are required to meet remotely or in a hybrid format	Address any friction points that may have emerged between team members
Address known vulnerabilities (e.g., distrust among team members; lack of resources/expertise)	Provide transparency and ongoing status updates to reduce ambiguity	Communicate appreciation to team members (partner to associate and peer-to-peer)
Establish a process for regular communication about a developing problem	Continue constructive routines like regular meetings	Thank external resources for their help and support
Identify back-ups for people in key roles	Don't forget about personal interaction and check ins	

The intentionality of addressing each of these components will help your team be ready to handle a wide range of challenges.

TNT: Debrief after micro-challenges

Micro-challenges are small frustrations and setbacks that legal teams experience on a more regular basis than big adversities. These are great resilience building opportunities. Research has demonstrated that how your team recovers from minor challenges is predictive of how it will cope with bigger ones.[28] Use micro-challenges as opportunities to deploy some of the strategies on the chart above. They will build your resilience muscles so that you're ready to flex when the bigger adversities strike. You can start by discussing what went well, what you would improve, and what specific actions helped or didn't help.

TNT: Get everyone on the same page

Resilient teams are consistently on the same page about direction, priorities, and roles.[29] If you asked everyone on your legal team to explain the direction of a matter, what clients or cases have priority, and what each person's role is in executing the work, would they all give you the same answer? Legal teams should regularly discuss and have a clear understanding of what success looks like and what top priorities are, with clear role clarity.

TNT: Make knowledge easy to find and understand

Knowledge management attorneys and business professionals play an important role in fostering team resilience. One way to build team resilience is by making knowledge (forms, documents, precedent) easy to find and understand. When there is a crisis, teams need to be able to access important information quickly. Here is what helps:

- Pay attention to the quality of the legal documents your team produces. High-quality documents are concise, clearly articulated, and answer important questions.
- Put documents on a shared platform that is easy to search and easily accessible for the entire team.
- AI tools can help your team create summary results, automate administrative work, and enable faster knowledge search.

Resilience in today's legal profession is more than just individual toughness or the ability to simply "push through". It is built when lawyers develop the skills to manage their energy, attention, and reactions, and when legal leaders intentionally create team environments characterized by trust, clarity, and psychological safety. The legal organizations that will thrive in the years ahead will be those that treat resilience not as a personal responsibility alone, but as a shared strategic capability.

References

1 World Economic Forum, Future of Jobs Report 2025: www.weforum.org/publications/the-future-of-jobs-report-2025/.

2 David M. Fisher and Jennifer M. Ragsdale (2019). "The Importance of Definitional and Temporal Issues in the Study of Resilience". 68(4) *Applied Psychology: An International Review*, 583-620. See also David Fletcher and Mustafa Sarkar (2013). "Psychological Resilience: A Review and Critique of Definitions, Concepts, and Theory". 18(1) *European Psychologist*, 12-23.

3 Alexis Jeannotte, Erin Eatough, and Gabriella Rosen Kellerman (2020). *Resilience in an Age of Uncertainty: Cultivating Resilient Leaders, Teams & Organizations.* Better Up Labs.

4 Karen van Dam (2013). "Employee Adaptability to Change at Work: A Multidimensional Resource-Based Framework". In *The Psychology of Organizational Change: Part III – Predicting Employees' Reactions to Change: Individual Factors.* (Shaul Oreg, Alexandria Michael, and Rune Todnem, eds.) 123-142. Cambridge University Press: Cambridge, England.

5 Jacqueline Brassey et al. (27 May 2022). "Addressing Employee Burnout: Are You Solving the Right Problem?" McKinsey Health Institute: www.mckinsey.com/mhi/our-insights/addressing-employee-burnout-are-you-solving-the-right-problem#/.

6 *Ibid.*

7 World Economic Forum, Future of Jobs Report: www.weforum.org/publications/the-future-of-jobs-report-2025/in-full/3-skills-outlook/

8 Erica Seville (2017). *Resilient Organizations: How to Survive, Thrive, and Create Opportunities through Crisis and Change*. London, UK: Kogan Page.

9 George W. Casey, Jr, (2011). "Comprehensive Soldier Fitness: A Vision for Psychological Resilience in the U.S. Army". 66(1) *American Psychologist*, 1-3. Note that the program was initially called Comprehensive Soldier Fitness but changed its name to Comprehensive Soldier and Family Fitness as the program evolved to train spouses and family members.

10 *Ibid.*

11 Martin E.P. Seligman (2018). *The Hope Circuit*. 326 New York, NY: Public Affairs. The MRT program was developed based on a number of programs created and empirically validated by the University of Pennsylvania, including the Penn Resilience Program (PRP), a parallel program called APEX, and also incorporated a number of positive psychology concepts. The PRP has been evaluated in at least 19

controlled studies and, while some inconsistent findings have been reported, the studies suggest that PRP significantly reduces symptoms of depression and anxiety and helps participants perform better. More importantly, in the studies that included long-term follow-ups, PRP resilience skill effects were found to last for two years or more. In addition, the research on the PRP also demonstrated that teachers who are trained in the PRP can subsequently teach resilience skills effectively, lending support to the train-the-trainer model developed by Penn and incorporated in the MRT resilience program. The research supporting these statements is as follows: Jane E. Gillham, Karen J. Reivich and Lisa H. Jaycox (2008). *The Penn Resiliency Program* (also known as the *Penn Depression Prevention Program and the Penn Optimism Program*). Unpublished manuscript, University of Pennsylvania; Jane E. Gillam et al. (1991). *The APEX Project: Manual for Group Leaders.* Unpublished manuscript, University of Pennsylvania; see also, Karen Reivich, Andrew Shatte, and Jane Gillham (2003). Penn Resilience Training for College Students: *Leader's Guide and Participant's Guide.* Unpublished manuscript, University of Pennsylvania; and Steven M. Brunwasser, Jane E. Gillham, and Eric S. Kim (2009). "A Meta-Analytic Review of the Penn Resiliency Program's Effects on Depressive Symptoms". 77, *Journal of Consulting and Clinical Psychology*, 1042-1054.

12 You can read more about how the program was created here: Martin E.P. Seligman (2018). *The Hope Circuit.* 311-327 New York, NY: Public Affairs; see also Karen J. Reivich, Martin E.P. Seligman and Sharon McBride (2011). "Master Resilience Training in the U.S. Army". 66(1) *American Psychologist*, 25-34. Also, personal conversation with retired Army officer Sylvia Lopez Johnson as to the number of MRTs trained.

13 Personal communication with retired Army officer Lauren Osinski as to the CSF2 program end date.

14 I would like to thank and acknowledge Dave Shearon for letting me use his own previous writings about the Army resilience training for this section, and for sharing the data he collected about his own work with the Tennessee Commission.

15 *Supra* note 2.

16 Gabriella Rosen Kellerman and Martin Seligman (2023). *Tomorrowmind: Thriving at Work with Resilience, Creativity, and Connection – Now and in an Uncertain Future.* New York: Atria Books.

17 Bradley L. Kirkman and Troy A. Smith (2026). "Team Empowerment and Team Resilience". 13, *Annual Review of Organizational Psychology and Organizational Behavior*, 77-106.

18 Edwine Barasa, Rahab Mbau, and Lucy Gilson (2018). "What is Resilience and How Can It Be Nurtured? A Systemic Review of Empirical Literature on Organizational Resilience". 7(6) *International Journal of Health Policy Management*, 491-503.

19 Judith S. Beck (2011). *Cognitive Behavioral Therapy Basics and Beyond*, 2nd ed., 172. New York: Guilford Press. See also Karen Reivich and Andrew Shatté (2002). *The Resilience Factor*, 168-185. New York: Broadway Books.

20 Albert Bandura (2009). "Cultivate Self-Efficacy for Personal and Organizational Effectiveness" in *Handbook of Principles of Organizational Behavior*, 2nd ed. (Edwin A. Locke, ed.) 179-200. UK: John Wiley & Sons.

21 Jane McGonigal (2015). *SuperBetter: The Power of Living Gamefully*. New York: Penguin Books.

22 Teresa Amabile and Steven Kramer (2011). *The Progress Principle: Using Small Wins to Ignite Joy, Engagement, and Creativity at Work*. Boston: Harvard Business Review Press. See also Remus Ilies, Joyce E. Bono, and Arnold B. Bakker (2024). "Crafting Well-Being: Employees Can Enhance Their Own Well-Being by Savoring, Reflecting Upon, and Capitalizing on Positive Work Experiences". 11, *Annual Review of Organizational Psychology and Organizational Behavior*, 63-91.

23 Sebastian Raetze (2020). "What Makes Work Teams Resilient? An Overview of Resilience Processes and Cross-Level Antecedents". In *Research Handbook on Organizational Resilience*, 232-246 (Edward H. Powley, Brianna Barker Caza, and Arran Caza, eds). Edward Elgar Publishing.

24 Scott Tannenbaum and Eduardo Salas (2021). *Teams That Work: The Seven Drivers of Team Effectiveness*. New York: Oxford University Press.

25 *Supra* note 16.

26 Amy C. Edmondson (1999). "Psychological Safety and Learning Behavior in Work Teams". 44(2) *Administrative Science Quarterly*. 350-383. You can download the full report by Paula Davis, titled "Lawyer Strong® —> Law Strong. Burnout and Psychological Safety in Law: National Survey Findings and a Practical Path Forward", here: https://stressandresilience.com/training-workshops-law/.

27 George M. Alliger, Christopher P. Cerasoli, Scott I. Tannenbaum, and William B. Vessey (2015). "Team Resilience: How Teams Flourish Under Pressure". 44, *Organizational Dynamics*, 176-184.

28 Richard J. Davidson and Sharon Begley (2012). *The Emotional Life of Your Brain. How Its Unique Patterns Affect the Way You Think, Feel, and Live – and How You Can Change Them*. New York: The Penguin Group.

29 *Supra* note 23.

Chapter 3:
Grief and trauma in legal practice – managing exposure in a loss-saturated profession

By Tom Spence

The hidden emotional landscape of legal work

The previous chapter explored resilience and mental agility as critical capabilities for navigating pressure, uncertainty and change in legal practice. These skills are essential. They enable lawyers to sustain performance, adapt under pressure, and respond effectively to the demands of modern legal work.

However, a broader context deserves attention. In many Western settings, grief and trauma remain under-recognized, often unnoticed until directly experienced. Understanding often arises not through education, but through exposure – sometimes only after significant experience.

In many cultures, this has not always been the case. Grief has been understood as something held collectively rather than managed individually – a recognition that our capacity to navigate loss is shaped not only by personal strength, but by the environments and relationships around us.

Professional environments do not sit outside of this dynamic; they reflect it. Lawyers are not only managing pressure – they are repeatedly exposed to conflict, loss, failure, and human distress. Behind transactions, disputes, and advisory work sit divorces, deaths, financial collapse, criminal harm, and organizational breakdown. Over time, this exposure accumulates.

Law is, in this sense, a loss-saturated profession. Legal education and early professional training rarely prepare lawyers to recognize or process these impacts. Curricula focus on analysis, argument, strategy, and technical skill, with little emphasis on the emotional and cognitive load created by repeated exposure to human distress. As a result, most lawyers enter practice equipped to perform under pressure, but not to manage its cumulative effects.

Yet the profession's culture rarely accounts for this. Professionalism is equated with composure and emotional neutrality, with lawyers moving swiftly from one matter to the next – the implicit expectation being not to dwell.

This works – to a point.

But suppression is not neutral. When exposure is not acknowledged or processed, it does not disappear. It shapes attention, narrows thinking, influences behavior under pressure and, over time, begins to affect judgment, leadership, and culture.

Suppression has cognitive, ethical and leadership consequences

Resilience enables lawyers to perform under pressure. But resilience alone does not account for the cumulative impact of repeated exposure to conflict, loss, and human distress.

This chapter builds on the resilience conversation by examining grief and trauma as operational realities within legal practice. It explores how repeated exposure shows up in individuals, teams, and organizations, the cost of silence, and why sustainable performance in law depends not only on individual resilience, but on a firm's capacity to recognize, regulate, and integrate the impact of what its people are exposed to.

Understanding grief in professional contexts

To engage meaningfully with grief and trauma in legal practice, it is first important to clarify what we mean by grief.

The word "grief" comes from the Latin gravis, meaning heavy or burdensome – a reminder that grief is a weight that can sit on our minds, bodies, and interactions. While often associated with bereavement, it is more broadly the response to the loss of something meaningful to us.

In professional life, grief can stem from lost clients or opportunities, reputational harm, ethical dilemmas, organizational change, or balancing personal loss with professional duties.

Grief manifests emotionally, cognitively, behaviorally, and physiologically. In legal contexts, there is often an expectation to remain composed, neutral, and decisive – but this regulation does not remove the burden; it simply absorbs it.

Grief as cumulative exposure

Legal work is rarely linear. Combined with personal life experiences of loss, this creates ongoing, often invisible accumulation.

The cumulative nature of grief in professional environments can produce:

- *Cognitive impacts* – decision fatigue, narrowed attention, impaired judgment.
- *Behavioral impacts* – irritability, over-control, withdrawal, conflict escalation.

- *Leadership impacts* – reduced empathy, ethical blind spots, impaired mentoring.

Unchecked, this accumulation shapes not only individuals but also team dynamics and organizational culture.

The contextual nature of grief

Grief is relational and environmental. Our ability to process loss is influenced by:

- Social norms around emotional expression;
- The presence or absence of supportive colleagues and leaders; and
- An organizational culture that either normalizes or suppresses emotional impact.

In many professional contexts, the expectation to "carry on" reinforces suppression, creating silent depletion across individuals and teams.

Grief as an operational reality

Understanding grief in legal practice means recognizing it as an operational factor, not just a personal experience. Repeated exposure affects attention, behavior, collaboration, ethical decision making, and leadership capacity. By integrating grief into professional life, organizations can design systems and cultures that:

- Support recovery without compromising performance;
- Prevent cognitive and emotional overload; and
- Enable teams and leaders to operate with clarity and integrity.

Grief literacy is therefore not a soft skill – it is a performance and risk management capability, essential for sustainable legal practice.

Recognizing grief as an operational reality leads us to trauma. While grief reflects our response to loss, trauma emerges when exposure overwhelms our capacity to process or integrate the impact – whether from a single event or cumulative pressures. Understanding this intersection is critical, as unacknowledged exposure shapes decision making, team dynamics, and organizational culture. The following section explores how trauma manifests in professional contexts and why law firms must design systems to support regulation and collective recovery.

Stress, trauma, and the continuum of exposure

In professional contexts, "stress" is often treated as distinct from trauma – something manageable, expected, and largely benign. However, physiologically, the distinction is less clear. The nervous system responds to pressure, threat, and intensity along a spectrum rather than in neatly separated categories.

This has important implications for legal practice. The pressures commonly described as "stress" – tight deadlines, high stakes decisions, client conflict, and sustained workload – activate many of the same biological systems involved in trauma responses. What the profession normalizes as pressure is, in physiological terms, repeated nervous system activation. While not overwhelming in isolation, their cumulative effect places sustained demands on attention, emotional regulation, and cognitive flexibility. Over time, repeated activation without adequate regulation can narrow thinking, reduce adaptability, and increase reactivity. The issue is not whether lawyers can cope in the moment – it is what repeated coping is doing to them over time. Stress, in this sense, is not separate from trauma but part of the same continuum of nervous system load, with effects that are often subtle yet significant.

Within this continuum, trauma can be understood as the point at which exposure – acute or cumulative – exceeds an individual's capacity to process or integrate the experience. It is not simply an emotional reaction, but a physiological and cognitive state that shapes perception, behavior, and decision making. In this sense, trauma is not an outlier event – it is a predictable outcome of sustained, unregulated intensity.

Most lawyers are not clinically traumatized, yet many are consistently trauma-exposed. Working across multiple emotionally, ethically, and cognitively intense matters, combined with baseline pressures, leads to cumulative activation without sufficient opportunity to regulate or reset.

In this light, trauma in legal practice is not exceptional or individual, but an operational reality. Recognizing it shifts focus from individual resilience to systemic solutions – firms must develop structures, cultures, and practices that support regulation, reflection, and collective resilience. Without this, resilience is endurance, not sustainability.

How suppression became the norm in legal culture

Law has long celebrated traits that serve the profession well: composure, intellectual clarity, objectivity, and control. Lawyers are trained to maintain distance, manage complexity, and deliver outcomes under pressure. These characteristics are rightly valued, particularly in high-stakes contexts where decisions carry serious consequences for clients, organizations, and society.

Yet, over time, these professional virtues have become conflated with emotional suppression. Composure – the ability to remain calm under pressure – has subtly shifted from a functional skill to an implicit expectation that emotional responses to loss, conflict, or distress should be hidden. The implicit rules absorbed during training and early practice are clear: remain functional, move quickly to the next matter, and manage any emotional impact privately.

This expectation is reinforced by professional education and practice structures. Legal training focuses heavily on analysis, strategy, and argumentation, with little attention given to the cognitive and emotional load of repeated exposure to conflict and loss. Law students and early-career lawyers are taught to excel under pressure, to compartmentalize, and to "stay professional", often without guidance on processing the human consequences they encounter. As a result, emotional regulation is frequently equated with emotional absence.

In the short-term, this approach appears effective. Lawyers continue to perform at high levels, managing heavy caseloads, complex negotiations, or sensitive client matters without visible disruption. Suppression can create an illusion of stability – teams deliver, matters progress, and deadlines are met.

However, the long-term consequences are significant. Suppression consumes cognitive bandwidth. Each unacknowledged emotional response – whether grief, frustration, or distress – requires effort to manage and conceal. Over time, this hidden load narrows thinking, reduces psychological flexibility, and limits the capacity to respond adaptively to new challenges. It contributes to irritability, emotional flattening, withdrawal, over-control, and disengagement. In essence, the very traits celebrated as professionalism can, when unchecked, erode judgement, leadership capacity, and collaborative functioning.

Culturally, suppression has become self-reinforcing. Lawyers observe senior colleagues managing intense matters without visible emotional impact, and they internalize the expectation that maintaining composure is synonymous with competence. Deviation from this norm is often interpreted as weakness, undermining willingness to seek support or acknowledge strain. The result is a professional environment in which cumulative exposure is rarely discussed, processed, or regulated.

The paradox is clear: what appears to sustain performance in the short-term – the relentless adherence to composure and emotional neutrality – quietly undermines it in the long-term. Cognitive and emotional load accumulates, decision making narrows, and the capacity for ethical discernment and leadership can be compromised. Suppression becomes both a coping mechanism and a risk factor.

Understanding this dynamic is essential. Recognizing that suppression is not neutrality, but a cognitive and organizational cost, allows firms to reframe professionalism. High performance does not require invisibility of emotion. Instead, it thrives when lawyers are supported to regulate, acknowledge, and integrate the impact of their work. Shifting from suppression to regulation is a cultural and structural challenge, but one that is critical for sustainable professional practice in a loss-saturated environment.

Impact of unprocessed exposure

When grief and trauma exposure go unacknowledged, the impact extends beyond the individual to teams and the wider organization. High-performing environments can continue to deliver strong outputs, while underlying cognitive, emotional, and relational capacity is gradually reduced. Over time, this can affect both performance and sustainability.

Unprocessed exposure manifests across three interconnected domains:

- *Cognitive* – decision fatigue, reduced attention, memory lapses, and narrowed thinking, limiting risk assessment and problem-solving.
- *Behavioral* – irritability, withdrawal, over-control or reactivity, undermining collaboration and communication.
- *Leadership* – diminished empathy, ethical blind spots, and reduced capacity to mentor, manage, and lead effectively.

These are not isolated symptoms – they are early indicators of system strain. Left unaddressed, they compound into organizational consequences:

- Rising attrition and loss of talent.
- Burnout and reduced overall capacity.
- Declining collaboration, engagement, and innovation.
- Greater potential for conflict and pressure on ethical decision making.

At this point, the issue is no longer individual wellbeing – it is organizational performance and risk. What is not processed does not disappear, it accumulates. In a profession characterized by repeated exposure to complex, high-stakes, and often emotionally charged situations, this cumulative load can gradually shape how individuals think, respond, and interact. High output can mask underlying depletion, creating the illusion of resilience while vulnerability increases.

Each unresolved matter, each unacknowledged human consequence, adds to a growing cognitive and emotional load. In a profession defined by repeated exposure, accumulation is not accidental – it is inevitable. Over time, this narrows judgement, fragments attention, and strains professional relationships. High output can mask this depletion, creating the illusion of resilience while underlying vulnerability increases.

Framing unprocessed exposure in this way highlights it as an operational consideration rather than solely an individual concern. The implications are not limited to wellbeing – they extend to judgement, collaboration, leadership effectiveness, and ultimately the quality and consistency of professional outcomes.

In legal practice, exposure to conflict, loss, and human consequence is inherent. Recognizing this allows firms to take a more proactive and structured approach – not by reducing expectations of performance, but by ensuring that systems, leadership practices, and cultural norms support sustained clarity, sound decision making, and effective collaboration.

This reframes the challenge. Sustainable performance is not achieved through endurance alone. It depends on a firm's ability to recognize, regulate, and integrate the impact of repeated exposure.

By shifting the focus from individual coping to systemic responsibility, firms can move from reactive management of strain to the deliberate cultivation of clarity, ethical integrity, and collective resilience.

Regulation vs suppression – developing a critical professional competence

In high-exposure legal environments, managing internal responses to grief, trauma, and loss is a professional competence. Lawyers encounter repeated exposure to human distress, conflict, and organizational disruption, and how they navigate these experiences shapes judgment, collaboration, and ethical clarity. Professional exposure is a continuum, not isolated events, and the same systems are engaged by both acute incidents and sustained pressure. Regulation is therefore not optional – it is an ongoing skill that maintains clarity, adaptability, and effectiveness across all aspects of practice.

Two very different approaches emerge: *suppression* and *regulation.*

1. *Suppression* seeks to remove emotional impact, often masking it beneath composure. While seemingly effective short-term, it comes at a cost:

- Consumes cognitive bandwidth, reducing capacity for complex decision making.
- Narrows thinking, increasing rigidity and reactive behavior.
- Weakens emotional awareness, empathy, and leadership capacity.

2. *Regulation*, by contrast, is an active professional skill. It does not mean therapy or overt emotional expression; it means:

- Acknowledging internal impact without becoming overwhelmed.
- Stabilizing attention and physiological responses.
- Returning to clear, flexible thinking that supports sound judgment.

Regulation preserves energy, allows efficient processing of exposure, and prevents cumulative load from silently eroding performance. Teams that regulate effectively maintain steadiness, anticipate risk, and preserve collaboration under pressure. Suppression, by contrast, leaves unresolved impact to resurface in narrowed thinking, irritability, or ethical blind spots. Regulation transforms unavoidable exposure into a manageable and sustainable part of professional life.

The one grain approach – practical navigation of grief and trauma

Without a structured way to manage cumulative exposure, even well-intentioned efforts at regulation can remain inconsistent or reactive.

To translate these principles into practice, a simple, structured approach can be helpful. Based on my experience working with legal professionals in loss-saturated environments, I use what I refer to as the One Grain Approach – a practical model developed in collaboration with my mentor, Rosemary Wanganeen,[1] for navigating cumulative exposure in a manageable and sustainable way.

The principle is straightforward. Meaningful change begins *one step at a time – one grain at a time*. You do not need to process the full weight of cumulative exposure at once. Progress begins with addressing a single unit of experience at a time – small, deliberate steps that, over time, restore clarity and reduce cognitive load. Even moving a single "grain" of your internal experience through the right process starts the shift. Over time, small grains accumulate, creating sustainable clarity, resilience, and integration.

Within the One Grain approach, the AAPI framework (Acknowledge,

Accept, Process, Integrate) provides the structured path for moving each grain through the "hourglass" of experience. See Table 1.

Table 1: The AAPI framework.

Step	Principle	Practical application
Acknowledge	Notice the cumulative impact of grief, trauma, or high-pressure exposure.	Leaders and teams actively notice patterns of strain, fatigue, or stress without judgment. Track recurring stressors across matters or clients.
Accept	Treat grief and trauma as operational realities, not personal weaknesses.	Normalize exposure and plan for its effect on attention, decision making, and collaboration. Signal to staff that these experiences are expected, not exceptional.
Process	Create structures to allow regulated reflection or decompression.	Implement structured debriefs, handovers, short pauses between matters, or peer support systems. Focus on cognitive load management – not therapy.
Integrate	Embed insights into firm culture, workflows, and leadership practice.	Update policies and procedures, formalize mentorship and support, signal acceptable pauses, and capture lessons from high-exposure cases to strengthen organizational learning.

Key insight: Sustainable change does not require resolving everything at once. Addressing even a single unit of accumulated experience can begin to restore clarity, reduce cognitive load, and improve professional effectiveness

This approach is designed to be practical, approachable, and scalable. It starts with the individual, yet supports team and organizational culture – aligning human experience with professional performance and supporting both individual capability and organizational effectiveness in high-pressure environments.

Practical skills for lawyers – managing exposure in practice

Lawyers operate in high-stakes, loss-saturated environments where repeated exposure to conflict, client distress, or human tragedy can accumulate unnoticed. Translating awareness of grief and trauma into practical skills allows legal professionals to maintain judgement, clarity, and sustainable performance. These practices are not about therapy – they are professional competencies that protect attention, decision making, and collaboration.

Because the nervous system does not sharply distinguish between everyday pressure and high-intensity events, small, consistent interventions play a critical role in maintaining cognitive clarity and preventing cumulative load. Key practical approaches include:

- *Structured pauses*. High-pressure work often encourages moving immediately from one file to the next, leaving little space for reflection or cognitive reset. Brief, structured pauses can dramatically improve regulation. This is particularly important given the continuous nature of stress activation in legal practice, where cognitive load can build even in the absence of a single defining event. A three- to five-minute mental reset before the next matter – breathing exercises, standing and stretching, or stepping outside – allow attention to return to baseline, preserve cognitive bandwidth, reduce reactivity, and enhance clarity for critical decisions.

  Even brief pauses that allow breathing to slow and attention to reset can help regulate the nervous system, lowering stress and improving focus. Over time, these brief pauses accumulate into meaningful cognitive and emotional resilience.
- *Debriefs*. Reflection is key to processing exposure, yet legal culture often discourages slowing down. Structured, short debriefs provide space to acknowledge what has occurred and recalibrate. Brief post-case discussions (10-15 minutes) focused on professional observations help process exposure, maintain team cohesion, and reveal patterns of cumulative strain.

  Debriefs can also reveal patterns of cumulative strain across cases or teams, allowing leaders to adjust workloads or provide targeted support before issues escalate.

- *Language and behavioral awareness.* The language used in legal teams shapes culture and emotional norms. Subtle shifts can normalize regulation without encouraging unprofessional disclosure. Subtle shifts in team language (e.g., "Let's reset before moving forward") and noticing signs such as irritability, fatigue, or perfectionism signal strain early, supporting regulation and timely intervention.
- *Early support.* Accessing professional or peer support is not a sign of weakness – it is a tool to preserve professional capacity. Encouraging use of peer support, mentoring, or firm-provided professional resources prevents cognitive overload, reduces burnout risk, and maintains ethical clarity.
- *Environmental considerations.* The physical workspace contributes to regulation and sustainable performance. Even small adjustments can make a difference that can meaningfully support sustainable performance. Simple design changes – such as access to natural light, quiet zones, or short walks – support attention restoration, reduce cognitive fatigue, and enhance emotional regulation.

Small, deliberate practices collectively strengthen regulation, preserve professional effectiveness, and transform cumulative exposure into sustainable performance. Integrating these approaches ensures lawyers and teams can maintain clarity, collaboration, and ethical decision making in a high-pressure, loss-saturated environment.

Collective resilience – a strategic reframe

Resilience research shows that individuals and teams can build skills to navigate pressure, uncertainty, and change – capabilities critical in modern legal practice. However, resilience alone does not fully address the unique exposure patterns of legal work. Lawyers manage high-pressure tasks while also encountering clients', colleagues', and organizational grief, trauma, and conflict. Understanding how these exposures shape professional judgement extends the resilience conversation.

Traditional narratives emphasize the individual lawyer who endures pressure, adapts, and continues to perform. Skills such as mental agility, stress management, and adaptive thinking remain foundational for sustainable practice.

Collective resilience reframes the conversation – individual performance and wellbeing are inseparable from the systems and environment around them. Lawyers thrive when teams and organizations actively support regulation, reflection, and recovery. In this view, resilience is not personal toughness alone – it is a relational and systemic capability shaped by leadership, culture, workflow design, and peer support.

Teams can bolster resilience by:

- *Normalizing discussion of pressure.* Acknowledge intensity without fear of stigma or judgement.
- *Encouraging early escalation.* Address challenges before they escalate into cognitive or ethical risk.
- *Supporting recovery after difficult work.* Structured debriefs, short resets, or peer support prevent accumulation of cognitive and emotional load.
- *Modelling regulation.* Leaders demonstrating steadiness and managing their own responses set the emotional bandwidth for the team.

Across cultures, healing and resilience have rarely been treated as purely individual tasks. Traditional societies emphasized communal support, ritualized reflection, and connection with natural rhythms. Modern research increasingly supports these insights – regulation is relational, and environments that allow pause, reflection, and connection improve cognitive clarity, emotional balance, and decision making.

The African philosophy of Ubuntu captures this principle: "I am because we are." In practice, an individual's ability to sustain judgement and performance depends on the surrounding system's capacity to support regulation, reflection, and recovery. Teams that foster collective resilience do more than protect individuals – they safeguard judgment, ethical clarity, and sustainable performance. Embedding structures, cultural norms, and leadership behaviors that support collective regulation strengthens a firm's capacity to navigate loss-saturated work without hidden accumulation of strain.

Strategic takeaway: Resilience is not solely a personal skill – it is a strategic, systemic property. Legal teams that embrace collective resilience, supported by appropriate structures, culture, and leadership behaviors, are better positioned to maintain performance, collaboration, and ethical clarity even under repeated exposure to loss, conflict, and high-stakes pressure.

Leadership and culture in law firms

Leadership shapes organizational culture, and in law firms, it is decisive. Culture is not just policies – it is what leaders model, tolerate, and reward. Leadership behaviors, priorities, and expectations set the norms for how teams operate, respond to stress, and navigate high-pressure environments.

Shifting how firms understand and respond to grief and trauma is fundamentally a leadership and change management challenge. Awareness alone does not change culture – practices become embedded when consistently applied, when accountability for team health is clear, and when leaders visibly model the behaviors they expect.

In grief-literate firms, leaders:

- Acknowledge the intensity of work without dramatizing it, signaling that attending to cognitive and emotional impact is a professional capability, not a weakness.
- Normalize pathways for support, including peer discussion, supervision, and structured debriefs, making these part of professional practice rather than remedial measures.
- Consistently embed pause, reflection, and recovery into workflows, demonstrating the connection between exposure management and sustainable performance.

Cultural change requires consistent practice, clear accountability and visible leadership

The organizational benefits are tangible – better decision making, earlier escalation of risk, stronger collaboration, higher talent retention, and enhanced resilience to cumulative stress. Exposure is treated as an operational reality, not an individual failing, fostering both accountability and support.

Research shows three conditions are critical to cultural transformation in law firms – consistency, accountability, and leadership. Leaders must apply these principles daily, ensuring that grief and trauma awareness is treated as a professional competence integrated into performance, collaboration, and ethical standards. Leadership, in this sense, is not only about strategy or outputs – it is about shaping systems and environments that enable lawyers to function optimally under high-stakes, loss-saturated work.

Steadiness in law – building grief-literate firms

Professionalism is not emotional absence – it is the ability to remain steady under pressure. Grief-literate legal environments are not softer – they are steadier, clearer, and ultimately more sustainable.

Resilience remains a critical capability in legal practice. The ability to adapt, recover, and perform under pressure will always matter. But in a profession defined not only by high-stakes work, but also by repeated exposure to conflict, loss, and human distress, resilience cannot rest solely at the individual level. The question is not whether lawyers are resilient enough – it is whether the environments in which they operate are designed to support that resilience over time.

Law will always involve loss. The strategic challenge for firms is whether they acknowledge that reality and build the capacity to regulate and integrate its impact, or allow it to shape judgement, behavior, and culture silently. Stress and trauma exist along the same continuum of exposure, and the consistent application of regulation determines whether that exposure sharpens or erodes professional judgement. Suppression may appear effective in the short-term, but over time it narrows thinking, reduces empathy, and erodes ethical clarity.

By recognizing exposure, embedding practical support, and shifting from suppression to regulation, firms strengthen both individual and collective resilience. Teams supported in this way sustain performance, escalate risk early, collaborate effectively, and maintain ethical clarity under pressure. The One Grain Approach offers a practical lens for this work – meaningful change begins one step at a time. Attending to a single "grain" of pressure, grief, or exposure allows individuals and teams to begin the shift toward steadiness, integration, and sustainable performance.

Across cultures, the capacity to navigate loss has rarely been viewed as purely individual. Modern legal practice echoes this insight – when firms create environments where experience can be acknowledged, processed, and integrated, lawyers are enabled not just to endure their work, but to sustain clarity, connection, and sound judgement within it. The Ubuntu philosophy captures this principle – individual performance is inseparable from the systems and teams that support it.

Grief-literate firms understand that high performance and emotional awareness are not opposites. By embedding regulation, reflection, and structured support into firm culture, organizations enhance judgement, ethical decision making, and long-term performance in a profession where human and commercial stakes are consistently high. In law, resilience sustains individuals; steadiness sustains firms. And it is steadiness – not mere endurance

– that allows legal organizations to thrive in a loss-saturated world. Even small, intentional steps – one grain at a time – can create lasting change for individuals, teams, and organizational culture alike.

Reference

1 Rosemary Wanganeen is a leading Aboriginal Australian grief and loss practitioner, founder of the Seven Phases to Integrating Loss framework, and chief executive officer of The Healing Centre for Griefology.

Chapter 4:
Neurodiversity in legal practice

By Danielle Gleicher-Bates and Emma Llanwarne, neurodiversikey

What neurodiversity means

As society has come to realize the need to better understand and embrace neurodiversity, so too has the legal sector. Modern-day legal practice necessitates a solid grasp of neurodiversity, in the contexts of both clients and the workplace.

So, what is neurodiversity? Neurodiversity encompasses all variations in "brain wiring" or, in other words, all neurotypes. This is a broad umbrella encompassing both "neurotypical" and "neurodivergent" minds. Neurocognitive functioning that fits in the "neuronormative" box – determined by the majority and influenced by what has historically been deemed socially "acceptable" – is what we call "neurotypical". Outside of that box, we find neurodivergence.

In recent years, society's understanding of neurodivergence has expanded. However, there is no exhaustive or universally agreed list of neurodivergent neurotypes. For the purposes of this chapter, we will focus on ADHD, autism and the Specific Learning Differences (SpLDs): dyscalculia, dysgraphia, dyslexia, dyspraxia/Developmental Co-ordination Disorder, and Developmental Language Disorder. Other neurodivergent neurotypes may include, for example, Tourette's, bipolar, sensory processing differences, and more.

ADHD, autism, and the SpLDs commonly co-occur with each other, and with health conditions. For example, autistic people are more likely to have a joint hypermobility syndrome, such as Ehlers-Danlos Syndrome connective tissue disorder. Mental health conditions such as depression or anxiety are also more common, primarily due to the stigma and barriers neurodivergent people face. Neurodivergence is also commonly misdiagnosed as a mental health condition.

Misconceptions and stereotypes are rife. The most common, across neurotypes, is that neurodivergence lowers intelligence, which is untrue.

What these neurotypes do have in common, however, is differences in executive function. Executive function is effectively the brain's built-in personal assistant, responsible for tasks like attention, prioritization, planning, emotional regulation, task initiation, memory, and self-assessing and moderating behavior. Whilst there are commonalities across neurotypes and amongst individuals with the same neurotype, there is still significant variation.

ADHD is characterized by differences in attention, concentration, physical and mental activity levels, motivation, and working memory. Common autistic areas of divergence include social communication and interaction, sensory processing, working memory, cognitive flexibility and interoception (our internal physical and emotional senses).

As the name suggests, the Specific Learning Differences diverge more narrowly. These differences can be very loosely categorized as linguistic (dyslexia, DLD), numerical (dyscalculia), and motor skills (dysgraphia, dyspraxia/DCD).

Differences in numerical and visuo-spatial processing, sequencing, working and long-term memory, and attention are associated with dyscalculia.

Dyslexia and DLD are easily confused, the latter being less well-known and researched. Whilst there is overlap between the two, i.e. differences in phonological processing, verbal learning and memory, DLD also features differences in grammatical understanding, written and spoken communication, and semantics, whereas dyslexia diverges in visuo-spatial processing and sequencing.

Dysgraphia diverges in the areas of written communication, working memory, fine motor skills, auditory and visuo-spatial processing, transcription, and sequencing. Dyspraxia/DCD is characterized by those shared differences, in addition to gross motor skills, sequencing, coordination, and proprioception (sensing force, the body's position and movement).

The disability cross-over

Before we go any further, let's address the elephant in the room – the tension between neurodivergence, disability identity, and disability in law. Not every neurodivergent person will be considered disabled for the purposes of the Equality Act 2010, nor will every neurodivergent (or neurotypical) person who is considered disabled under the Act self-identify as disabled. Self-identification is a personal preference, and of course, someone may self-identify as disabled but not satisfy the legal requirements. Ultimately, flexibility and accommodation are encouraged wherever possible. Inclusion benefits everyone.

In any case, the principles of this chapter can largely be applied in respect of both neurodivergence and disability. There are some nuances, of course.

Strengths-based thinking vs deficit-based assumptions

The neurodiversity paradigm promotes a strengths-based view of neurodivergence, rejecting the traditional deficit-focus – a distorted lens through which challenges are magnified, to the exclusion of strengths. Neurodivergent individuals, like anyone else, have areas of both strength and challenge. The difference is in distribution, with neurodivergent skill profiles typically having more pronounced peaks and troughs, certainly not flat-out inability. Unsurprisingly, the deficit-focus feeds into harmful stereotypes and stigma.

The inadequacies of the deficit-focus do not stop there, though. It fails to account for the nuance of those peaks and troughs entirely – that is, neurodivergent strengths and challenges can be contextual, even paradoxical. For instance, hyperfocus is often hailed, with good intentions, as a superpower. But, that very same ability can be inconvenient (try steering involuntary hyperfocus away from the "wrong" thing) and harmful (when you tune everything out, including your own hunger and thirst cues).

Identity-first vs person-first language

Following on from the deficit-focus and disability identity, the language an individual uses to self-identify comes down to personal preference. But, what do we mean by this, and how should you refer to someone else? The language we use to refer to neurodivergence (or disability) can be broken down into "identity-first" or "person-first". Using identity-first language, you would say: I *am* dyslexic, she *is* ADHD/an ADHDer, they *are* dyspraxic. Person-first language looks like: you *have* dysgraphia, he *has* autism, they *have* dyscalculia.

The former tends to be the preference among the wider neurodivergent community, as it discourages seeing an individual and their neurotype, and the challenges or barriers they face, as separate entities and experiences, or their neurotype as a defect to be eradicated or "cured". Instead, it encourages acceptance of neurodivergence as an integral part of who someone is. Person-first language suggests a degree of separation and distance between an individual and their neurotype. This approach discourages defining someone by their neurotype, which some people prefer, and others feel does not reflect the reality or impact. It is a matter of personal choice and it is important to respect an individual's preference.

Why law attracts – and challenges – neurodivergent thinkers

The intellectually challenging nature of law can be particularly rewarding when you think differently. Legal practice enables neurodivergent people to play to their strengths and preferences in a number of ways. We will take a look at the specific skills later on.

Despite the stereotypes about law, the sector provides a variety of opportunities attractive to neurodivergent thinkers. The multiple branches of the profession and range of roles mean there are options to suit almost anyone – whether that looks like fixed, regular hours or total control of your own practice. Self-employment, employment, consultancy, working in-house... there is no shortage of choice. Of course, this depends on the area of law you work in. The diverse range of practice areas offer varying demands, from the fast-paced and unpredictable, to the comparatively stable and consistent. Whether you are someone who needs constant change to stay motivated, or you baulk at the thought of last-minute case preparation, there is likely a fit for you.

For many neurodivergent people, the predictability and certainty of the law itself is what draws them to become a lawyer. In a society that is not considerate of your needs and has many unspoken and unwritten rules, many of which may not make sense to you, the relative stability and security of law can be enticing. Law can of course be rigid and restrictive, and pathways to progression tend to be carved out early on, and vertical rather than horizontal. Vertical progression typically offers additional responsibility, management, and remuneration, which may not offer the same incentive or sense of satisfaction for someone who is more interested in becoming highly specialized and niche.

However, as a very traditional profession, those unwritten and unspoken rules can be challenging. Navigating a profession like law is difficult for anyone, but it can be multiplied when factoring in notions of "professionalism". Not only are these ideals often implicit, but neurotypical-centric, rendering neurodivergence non-conforming by default. Although the legal profession has come a long way in relation to diversity, equity, and inclusion, we are not at the finish line yet, and despite encouragement to bring our authentic selves to work, it is not always safe to do so. It is unsurprising then when an internal conflict arises between deciding to disclose neurodivergence, or to be "openly" neurodivergent, and the need to actively work on self-promotion and business development.

Disclosure – choices, risks, and boundaries

Whilst the decision to disclose neurodivergence should only be made by the individual in question, it is essential that everyone appreciates this choice is neither simple nor binary. It may be influenced by numerous factors, and it can be difficult to ascertain whether the potential benefits outweigh the potential risks. In an ideal world, it would not be necessary to factor in the risk of discrimination and stigma, but, in reality, it is a legitimate concern, particularly if you have past experience of them. In addition, internalized ableism – the adoption of external ableist beliefs about yourself – can discourage disclosure.

Whether you are personally considering sharing you are neurodivergent, or looking to better understand colleagues and clients who may be deliberating this question, there are some general considerations to bear in mind. The point is not to scare anyone off from disclosure but to empower individuals to make informed decisions that are right for them in the circumstances, to promote better understanding all-round, and foster environments conducive to disclosure. This is especially important in the context of clients whose reluctance to disclose, from the outside, may not seem rational or proportionate to the potential cost to them.

Why? What outcome are you seeking? Does pursuing this outcome come with any risk or cost to you, and is it outweighed by the benefit? This will guide you later on. For instance, if the aim is to request reasonable adjustments, that influences who it is best to disclose to and what you share with them, which is also context-dependent.

Who? Think about the person or people to whom you are considering disclosing. Do you want to limit disclosure to a specific person or people? What is your relationship? Is trust established? Is it long-term or temporary? Are they supportive and knowledgeable about neurodivergence or disability? Are you aware of any use of stigmatizing language, behavior, or other indicators that they may respond dismissively, negatively, or discriminatorily?

What? Decide exactly what you are and are not comfortable disclosing beforehand, including whether that depends on the person. This will likely depend on the context too. Establishing your limits ahead of time can help with self-confidence, upholding personal boundaries, and preventing over-sharing under pressure. It is important to recognize that in order to obtain reasonable adjustments, you will be required to disclose some information.

When? Consider the timing of disclosure. Is there any urgency or a deadline? Is there a point at which it is more or less beneficial to disclose?

How? Is there a particular mode of communication you would like to use? E.g. email, an informal conversation. Would you benefit from someone else's support when you disclose, such as a friend, relative, or colleague? Is there a process or procedure to follow?

Psychological safety is key, even more so for anyone who has experienced trauma, discrimination, bullying, or harassment, all of which can present further barriers to disclosure.

Reasonable adjustments

As we have touched on, disclosure is usually required in order to obtain reasonable adjustments. However, reasonable adjustments can and should be made anticipatorily where possible as part of making accessibility and inclusion the starting point rather than an afterthought.

There is no definitive list of reasonable adjustments to make for someone who is neurodivergent, primarily because their needs are highly specific to them, often contextual, fluctuating, and influenced by environmental factors. This is increasingly true where there is any co-occurrence of neurotypes or otherwise. Additionally, not everyone will find the same adjustments helpful.

There are, however, common categories of adjustments to think about, with some examples:

- *Policy and procedure.* Creating a neurodiversity policy, adjusting existing policies and procedures.
- *Physical environment.* Heating, lighting, ventilation, use of space, clear signage, ergonomic and kinesthetic furniture, quiet spaces, acoustics.
- *Practical and organizational.* Reminders, movement and rest breaks, regular reviews, remote or hybrid working, flexi-working, staggered start and end times, admin support, providing information in advance, breaking tasks down into steps, extra time and deadline extensions, templates and precedents, do not disturb/focus hours, coaching, mentoring, accountability buddies.
- *Sensory supports.* Colored paper, screen tinting, colored overlays, noise cancelling headphones, fidgets, ear plugs, weighted pads or clothing, heat/cold packs, changes to dress code.

- *Communication.* Written instructions, communicating complex numerical information in multiple formats, e.g. as a diagram, and verbally, clear and explicit communication, specific modes of communication.
- *Assistive technology/tools.* Text-to-speech, dictation, grammar/spell checking, automation, time and task management apps, mind mapping software.
- *Interpersonal.* Neurodiversity training for teams to bridge differences and foster understanding, employee networks and socials.

For clients, additional or alternative adjustments may be available. For example, special measures in criminal cases can include intermediaries and communication aids, amongst others.

Practicing as a neurodivergent lawyer

In addition to the hard skills we typically associate with practicing law, lawyers rely on a broad range of soft skills. The most obvious is a keen sense of right and wrong, underpinning the professional ethics and integrity required in this position of trust. Foundational to that trust, emotional intelligence combined with effective communication allows lawyers to build rapport, persuade, exercise appropriate judgment, and sensitively tailor client care. Naturally, the ability to creatively problem-solve and think critically enables resolution of the most complex legal issues, aided by attention to detail. Resilience, flexibility, and adaptability are essential in a profession where unpredictability and high pressure are the baseline. Finally, the underdogs of soft skills – organization and time management – act as the scaffolding holding it all together.

Misconceptions and stereotypes would have you believe that being neurodivergent and a lawyer are mutually exclusive. Fortunately, this could not be further from the truth. It is no coincidence that the soft skills that make a good lawyer overlap with a number of common neurodivergent strengths.

Ironically, a number of the differences that neurodivergent people are stigmatized for lend themselves well to legal practice. When your brain interprets, processes, and learns information differently, you naturally think outside of the box and have a unique perspective, enhancing creative problem-solving and critical thinking. For instance, dyslexic big-picture thinking, autistic pattern recognition, and dyspraxic strategizing.

Many neurodivergent people excel at communication, whether they instinctively favor clarity and directness over social conformance, or are compelling story-tellers able to captivate any audience. Resilience, flexibility, and adaptability are typically not developed through choice but overcoming a long line of obstacles in a world built in conflict with neurodivergent needs, frequently encouraging an already strong sense of justice. Consequently, working under pressure often comes naturally, not least for a number of ADHDers whose high energy translates into being fast-acting and thinking. Emotional intelligence can be expressed through deep empathy, authenticity, and strong rapport-building, contrary to common stereotypes. For a lot of neurodivergent people, working on something in which they are passionately interested and care deeply about makes it easy to hyperfocus and employ meticulous attention to detail.

Soft skills can still pose challenges and barriers. Without adequate sector-wide education and training to increase understanding and acceptance of neurodivergence, the same communication differences that serve neurodivergent lawyers well can be misinterpreted negatively based on neuronorms. If you are comfortable doing so, email signatures can include a polite note alerting to differences. You do not necessarily need to mention your neurotype. It can be as simple as "I favor clear, direct communication" or "Despite my best efforts, I occasionally miss spelling errors and appreciate notification of them if important".

Differences in executive function can make managing organization and time management a fine balance which, depending on the person, may tip in either direction – rigidity or laxity. Here, accommodating these differences where possible and utilizing practical supports, tools, and technology can make all the difference – e.g. protected time to focus, reminders, task management apps, and booking appointments to accommodate schedule preferences. For neurodivergent people, emotional intelligence, attunement and depth often come with difficulty in turning down or regulating the "volume". This intensity can quickly become draining on the individual but can be managed – for instance, by limiting particularly emotionally charged work to certain times, and setting other personal boundaries, both with yourself and others.

Requesting reasonable adjustments

Requesting reasonable adjustments will realistically require some level of disclosure. Much like the process of deciding whether or not to disclose your neurodivergence, requesting reasonable adjustments often involves forethought and some preparation. The considerations in the disclosure section will assist in this.

Before you request reasonable adjustments, it can be helpful and increase your chances of success if you do some preparation in advance. Depending on the circumstances, including what you are requesting, in addition to whether this is a fresh disclosure or request, you may need to provide some form of evidence of your neurodivergence/disability. Although the focus is on your needs rather than a specific diagnosis or label, it can be more difficult if you have not been diagnosed, but do not let this put you off. Global problems accessing assessment, diagnosis, and support are increasingly recognized, with some organizations even offering to pay for private assessment.

Unless you think it is unlikely that you will request reasonable adjustments again, it will probably save you time and effort in future to create a file compiling your evidence and information on your needs, e.g. the specific reasonable adjustments (and any specific context as required), as well as any general areas in which you require adjustments. There are resources online with examples of reasonable adjustments. If you have created a "menu" or list already, you do not need to recreate it, but remember you may require context-specific or new reasonable adjustments you had not considered before.

Before making your request, look into whether there are any procedures or policies you need to follow, or whether there is a specific team or person to contact. It may be helpful to get in touch with them before making a request, particularly if you will need reasonable adjustments in circumstances you have not navigated before, or an "unknown", e.g. an undisclosed recruitment process.

This preparation does not need to be time-consuming or extremely in-depth. The purpose is making it easier for you, enabling you to feel confident and comfortable advocating for yourself and empowering you to stand firm or negotiate when necessary. Preparation can increase the chances of a request being successful, by enabling better understanding, and decreasing the chances of it being dismissed without finding a solution.

Masking, burnout, and imposter syndrome in legal environments

Masking, imposter syndrome, and burnout are not unique to neurodivergent people. Whether consciously or not, if you have ever changed the way you act or appear in order to fit in, you have masked. Similarly, anyone can fall victim to the chronic, baseless self-doubt and fear of exposure characteristic of imposter syndrome. Despite the very real mental, physical, and emotional exhaustion it causes, burnout is described by the WHO not as a medical condition but an "occupational phenomenon".

This is an all too familiar trifecta in law. What is it about legal environments that allows them to thrive? Toxic working practices and environments, compounded by the pressures of high caseloads, time-paucity, and cuts to funding, push lawyers to their limits. Add to grind and hustle culture the high stakes, competitive and adversarial nature of law, highly emotionally charged situations, and for some, frequent exposure to distressing material. Legal environments have all the ingredients – a recipe for masking, burnout, and imposter syndrome.

Being neurodivergent can make them more likely – not necessarily directly, but as a result of societal attitudes and treatment of neurodivergence. The three can occur independently but also fuel each other in a vicious cycle. Masking is often a protective mechanism – a concealment of neurodivergence – to avoid stigma, discrimination, bullying and harassment. However, masking all or most of the time can impact self-esteem, confidence, and mental health. Mix in the cumulative negative experiences neurodivergent people are subjected to throughout life, and society's constant gaslighting – accusations of a lack of effort, intelligence, willpower, and ability, or wanting "special treatment", to name but a few – and it's not hard to see why someone may start to doubt their own ability, perception, and experiences, and absorb ableist beliefs. When you really care about something and believe you are the problem, it is not unusual to try harder, or over-compensate, despite it being unsustainable in the long-term, and an almost certain route to burnout.

On a personal level, masking, imposter syndrome, and burnout result in poorer mental health, decreased capacity cognitively, physically, and emotionally, illness, and even having to leave or change jobs. It can be hard to get back on your feet and regain self-confidence without falling back into over-compensation or the bigger vicious cycle. Masking, imposter syndrome, and burnout can lead to reduced productivity, poor performance, increased absence and presenteeism, lowered morale, and reinforce unhealthy workplace culture. Ultimately, this can pose a risk to clients.

Managing your own working style with insight and self-compassion

Fortunately, there are steps you can take to protect yourself as a neurodivergent lawyer. By accommodating your own needs and playing to your strengths with awareness, acceptance, and compassion, you can avoid becoming stuck in toxic cycles.

Once you have a solid understanding of where your strengths lie, what challenges you, and any barriers (personal, systemic, structural or otherwise), you can begin to mold your working style. This assists in identifying specific reasonable adjustments, or at least, areas in which you require them. It is not always possible to predict exactly what you need until a situation crops up. However, it can be helpful to know that you typically require adjustments in a particular domain, e.g. in relation to organization. Creating a personalized "menu" or list is useful preparation and prevents being caught off-guard.

It is equally important to factor in working to your strengths wherever possible, e.g. prioritizing cognitively demanding tasks at times of day when you concentrate best, in addition to building in protective mechanisms to prevent those same things becoming harmful. Using the earlier hyperfocus example, you might set alarms at regular intervals for movement and rest breaks, and reminders to eat and drink.

To do this successfully, self-acceptance is non-negotiable and goes hand-in-hand with self-compassion. It is not uncommon, especially after late-diagnosis, to grieve and feel anger. For instance, regarding the challenges you have faced, have yet to face, and even of the person you thought you were, or would be. It can be mixed in with internalized ableism, an acceptance of external ableist beliefs about yourself, which often leads to over-compensation, and is a driver for masking, imposter syndrome, and burnout by attempting to maintain the unsustainable. Without self-acceptance, it is unlikely that you will give yourself the compassion you deserve, or consequently, work with your brain, instead of against it.

The importance of having a strong support network, made up of both allies and other neurodivergent people, cannot be understated. It is pivotal to self-confidence and acceptance to surround yourself with people who can relate to your experiences and have navigated the same obstacles, in addition to those who do not share your experiences but have your back nonetheless, and are crucial to making change.

Working with neurodivergent colleagues and clients

A supportive environment is one in which neurodivergence is respected, accepted, and empowered. A very simple change we can all make is to ensure the language we use is inclusive, avoiding language that pathologizes or stigmatizes. Similarly, we should be careful to prevent the pendulum swinging the other way, and inadvertently creating unrealistic (including superhuman) expectations of someone, whilst minimizing the systemic barriers they face.

Allyship is critical to creating a supportive, inclusive environment for neurodivergent people, fostering cohesion and a sense of community and belonging. These are all necessary for effective working relationships with both colleagues and clients. Effective allyship is a long-term and continuing process, but as a quick start guide, here are seven steps you can take:

1. *Presume positively, e.g. competence and ability.* This requires accepting that someone may think or do things differently or "incorrectly" according to convention, or require adjustments, ultimately achieving the same aim. What works for one person may not for another, and does not indicate anything about ability or competence.
2. *Listen to lived experience.* Professional expertise has its place but not to the exclusion of input from those with first-hand experience. Listening is critical to build understanding, trust, and empathy, and to preserve autonomy and dignity.
3. *Educate yourself – take responsibility for learning.* Do not expect or rely on those with lived experience to educate or inform you. Whilst many people are happy to help, be mindful of the burden and cost to them.
4. *Amplify voices.* Highlight, seek out, and provide a platform for the voices that ordinarily would not be heard or listened to.
5. *Speak up.* When something isn't right, say so. It can be difficult and risky for impacted individuals to raise issues. Bullying, harassment, and discrimination should never be tolerated. Importantly, this does not mean speaking for, or over, anyone.
6. *Enable through empowerment.* This is an ongoing process that boils down to dismantling barriers and avoiding paternalism. It includes making reasonable adjustments, and considering accessibility and inclusion. It can be more informal too, e.g. moral support. Conversely, actions like micro-management are disempowering.
7. *De-center yourself.* By de-centering the majority as the starting or reference point, we naturally consider other perspectives, and move away from accessibility and inclusion being an afterthought, towards being the baseline. De-centering also facilitates challenging social norms like neuronormativity.

Making reasonable adjustments

It is easy to think reasonable adjustments are confined to formal processes under the territory of HR or occupational health, specific provisions in court like special measures, or even to explicit requests. However, with some thought, making reasonable adjustments can be integrated into everyday practice, by considering accessibility and inclusion from the outset, whatever you are planning or doing. Follow the principle of "nothing about us, without us" and refrain from making any decisions without the input of those impacted. Maintaining autonomy and dignity are top priorities.

This proactivity will also assist with ensuring anticipatory reasonable adjustments are made. The process begins with patience, understanding, and respect – reasonable adjustments are not special treatment or an unfair advantage, but a means of addressing the barriers individuals face primarily because society, including the workplace and legal system, is not designed with neurodivergent or otherwise disabled people as a priority. The purpose is to enable individuals' full participation and empowerment to realize their potential. It is important to tackle attitudinal barriers that arise in response to requests for or implementation of reasonable adjustments.

Early identification of individual needs permits early action and implementation. The sooner you know, the sooner you can dismantle or reduce the barriers for someone. When an individual discloses they are neurodivergent or disabled, or requests reasonable adjustments, listen carefully, and take what they say on board and seriously. Lived experience is invaluable – individuals are the experts of their own experiences – and whilst this input can be supplemented by professional advice, it should not be completely excluded or overridden. Listening to lived experience is especially important in relation to any reasonable adjustments an individual has already tried and found ineffective, saving time, effort, and potentially money.

Signposting to appropriate services such as occupational health, Access to Work, and even diagnostic services can bolster the support available to an individual. It is important to remember that not everyone can access the services and resources they need, or will know what they require. This process should be collaborative, flexible, and ongoing, enabling continued assessment of the effectiveness of reasonable adjustments to find the right solution.

As for what not to do, anything that disempowers, dismisses, or discriminates is a no-go. This includes forcing reasonable adjustments onto someone which they do not agree with, in addition to making decisions or speaking for them, unless agreed. Comments suggesting neurodivergence or disability is an excuse, or that reasonable adjustments are unnecessary, unfair, or a burden or inconvenience, are never acceptable. Ensure you do not disclose someone's neurodivergence, disability, or reasonable adjustments without their consent, inadvertently or otherwise. Finally, remember there are significant barriers in accessing assessment, diagnosis, and support, as well as substantial service and funding cuts, before refusing reasonable adjustments outright without exploring all options.

Serving clients' best interests and needs

It goes without saying that reasonable adjustments, in addition to wider accessibility and inclusion, serve clients' best interests and needs. Beyond the practical benefits to clients, they are core to ensuring access to justice, fairness, and avoiding discrimination. Combined with understanding, empathy, and patience, prioritizing and accommodating clients' needs can facilitate building rapport, trust, and openness, in addition to enabling their full participation and engagement.

Familiarizing yourself with individual neurodivergent neurotypes and how they may outwardly present can lead to better outcomes, improved advice and representation. Depending on the precise service being offered, it may be appropriate to enquire about neurodivergence and reasonable adjustments in any client onboarding process, or provide information setting out what to expect as a client in addition to material about reasonable adjustments.

Being proactive regarding reasonable adjustments and demonstrating a strengths-based understanding of neurodivergence could be the reassurance that clients wary of disclosure or requesting reasonable adjustments need. Not everyone will know what to expect as a client, what adjustments they need, or are available. Individuals may worry that their neurodivergence will be weaponized against them or lead to discrimination, particularly if they have had similar experiences before.

Identifying neurodivergence and reasonable adjustments as early as possible in the client relationship is preferable, enabling appropriate measures to be put in place as soon as possible. This is especially pertinent where the court or other third parties need to be notified in advance. Proactivity and timeliness are even more important when neurodivergence is suspected, requiring expert assessment and reports, or where there is already a diagnosis, an assessment of specific needs is necessary.

Where neurodivergence is relevant to the legal matter itself, early identification and intervention can be life changing. The impact may not necessarily be on the outcome of the matter, but may otherwise alter the trajectory of an individual's life. For instance, in criminal or family proceedings, where someone is able to gain access to services, support, or treatment they would otherwise not have, and prevent re-offending or the need for future intervention into family life.

Chapter 5:
Time management and prioritization

By Nikki Alderson

Introduction

The legal profession is built around time. Commonly measured in six-minute units, time is recorded and billed, and time-based targets scrutinized. Yet, despite the central importance of time within legal practice, many lawyers feel they have very little control over it, and certainly never enough of it. In coaching sessions, one of the most common challenges that solicitor and barrister clients raise, when discussing their careers, productivity, and wellbeing, is time. The phrase "there simply are not enough hours in the day" crops up regularly in conversations across the profession, as if a categoric fact rather than an internal feeling.

Almost 80 percent of legal professionals surveyed in 2025 reported experiencing feelings associated with burnout at least "sometime" within the past year.[1] In the same year, according to a lawyer burnout and time-use survey, nearly half of lawyer responders spent seven or more hours each week on administrative or non-specialist tasks, such as summarizing documents and managing timelines, reducing the remaining time available for high value legal work such as analysis, strategy, and client advice.[2] Taken together, these figures reveal something important about modern legal practice. The challenge is not simply the volume of work lawyers face. It is how their time is fragmented, interrupted, and often dictated to by external demands.

Yet time is constant, of course. Every professional receives the same 24 hours in a day. The solutions lie in how those hours are managed, structured, and protected. For many lawyers, the issue is not the absence of time but the absence of time ownership. Competing deadlines, demanding clients, internal expectations, and constant digital communication create the sense that time belongs to everyone else. The result is a working pattern where lawyers spend much of the day reacting rather than deciding.

This chapter explores why lawyers struggle with time, burnout avoidance, and how to manage competing stakeholders without sacrificing focus, wellbeing, or professional standards. It also introduces practical solutions that help busy legal professionals manage competing stakeholders and deadlines to regain control of their time. Demonstrably, time ownership is not about squeezing more work into the day. Understanding how to regain ownership of time has become one of the most important professional skills a lawyer can develop. It is about making conscious choices about what deserves attention, what needs to be actioned and when, and how that can be delivered effectively.

Why lawyers struggle with time

The legal profession operates within a culture that places significant pressure on time. Billable hour targets, client expectations, and the unpredictable nature of legal work create an environment where time feels frequently under threat. In many firms, lawyers are expected to bill around six to seven-and-a-half hours per day, which often requires working approximately ten hours per day once non-billable work is included.[3] Workload stress is widespread, with 74 percent of lawyers reporting high stress related to workload demands.[4] However, many of the challenges lawyers face with time arise not only from workload but also from the way time is perceived and discussed.

The myth of "not enough hours"

Saying there are not enough hours in the day implies that time itself is the problem. In reality, time is fixed. What can change is how it is allocated, protected, and prioritized. Language matters too. When professionals repeatedly say they do not have time, they reinforce the belief that time is something external and uncontrollable. This removes personal agency and places responsibility elsewhere.

Time "ownership", as opposed to "management", requires a shift in mindset. Rather than saying there is no time, the more accurate statement is that something else has been prioritized, whilst other priorities have been downgraded. We can achieve a better sense of our own agency when we own as opposed to manage time. This does not mean lawyers are free from pressure or unrealistic demands. The profession contains genuine constraints and deadlines. However, recognizing where choice still exists, even if only in a small tweak of language, is an essential step in regaining control.

Cultural pressures within the profession

Likewise, the structure of legal practice contributes significantly to time pressure. It is not uncommon to see busy-ness worn as a badge of honor, rather than something that can actually threaten the ability to do a good job or maintain a positive state of health and wellbeing. Long working hours are common, with many lawyers routinely working 60-80 hours per week in high pressure environments.[5] Compounding matters, billable targets reward hours worked and presenteeism rather than necessarily the effectiveness of those hours. Lawyers may feel compelled to remain constantly available to demonstrate commitment or responsiveness. This creates a culture where stepping away from work can feel uncomfortable, even when it is necessary for focus and indeed recovery. A recent Wellbeing at the Bar report revealed that 27.2 percent of respondents felt they were not managing well with their workloads, with inevitable consequences to productivity and focus.[6]

Junior lawyers often feel particularly exposed to these pressures. Due to power imbalances, whether real or perceived, they may be reluctant to question instructions, re-negotiate deadlines or clarify priorities. The idea of sitting down with managers or seniors to discuss task lists and capacity with a view to asking what might be de-prioritized can feel a bridge too far. The result is a growing list of tasks that appear equally urgent. Over time, this constant pressure can erode the ability to not only prioritize but also function effectively. According to a 2022 report commissioned by the Bar Council, "Life at the Young Bar", approximately one in six young barristers indicated a desire to leave the profession due to heavy workloads and fears of burnout.[7]

The impact of remote and hybrid working

The pandemic fundamentally altered how lawyers work. Remote working brought greater flexibility for many professionals, and studies showed that working from home had the potential to significantly boost productivity.[8] The downside was that it also blurred the boundaries between professional and personal time. Whilst the commute disappeared, the working day expanded to fill the gap. Emails were answered and phone calls taken earlier in the morning and later in the evening. Meetings increased. Informal conversations that previously happened quickly in person turned into scheduled, often back-to-back, and seemingly incessant, calls.

Many lawyers discovered that flexibility did not automatically lead to better time management. Almost 60 percent of Life in the Law 2020/21 Survey participants reported being more concerned about increased pressures around work–life balance. Participants reported difficulty in maintaining boundaries, keeping motivated, and being able to concentrate on tasks.[9]

The role of digital communication

The digital age has transformed professional life. Emails, messaging platforms, and collaboration tools enable rapid communication and efficient document sharing. But while technology allowed work to continue during the pandemic, it also created a sense of constant availability. Without clear boundaries the digital working environment risks encouraging constant reaction, that "always on" pressure. Even today, these same tools continue to create interruptions. Every notification invites attention. Every message has the ability to demand an immediate response.

The difficulty is that digital communication rarely distinguishes between urgency and importance. Everything arrives in the same inbox, competing for attention. When lawyers spend large portions of the day responding to incoming requests, meaningful progress on important work becomes harder to achieve. Almost 65 percent of participants in Law Care's Life in the Law study agreed or strongly agreed they needed to check emails outside of regular hours, and 28 percent felt the need to be available to clients 24/7.[10] Emails, instant messages, and pinging notifications sound their arrival throughout the day. This constant digital noise of modern professional life comes with consequences too. Cognitive research indicates that, after an interruption, it takes an average of 23 minutes to fully regain focus on that same task.[11]

Annabel,[12] mid-ranking, well respected barrister, struggled with her own unhelpful use of technology so much post-pandemic that she diagnosed herself as having a WhatsApp addiction, describing the debilitating consequences of constant, and repeated, checking of the app during the working day. Desperate times called for desperate measures, given the obvious knock-on consequence to her work productivity. She would get her friend and colleague to lock her phone away for her in her desk to ensure she had no access to it throughout the working day to avoid this detrimental habit.

Focus, energy, and avoiding burnout

Time management discussions often focus on scheduling. Yet productivity also depends on energy. A diary filled with carefully planned tasks is only effective if the individual has the mental capacity to complete them. Persistent time pressure can gradually erode energy levels. When professionals feel constantly behind schedule they may extend their working hours, reduce breaks, and sacrifice recovery time. Whilst initially this can appear productive, over time it becomes unsustainable.

The relationship between time pressure and burnout

When professionals feel permanently behind, the stress response remains activated. Deadlines begin to feel relentless and recovery time becomes limited. Over time, this pattern can contribute to exhaustion, reduced concentration, and declining job satisfaction. Understanding the causes of time pressure is therefore not simply a productivity exercise. It is also a wellbeing priority.

Recognizing early warning signs is essential. Burnout is characterized by exhaustion, reduced professional efficacy, and emotional detachment from work. Nearly 60 percent of legal professionals reported poor mental wellbeing, according to a survey of over 1,500 professionals in the legal sector, and around 34 percent of them having considered leaving the profession due to burnout, impacting on long-term talent retention and career satisfaction.[13]

In order to stay well within the legal profession, a structured plan was found to be essential to preserve wellbeing for Harriet, partner in a law firm, who came to me when she had "had enough". She was unhappy, unfulfilled, overworked, burnt out, stressed, fed up, under appreciated. She hadn't had a holiday for well over a year, was working every weekend and felt trapped on a treadmill of "living someone else's dream", not wanting to continue, but feeling pressured to do so for fear of letting herself or her family down. These are certainly not isolated experiences. Harriet was giving serious consideration to a change within her existing role or even an all-out career change. Either way, she recognized that, in order to do so, she would need a structured plan to preserve her mental health in the short-term, and indeed went about making one – setting boundaries around working hours and the volume of work brought home to work on at evenings and weekends.

Protecting energy as well as time

Time ownership involves better energy-protection as well as task management. "Me time" should not be considered indulgent but instead simply that it makes good business sense. There is a reason on airplanes that, before helping others, we are asked to first fit our oxygen masks. On the same point, it is not possible to pour from an empty cup. Some practical examples for protecting time and energy include:

- Scheduling focused work during periods of peak concentration.
- Taking short breaks between demanding tasks.
- Ensuring adequate recovery outside working hours.

These practices support sustained performance rather than short bursts of overwork.

Suzy's example touches on a number of these different aspects. Having done a coaching exercise together, she identified that her life balance was exceptionally low down on the list of priorities. She challenged herself to push past her original approach which was to say, "Well that's just the way it is – I haven't tried anything but get on with it." She didn't know how to ask for support, hated doing so in fact, and had become conditioned into thinking that to do otherwise was a sign of weakness in the cut-throat corporate world. That said, with some gentle coaching encouragement, she felt empowered to ask for help both up the chain from bosses, and down, by delegating certain tasks to more junior members of the team. For the first time in around ten years, she enjoyed not working as late for a whole week, and things improved.

The role of routines

Routines provide stability in busy professional environments. Morning planning rituals, structured breaks, and end of day reviews can all contribute to a sense of control. For example, beginning the day by identifying the three most important tasks creates clarity before emails and messages begin to compete for attention. Identify those tasks before opening the inbox. Similarly, factoring in a 15-minute window to conduct a brief review at the end of the day helps professionals celebrate the things they have achieved that day whilst preparing to hit the ground running the following morning.

A barrister client, Julia, seeking to regain a sense of control, found that when she learned to say no, her sense of wellbeing improved immeasurably as she prioritized her own needs over others and established boundaries within her working day. After one particular session of embedding her changed habits, she reported feeling better and more relaxed already.

Single tasking

Multitasking is often seen as a valuable professional skill. In reality, it frequently reduces efficiency and creates a sense of doing lots of things badly rather than a few things well. Switching attention between tasks requires cognitive effort. As mentioned, each interruption increases the time required to regain focus. Single tasking, where attention is directed fully toward one activity at any one time, often leads to faster and higher quality outcomes, and allows lawyers to engage deeply in complex technical work.

Tracy, senior associate and career break returner, observed through coaching sessions that, with the right focus, she was able to achieve more quality time at work working or at home playing with her children, if the focus was purely that – work or children respectively.

Managing competing stakeholders and deadlines

Legal professionals rarely work in isolation. Partners, clients, colleagues, and external professionals all have expectations. As a result, many lawyers experience the challenge of multiple stakeholders requesting work at the same time. The key skill is not simply completing the work but managing the expectations surrounding it.

Recognizing stakeholder-driven urgency and the importance of communication

Often, urgency arises not from the work itself but from how it is communicated. A request may arrive with the phrase "as soon as possible" or "when you have a moment". Without further clarification, these phrases can create uncertainty. Effective communication is central to time ownership. A common mistake I observe in lawyer clients is assuming that every request is equally urgent, leading to an overwhelming list of immediate tasks. In reality, many stakeholders are open to negotiation when timelines are discussed openly. It is worth considering how best to communicate what is truly needed. When lawyers clearly explain their existing commitments, stakeholders can make more informed decisions.

It is hugely valuable therefore to establish clear communication protocols around deadlines and expectations. For example, create realistic expectations for clients by communicating honest timelines around current capacity, demonstrating professionalism, whilst seeking from them revised consideration around the genuine urgency, or otherwise, of their request. Alternatively, think of your own deadline, and add on a day or two. Communicate this to whoever needs to know – client, manager, co-worker – and see if there is any push back. Lawyers often believe they have to turn things around by return, but actually when they start communicating deadlines they have set themselves, they soon realize many are self-inflicted and unhelpful, as opposed to client-led or demanded.

Boundary-setting as a professional competence

Boundary setting can sometimes be misunderstood as inflexibility, unhelpfulness, even refusal. In reality, it should be considered a core professional skill. Many clients start their coaching journey accepting they have people pleasing tendencies and have fallen into the trap of saying yes to everything, which consequently sees them doing everything badly rather than a few things well. Clear boundaries protect the quality of legal work. When lawyers attempt to complete too many tasks simultaneously, the risk of mistakes increases.

Setting boundaries does not mean rejecting responsibility. It means ensuring work is completed to an appropriate standard. Professionals who communicate boundaries effectively are often perceived as organized and reliable. Plus, knowing how to respect your own boundaries and time sends a clear message to others to do the same.

Jo, a barrister struggling to use her time productively, saw the need for structure and efficiency to help. She achieved this by creating clear demarcations between work and non-work to readily identify the start and end of the working day. In less than a week, she was reporting huge benefits to both productivity and wellbeing, feeling more relaxed, balanced, and calm, which meant she found things easier and more enjoyable.

Likewise, Angela, a career break returner, initially struggled with setting out her stall when it came to managing client expectations, being all too aware of the expectation that lawyers are "always on". By setting her own limits around email sign off and out of office notifications, she soon realized others became more respectful of her boundaries too.

Practical, sustainable solutions for busy legal professionals

While mindset shifts are important, sustainable time ownership also requires practical, systemic solutions. Ultimately, the goal of time ownership is not simply increased productivity. The aim is to create working patterns that support long-term professional effectiveness and wellbeing.

Time ownership begins with the recognition that not all tasks deserve equal attention. Rather than reacting automatically to incoming requests, find benefit from pausing to assess the true importance of each task. This requires conscious decision making, asking questions such as:

- Is this genuinely urgent?
- What will happen if this is completed tomorrow rather than today?
- What other priorities will be delayed if I focus on this now?

Time ownership places the lawyer back in the role of decision maker rather than first responder.

Distinguishing "urgent" and "important" and re-ordering priorities

When lawyers develop clear prioritization systems they often experience:

- Improved concentration;
- Reduced stress;
- Better quality work; and
- Greater professional satisfaction.

One of the most powerful shifts in time management occurs when lawyers learn to distinguish between tasks that are urgent and tasks that are important. Urgent tasks demand immediate attention. Important tasks contribute to long-term outcomes, strategic progress, or professional development.

The challenge is that urgent tasks are often louder. Emails arrive. Messages appear. A colleague requests a quick review. These tasks can feel pressing even when they do not contribute significantly to long-term goals. Without a clear framework for prioritization, urgent work will dominate the day.

The "4Ds" prioritization framework

Several practical frameworks can support this decision-making process. One of the most widely recognized is the "urgent and important" matrix, sometimes known as the Eisenhower time management matrix.

Tasks fall into four categories:

1. *Important and urgent.* These tasks require immediate attention. Deadlines that cannot move or urgent client matters fall into this category.
2. *Important but not urgent.* This is where strategic work lives. Business development, professional development, and proactive planning are often important but easily postponed.
3. *Urgent but not important.* These tasks may feel pressing but do not necessarily require your direct attention. Delegation is often appropriate.
4. *Neither urgent nor important.* These tasks provide little value and can frequently be removed altogether.

Put another way, with every task request, perform the "4Ds" priority sense check:

1. *Do:* Is this something you have to do, and do now? This is both urgent and important and needs to be done straightaway.
2. *Diarize:* Is this something you have to do, but it can wait? This is important but not urgent, and hence capable of being diarized.
3. *Delegate:* Is this something that, whilst important, is not something that you yourself need to attend to? If so, think about to whom you can delegate this task. Many professionals hesitate to delegate because they believe it will take longer to explain the task than to complete it themselves. While this may occasionally be true in the short-term, effective delegation builds team capability over time. It also allows lawyers to focus on work that genuinely requires their expertise, improves their own leadership skills, whilst providing less experienced team members with a greater degree of responsibility, bringing them on faster as a result.
4. *Delete:* For all the other time-sapping activities that are neither urgent nor important – and in this category I often see clients tumbling down social media rabbit holes which they accept are an utter waste of time – get rid of them completely. Strike them off the list. Delete them.

Many lawyers spend a vast amount of time responding to urgent requests while neglecting important work that supports long-term progress. The goal of the 4Ds time ownership assessment is to rebalance this unhelpful practice.

Abigail, a self-confessed perfectionist, was struggling with delegation, with the inadvertent consequence that, by covering for others, colleagues began to look more capable than her, and she was suffering overwhelm and burnout. Recognizing the need for her team to "fail to learn", she practiced delegation. Whilst unsettled about relinquishing a degree of control, she reaped the rewards of this practice and soon saw positive results in terms of her own career progression as well.

The 4Ps – planning around priorities, pausing, and being present

Another useful concept is the idea of planning around priorities rather than noise. The Four Ps provide techniques to create space for focused work, and can be summarized as follows.

1. Plan

Structuring the day, and week, around important work rather than simply reacting to incoming demands, and keeping them under review, is a powerful tool for managing competing demands. Planning allows lawyers to identify pressure points early and communicate proactively with stakeholders. Weekly planning also provides an opportunity to ensure important tasks are scheduled rather than postponed indefinitely. A bit of color coding in a calendar never goes amiss either!

Marzena, consummate lawyer list-writer, acknowledged that her lists were often unachievable and provided her with the constant fear of being behind or failing. Instead of devising such long task lists, she devised a five-minute daily review at the end of each working day when she would run through the important tasks and double-check she was on track. As a result, she performed more productively in the workplace, procrastinated far less, and remained much more calm and positive.

Similarly, the poor working conditions of Isabelle, international barrister, became exacerbated by an inability to identify what her working day should look like and how she could communicate this effectively to clerks. She was too busy, taking on more work than she could manage, and was fast becoming drained, exhausted, and overwhelmed. A clear plan of her day and week, with well-established and non-negotiable boundaries around working hours, enabled her to regain control and composure, having an obvious knock-on beneficial effect to her wellbeing, both physically and emotionally.

2. Prioritize

Identify which tasks truly require attention today and which can be scheduled for later. Find a daily prioritization ritual that works for you. For example, at the beginning of each day, or for 15 minutes before logging off at the end of the working day, identify a small number of key priorities. This might involve selecting three tasks that must be completed before the end of the day. By focusing attention on a limited number of priorities, lawyers reduce the risk of becoming overwhelmed by a long task list. To decide in what order to put tasks, apply the Brian Tracy *"Eat that Frog"* approach – treating those big, awful, and time-consuming tasks as if needing to eat a live frog. Better to get that done first on the list, then any task thereafter will feel easy!

Finally, in situations where workload exceeds capacity, de-prioritization may also be necessary. Open discussions with supervisors or colleagues can help identify which tasks must take precedence.

"It's not in my pay grade" became a non-negotiable mantra for Helen, a career break returning client, as a means by which to categorize things into priorities and become more emboldened around saying no.

3. Pause

Before responding to new requests, take a moment to assess their significance. Draw breath and pause before giving a more considered answer.

4. Be Present

When attention is constantly divided, decision making becomes reactive, errors become more likely, and complex legal analysis becomes harder to sustain. In contrast, when lawyers create uninterrupted periods of focus, quality of thinking improves significantly. Presence allows professionals to engage fully with the task in front of them. It supports clearer judgment and more efficient progress. Use the Pomodoro technique (short, 30-minute timed bursts of concentrated task activity) or longer time-blocking chunks for other tasks requiring deeper dive concentration. Be fully present in whatever task is being undertaken at any one time. Unplug from digital devices where necessary.

I see clients, particularly working parents, attempting to wear too many hats all at once and achieving neither peace nor productivity as a result. Focus on the task in hand in isolation. If you are with friends or family, be with them fully, not checking your work phone for emails. When at work, be fully tuned in, not constantly checking WhatsApp messages, for example, for updates on childcare arrangements.

Emma found time-blocking an effective method of time management. She found self-imposed pressure to work in those blocks ensured she remained focused and got tasks done quicker. It also provided a huge sense of achievement, improving her self-confidence and more workplace calmness and contentment.

Structured weekly reviews

A weekly review provides the foundation for effective planning. Consider it your weekly time audit. During this process:

- Review completed work from the previous week;
- Identify existing deadlines and upcoming meetings;
- Schedule time for important longer-term projects; and
- Assess capacity, particularly for new work.

This structured reflection ensures that goals stay in sharp focus, important tasks stay visible, and things can also be easily reviewed. Then do similar on a daily basis for each of the tasks required that day. To start you off, download the free weekly/ monthly review exercise from my website.[14]

Technology boundaries

Technology has enormous potential to improve efficiency. Artificial intelligence tools, document automation, and digital research platforms can significantly reduce administrative workload. However, as has also been demonstrated, technology can also create distraction. Setting boundaries around digital communication can help professionals maintain focus. Examples include:

- Scheduling specific times to check email;
- Disabling all, or at least non-essential, notifications; and
- Using digital tools to organize tasks rather than simply store messages.

When used intentionally, and with a focus on lawyers "controlling the controllable", technology becomes a support rather than a source of interruption.

Supporting career break returners

Finally, for lawyers returning from career breaks, structured time systems can be particularly valuable. Returning professionals may initially feel pressure to prove their commitment or catch up quickly with colleagues. Clear prioritization systems help maintain focus on high value work rather than reactive tasks. Support from clerks, practice managers and colleagues can also play an important role in managing workload expectations during this transition.

Andrea is a great example, struggling with the challenges of the 5pm nursery collection deadline, digital distractions and open plan office, complete with frequent interruptions to her work from more junior colleagues seeking guidance. She soon devised a "stop and go" plan – ear buds in or out – which signaled when she could and could not be disturbed; her very own personalized "Do not disturb" sign for the office.

Likewise, Michaela, a senior associate career returner, observed that this challenge seemed to increase with changes in priorities and working arrangements oftentimes "forced" upon her due to nursery closing times etc. She soon acknowledged the need to re-set the firm's expectations of her working hours on her return, and re-established boundaries to accommodate the need to leave at a certain time.

Conclusion

Time is one of the most valuable resources available to legal professionals. Yet within the demands of modern practice, it can easily feel out of reach. The shift from time pressure to time ownership begins with recognizing that, while time itself is fixed, how it is used remains entirely within our influence.

Small changes in how time is approached can produce significant results over the course of a legal career, even, for example, by undertaking a simple language reframe, from "time management" to "time ownership". Plus, being reassured that ownership is not a single decision – it is an ongoing professional skill. By distinguishing urgency from importance, communicating effectively with stakeholders, protecting energy, and implementing practical planning systems, lawyers can regain a sense of control over their working day.

Time ownership does not eliminate pressure entirely. Legal practice will always involve deadlines, complexity, and competing demands. However, with the right mindset and systems in place, professionals can, as we have seen, navigate these challenges with greater clarity and resilience.

References

1 Rev: *4 in 5 Lawyers Are Burned Out: Can AI Be the Lifeline? Survey Results, 2025.* www.rev.com/blog/lawyer-burnout

2 Rev: *Time Management For Lawyers: Proven Strategies*, 2025. www.rev.com/blog/time-management-for-lawyers

3 www.fishbowlapp.com/post/how-many-hours-per-day-on-average-do-you-have-to-work-to-bill-7-hours-per-day

4 https://communities.lawsociety.org.uk/Uploads/x/c/u/resilience-wellbeing-survey-updated-infographic-2019.pdf

5 www.lawcare.org.uk/wp-content/uploads/2025/09/lawcare-lifeinthelaw-v6-final-1.pdf

6 www.barcouncil.org.uk/resource/bar-council-s-wellbeing-at-the-bar-report-2025.html

7 www.barcouncil.org.uk/resource/life-at-the-young-bar-report.html

8 www.kcl.ac.uk/news/study-shows-working-from-home-has-potential-to-significantly-boost-productivity.

9 www.lawcare.org.uk/wp-content/uploads/2025/09/lawcare-lifeinthelaw-v6-final-1.pdf
10 https://lawcare.org.uk/life-in-the-law/
11 Mark, G. (2018). *BrainBased Tips for Sharpening Your Focus* (UC Irvine research cited). www.forbes.com/councils/forbescoachescouncil/2018/12/11/brain-based-tips-for-sharpening-your-focus/
12 All case study names have been changed to preserve client confidentiality.
13 https://lawcare.org.uk/wp-content/uploads/2025/09/Life-in-the-Law-2025.pdf
14 www.nikkialdersoncoaching.com/free-downloads/

Chapter 6: **Decision making under pressure**

By Jean-Baptiste Lebelle and Alice Boullier de Branche, A&O Shearman

Decision making lies at the heart of a lawyer's work. It can take place under pressure, in urgent circumstances, and often with incomplete information. In a legal world where the pace is relentless, where the stakes are high, and where a culture of constant availability is deeply ingrained, the ability to make good decisions is one of the most critical skills for a legal professional. Yet this skill is rarely taught as such, and it is often regarded as an innate talent rather than as an ability that can be developed and refined.

Lawyers must constantly and daily make decisions across very different registers. Internally, as managers, they face ongoing trade-offs – whether or not to hire in order to meet the needs of associates who demand additional resources, or conversely to avoid taking risks and preserve the profitability of the team and, more broadly, of the firm. They must listen to their team's requests and consider raising compensation, even when it would be difficult to increase billing rates in a context where clients are increasingly reluctant to accept such increases, knowing that retaining talent is a strategic imperative. They must sometimes agree to let an associate attend training when a major hearing is being prepared and every resource counts.

In their relationship with clients, the decisions are no less complex. The lawyer must choose a course of action to advise the client, weighing the risk that such a decision entails. The lawyer must sometimes decline a matter because it will not be profitable, because the firm lacks the internal resources to handle it, or because it will not be possible to deliver within the required timeframe. In the guidance the lawyer provides, there is always a decision at play when choosing the advice considered most suited to the client's needs – the one that will present the best balance between benefit and risk.

This chapter offers tools for developing this essential skill. Decision quality is closely linked to the wellbeing of the professional and to the work environment. Studies show that boundaries between professional and personal life are increasingly porous for lawyers, which has direct consequences on their capacity for judgment. It is therefore essential to approach decision making not only from a technical standpoint, but also from the perspective of health, balance, and organizational culture.

Decision-making quality is inseparable from the lawyer's physiological, emotional, and cognitive state. Under sustained pressure, decision making becomes not only a matter of expertise and judgement, but also one of energy regulation, attention, and rhythm. This framing is essential to understanding why identical legal skills can lead to very different outcomes depending on context.

Common decision-making traps for lawyers

Lawyers are exposed to specific unconscious cognitive biases linked to their training and professional culture. Recognizing these biases is the first step toward neutralizing them.

We all have cognitive biases. They are mental shortcuts that help us make daily decisions in a world saturated with information. When a lawyer learns that the opposing party is a former client of the firm, the lawyer instinctively identifies a risk of conflict of interest, without needing to consult the ethical rules in detail. These automatic mechanisms, inherited from our evolution, are most of the time useful and effective. However, in the context of legal practice, these same shortcuts can become misleading. Hasty decisions made on the basis of these biases (confirmation bias, anchoring bias, availability bias, overconfidence, loss aversion) do not always lead to the best solution. Confirmation bias, for example, can lead a lawyer to favor arguments that confirm an initial theory while neglecting contrary evidence. Anchoring bias can cause the lawyer to remain fixated on an initial risk assessment without reassessing it in light of new information.

When a lawyer is subject to stress, whether more or less intense, the ability to identify these biases that can impair decision making is diminished. The legal profession has been identified by the American Bar Association as having poor mental health outcomes due to high expectations, constant client demands, and the culture of long working hours. Under such conditions, cognitive functions are significantly impaired. If the lawyer is subject to such intense stress, judgment can be profoundly affected – chronic fatigue, difficulty concentrating, irritability, and sleep disturbances are all warning signs that decision-making capacity is compromised. Chronic stress not only compromises personal well-being – it also jeopardizes professional effectiveness, leading to decreased productivity, increased errors, and deteriorated professional relationships.

Deciding under pressure, the role of wellbeing

The physical and mental health of the lawyer directly influences the quality of decisions. Fatigue, chronic stress, and lack of time impair the cognitive and emotional capacities essential to judgment. Warning signs must be identified and addressed before they have a lasting impact on performance.

Prolonged pressure activates the sympathetic nervous system, increasing vigilance and reactivity while reducing access to the prefrontal cortex, where judgement, planning and strategic reasoning occur. When lawyers remain in a state of sustained hyperactivation, decision making becomes more automatic, defensive, or excessively conservative. Brief regulation tools – such as controlled breathing, micro-pauses, or physical movement – support a return to cognitive flexibility at critical moments.

It is well established that the quality of the work environment constitutes a major determinant of individual and collective performance. The work of Amy Edmondson[1] on psychological safety demonstrates that teams in which members feel free to speak up without fear of judgment exhibit significantly higher levels of engagement, productivity, and innovation capacity. Similarly, research conducted in the field of workplace wellbeing[2] confirms that an organizational climate built on benevolence, inclusion, and authenticity promotes not only talent retention but also creativity and collaborative problem-solving. Finally, a 2019 study from the University of Oxford[3] demonstrated that happy employees are 13 percent more productive – a finding that also holds true in the legal sector. It is therefore essential that the law firm in which professionals practice provides an environment where wellbeing is an integral part of the strategy. Lawyers who maintain a healthy balance benefit from better mental and physical health, greater professional satisfaction, and enhanced creativity.

Pressure is more easily resistant in such an environment, and decision making takes place under better conditions. As a result, decisions are of higher quality. Research by Leslie Perlow at Harvard Business School[4] has shown that teams that collectively agree on predictable rest periods not only experience less burnout but also achieve better outcomes for their clients. This demonstrates that wellbeing is neither a luxury nor a hindrance to performance, but rather a driver of decision quality.

This environment of wellbeing must be championed and embodied by management. Leaders must serve as role models for wellbeing, to the extent possible, since they are often the most exposed and the most subject to pressure. But precisely because they hold this position, their exemplary conduct has a multiplier effect across the entire organization. Leadership is decisive in this transformation – leaders must adopt healthy behaviors, openly discuss their own limitations, and actively support their team members in managing their workload. The tone set at the top reverberates throughout the organization. Management that leads by example in terms of stress management and respect for rest periods creates conditions in which every lawyer can make informed decisions, even under pressure.

Balancing risk, judgment, and incomplete information

Lawyers must frequently decide without having all the information, which requires accepting uncertainty as a normal component of practice. Distinguishing reversible decisions from irreversible ones makes it possible to calibrate the depth of analysis.

When called upon to make a decision, the lawyer must be able to assess the consequences and risks associated with each option and then adapt the depth of analysis to the significance of the issues at stake. Thus, a readily reversible decision does not call for the same degree of scrutiny as an irreversible one, such as the recommendation to abandon legal proceedings or to accept a final settlement.

The reality is that lawyers often do not have all the information and cannot always obtain it. The legal practice environment is characterized by unpredictable client demands, urgent deadlines, and a culture of constant availability that often make it impossible to wait for perfect information. Lawyers must act and decide with this lack of information, accepting that uncertainty is an integral part of their profession. The concept of "optimal busyness" – which recognizes the natural flow of professional and personal demands – offers a useful framework for approaching this reality. Rather than seeking a perfect state of information, which is illusory, the lawyer must develop the ability to identify essential information, rapidly assess its reliability, and make an informed decision within the allotted time. Managing client expectations through transparent communication is a valuable tool here – by clearly explaining the limits of available information and the associated risks, the lawyer strengthens trust while protecting against unrealistic expectations.

Research on optimal busyness shows that performance and satisfaction peak when professionals are sufficiently challenged while retaining a sense of control. Excessive workload without recovery leads to tunnel vision, rigid thinking, and poorer judgment, while insufficient challenge leads to disengagement. Decision quality therefore depends less on constant availability than on maintaining a sustainable zone of activation.

When perfectionism becomes a disability

The demand for excellence can become paralyzing when it turns into dysfunctional perfectionism. The pursuit of the perfect solution leads to wasted time, missed opportunities, and increased stress. Learning to tolerate imperfection and to make decisions that are good enough is a key skill.

Lawyers make decisions every day. They work extremely hard and therefore have little time to allocate to each decision-making process. They must learn to be efficient and to optimize their time. To do so, they must be highly rigorous in gathering as much available information as possible, even though they often do not have access to all the information. But they must not, for all that, fall into perfectionism, at the risk of wasting precious time without reaching a better decision. As the saying goes, "Perfect is the enemy of good".

Lawyers strive for excellence and are distinguished by their intellectual rigor. But they must take care not to turn these strengths into handicaps. The rule of focusing on the tasks that generate the greatest value is a powerful tool for maximizing impact while minimizing unnecessary effort. By relentlessly pursuing perfection, they lose time and energy, when they are perfectly capable of producing work of very high quality without it being perfect. Under pressure, time is often short. One should therefore not aim for perfection but rather for the best one is capable of given the context – time pressure, budget constraints, lack of human resources, the pressure of what is at stake, media pressure, and so on. The forms of pressure are multiple and cumulative.

Research shows that professionals who can become "addicted" to the feeling of being constantly busy end up prioritizing short-term productivity at the expense of their capacity for reflection and their real effectiveness. This dysfunctional perfectionism fuels cycles of overwork and burnout. To avoid these pitfalls, lawyers must learn to recognize the signs of excessive demands and take proactive measures to restore balance. Delegation is an essential lever here – it both manages workload and provides more junior lawyers with the opportunity to develop their skills.

This attachment to constant busyness often creates the illusion of effectiveness while eroding the capacity for reflection, perspective, and sound judgement. Under pressure, the pursuit of perfection combined with chronic urgency diverts energy away from the decisions that truly create value.

Learning to aim for decisions that are sufficiently robust rather than perfect is therefore a core professional skill.

Collaborative decision making and collective responsibility

Involving multiple stakeholders in the decision-making process deepens analytical rigor and fosters shared ownership of outcomes. However, this approach carries risks of diluted responsibility and conformity that must be anticipated. Clarifying roles and managing disagreements are essential to its effectiveness.

Collaboration is important in legal decision making – it generates greater intellectual richness and innovation in deliverables. When several lawyers compare their analyses, individual biases are better identified and neutralized, and the proposed solutions are more robust. The challenge of quality decision making in the legal profession is not merely an individual concern. It is a collective responsibility that demands a fundamental shift in culture, leadership, and professional norms. Peer support networks, mentoring programs, and regular exchanges constitute invaluable sources of advice and emotional support, particularly for junior lawyers and those who are new to the profession.

Organizations play a decisive role in the decision-making quality of their teams. Leadership must adopt healthy behaviors and implement policies that promote peer support. Firms that take this responsibility seriously go beyond symbolic gestures – they embed policies that prioritize reasonable working hours, reward results rather than mere presence, and provide robust access to mental health and wellbeing resources. Collective responsibility means that every member of the firm, from senior partners to trainees, has a role to play in building an environment conducive to quality decisions. By encouraging collaboration and mutual support, firms create a sense of belonging and shared purpose that strengthens both individual and organizational resilience.

Standing by decisions and revisiting them when needed

Once a decision has been made, the lawyer must fully own it while remaining capable of revising it if necessary. This ability to stand behind one's choices is fundamental in a profession where personal responsibility is engaged at every moment. The lawyer who constantly second-guesses past decisions becomes trapped in a cycle of hesitation that paralyzes future action and erodes confidence.

However, owning a decision does not mean clinging to it stubbornly. Regular self-assessment is an essential component of sustainable practice. The decision debrief – a structured exercise that involves revisiting decisions taken in order to analyze their outcomes, motivations, and the alternatives considered – makes it possible to draw lessons for the future. This practice of continuous reflection lies at the heart of the concept of dynamic balance, which requires ongoing adaptation to the evolving demands of work and personal life. Lawyers must regularly assess their own wellbeing, reflect on their personal limits, and clarify their priorities.

The decision debrief is all the more valuable because it can be practiced individually or collectively. In a team setting, it allows lessons learned to be shared, strengthens cohesion, and normalizes the fact that every decision involves a degree of uncertainty. Openly acknowledging that a past decision could have been better is not an admission of weakness, but a sign of professional maturity. This openness helps dismantle the stigma around seeking help and normalizes the challenges that many lawyers face.

Optimal busyness applies to decision making

Optimal workload in the context of decision making aims for a balance in which the lawyer is stimulated without being overwhelmed, thereby preserving the quality of judgment. Alternating between periods of intensity and periods of cognitive recovery is essential. Recognizing warning signs allows intervention before performance deteriorates.

This concept directly relates to that of "optimal busyness" developed in research on workplace wellbeing. Optimal workload does not consist of maintaining a fixed ratio between working time and personal time but requires continuous self-assessment and adjustment. The goal is to reach a state in which the lawyer feels stimulated and engaged by the work, but without being overwhelmed or chronically stressed. Research shows that professionals are most satisfied when they have enough organizational control to feel challenged, without the workload becoming so excessive as to cause fatigue or burnout. This state is associated with energy, focus, and a sense of progress, rather than exhaustion and disengagement.

Applying optimal busyness to decision making requires continuous self-assessment. Cognitive signals (difficulty focusing), emotional signals (irritability, impatience), and physical signals (fatigue, tension) indicate when decision capacity may be compromised. Recognizing these signals early allows lawyers to pause, delegate, or adjust before judgment deteriorates.

Applied to decision making, this principle means that the lawyer must be attentive to the signs of decision overload – persistent exhaustion, irritability, and difficulty disconnecting from work are all signals that capacity for judgment is under threat. Corrective measures may include setting firmer boundaries, delegating tasks, or seeking support from colleagues and mentors. Intentional alternation between periods of intensive analysis and recovery time protects the cognitive and emotional resources necessary for quality decisions. Flexibility allows for periods of intense focus, balanced by genuine opportunities for rest and renewal.

Optimal busyness is not solely an individual responsibility. Leaders play a decisive role by modelling sustainable rhythms, clarifying priorities, and legitimizing recovery. By doing so, they create conditions in which high-quality decisions can be made consistently, even under sustained pressure.

Practical tools for deciding under pressure

Concrete tools exist for structuring decision making under pressure. Analytical frameworks, stress management techniques, and rituals for stepping back improve the quality of judgment in the most demanding situations.

In terms of structuring the decision, task prioritization and focusing on activities that generate the greatest value are powerful tools for maximizing impact while minimizing unnecessary effort. Allocating specific periods for focused work, client meetings, and administrative responsibilities makes it possible to establish a structured routine that supports both efficiency and personal fulfilment. Regularly reviewing and adjusting these schedules is essential to maintaining a healthy balance.

In terms of stress management and physical wellbeing, sleep, exercise, and nutrition are indispensable foundations of decision-making capacity. A meta-analysis published in 2018 in the journal *Sleep*[5] demonstrated that sleep deprivation impairs cognitive performance, decision making, and emotional regulation, all essential skills for lawyers. Regular physical exercise reduces stress, improves mood, and builds resilience. Making conscious choices about nutrition, such as opting for balanced meals and staying properly hydrated, supports energy and cognitive function throughout the day. Incorporating regular physical activity, even in the form of short walks during the day, has a significant positive impact on physical and mental health.

Conclusion

The ability to decide under pressure is not an innate talent, but a skill that can be cultivated and developed. By understanding the mechanisms of decision making, identifying one's own biases, and adopting structured methods, the modern lawyer can transform a source of stress into a genuine competitive advantage. This decisional mastery also depends on a protective lifestyle and an organizational environment that values the quality of judgment over mere reactivity.

The pursuit of an optimal workload in decision making, where engagement and control are balanced, offers a sustainable vision of professional excellence. The pursuit of this optimal balance, where challenge and control are in equilibrium and where time is managed with intention, points toward a promising future for legal practice. By prioritizing wellbeing, embracing innovation, and fostering a supportive professional culture, lawyers can regain control of their time, improve their performance, and build careers that are both successful and sustainable. This decisional mastery, combined with technical excellence and personal wellbeing, constitutes one of the hallmarks of the accomplished professional.

In this perspective, high performance should not be understood as endurance or constant availability, but as sustainable mastery. Lawyers who operate within an optimal zone of busyness make clearer, faster, and more defensible decisions over the long-term, benefiting both their clients and their own professional sustainability.

References

1 Amy Edmondson, *The Fearless Organization: Creating Psychological Safety in the Workplace for Learning, Innovation, and Growth*, Wiley, 2018.

2 National Task Force on Lawyer Well-Being, *The Path to Lawyer Well-Being: Practical Recommendations for Positive Change*, American Bar Association, August 2017.

3 De Neve, J. E., Krekel, C. and Ward, G., "Happy Workers Are More Productive: Evidence from the Oxford/BT Study," Saïd Business School, University of Oxford, 2019. www.ox.ac.uk/news/2019-10-24-happy-workers-are-13-more-productive

4 Leslie A. Perlow and Jessica L. Porter, "Making Time Off Predictable – and Required", *Harvard Business Review*, October 2009. https://hbr.org/2009/10/making-time-off-predictable-and-required

5 Wild, C. J., Nichols, E. S., Battista, M. E., Stojanoski, B. and Owen, A. M., "Dissociable effects of self-reported daily sleep duration on high-level cognitive abilities". *Sleep*, Volume 41, Issue 12, December 2018.

Chapter 7:
How to have difficult conversations

By Susan Heaton-Wright, founder, Superstar Communicator

Recently, a client of mine was avoiding having a difficult conversation with a client. He would flatter this individual, thank them profusely for sending information, yet he openly admitted to procrastinating about having an honest conversation with him. As you can imagine, the delays and subsequent conversation resulted in misunderstandings, frustration, and ultimately, a lost client.

This is a perfectly normal response to difficult conversations; we avoid them or we confuse the other person, either by being over kind or over direct. Most legal guidance on difficult conversations focuses on *what* to say. However, the *way* you conduct the conversation plays a major role in how it lands with the other person or people.

Difficult conversations are not just about content – they are a performance of clarity, control, and credibility under pressure. This is the core message from this chapter, which will cover the importance of difficult conversations and a number of models you can use to make this process easier. I have also included short exercises for you to reflect and practice.

Why difficult conversations define legal careers

As professionals, you regularly have conversations with clients, colleagues, and your leaders. Sometimes they are positive and constructive. However, the reality is that there are times when the conversation is awkward – not what the client wants to hear. Difficult. Unless we are able to have these conversations, to have the courage to lead them, to deliver messages that the client might not wish to hear, we are missing an opportunity to be an effective lawyer.

These conversations can include:

- *Delivering bad news to a client.* This could be anything from the other 'side' not agreeing with specific points of a negotiation; information being dismissed in court; counter claims – the list is endless. But unless you convey this information clearly to the client, they will not have the correct information. This is particularly important if the client is stressed or angry.

- *Managing unrealistic expectations.* A client might demand everything, or at least more than is reasonable. They might be requesting details that break the law. They might demand to win at any cost. Creating a framework where the client's expectations are met, within the law, is an important conversation to have. Your professional reputation is at risk if you agree to openly break the law. And there is a possibility that the client will demand to see someone else – possibly at another firm – who will do as he or she wishes. That is for your conscience to deal with.
- *Challenging a senior colleague.* The legal profession is hierarchical within its career structure. Partners and more experienced lawyers in the firm are quite rightly respected and this is reflected in their fees. However, there might be an occasion where you have observed an error – the senior person has omitted something essential to share with the client or perhaps you have some information that contradicts what the senior colleague is advising on. It takes courage and confidence to have these conversations – but, if done well, they set you up as someone to watch.
- *Challenging a colleague or someone you are managing.* This could be down to errors they have made, they have arrived late for a meeting, or even that their clothing and appearance is inappropriate for client meetings.

Reputation is built in moments of pressure. If we are able to act in a professional and effective manner in these situations, we grow our professional reputation. This includes having the courage to have these conversations. Clients remember *how* you handled the conversation, not just the outcome.

Exercise:
Reflect on difficult conversations you have observed, been on the receiving end of, or even had to deliver yourself. How did you feel? What was the outcome? Would you do anything differently?

What makes conversations "difficult"?

We could procrastinate, we could avoid the conversation, we could 'sugar coat' the message so that the other person is confused and doesn't appreciate the challenge or problem. Or we go in like a bull in a china shop, with our size 11 shoes, causing chaos, anger, and raised emotions.

These conversations have:

- *High stakes.* We put greater weight and emphasis on these significant cases.
- *Strong emotions.* I have already mentioned the client who wishes to win at all costs, or the client who is already very stressed or angry. We might be afraid of the outcome or anxious that we might make the wrong decision.
- *Power imbalance.* This is especially the case when we need to have a conversation with a senior colleague or a client
- *Uncertainty or conflict.* Quite often, difficult conversations will involve conflicting opinions.

Pressure = Stakes + Emotion + Perception of Risk.

Introducing The SuperStar Communicator™ approach to difficult conversations

As part of the work I do with talented professionals, I created the SuperStar Communicator™ methodology, which breaks down the process of any communication you have with others, whether they are written, face-to-face or even virtual conversations. This methodology is invaluable as part of the process of preparing for the conversation.

Whenever you are preparing for a conversation, undertake the following steps to be fully prepared.

Element 1: Purpose

- What is the outcome you want?
- What must be understood, decided, or changed?
- What matters to them?
- What are they worried about?
- How could you provide solutions?

Element 2: Content

- Opening sentence.
- Message – there could be a key message in the conversation, such as a time constraint or legal issues.
- Any evidence to back up your conversation.

- Case study: these are invaluable in being able to explain a specific situation or to reassure the client or colleague of your credibility.
- Call to action: make this clear at the end of the conversation. This is the "What we need to do".

Element 3: Preparation
- Self-preparation.
- Preparing the structure of the conversation.
- The environment where the conversation will take place.
- Any supporting evidence.
- Preparing the other person with either a clear agenda or the purpose of the conversation beforehand.

Element 4: Performance
- Demonstrating credibility.
- Non-verbal communication, including facial expressions.
- Body language.

Element 5: Voice
- Tone of voice – ensuring you sound confident.
- How easy it is for other people to listen and engage with you, otherwise others will be distracted.

We will be re-visiting all of these steps throughout this chapter, reinforcing their importance whilst relating these to difficult conversations.

The conversation grid

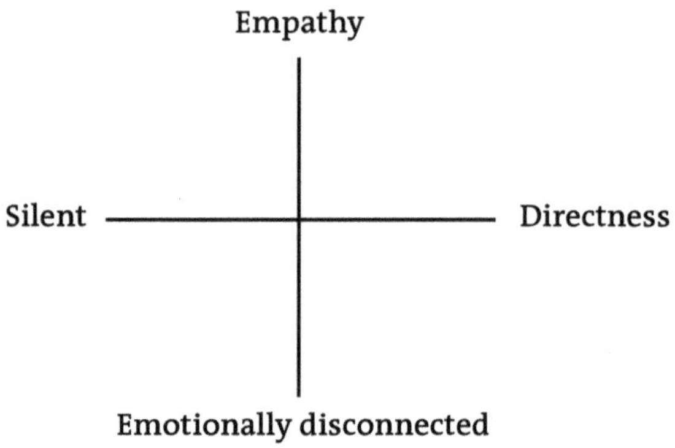

This is a useful illustration to demonstrate how we risk getting the tone and intention wrong in a conversation. Let's look at the different sections of the grid. The vertical line indicates levels of empathy or lack of emotion whilst the horizontal line shows the amount you say.

For example, if you are silent, you are risking other people not appreciating or understanding a specific challenge or risk, whilst if you are very direct, you not only risk upsetting someone, they could also respond by being angry.

Let's look at the four quadrants.

1. *Top Left:* Silent but empathetic. Perhaps you don't want to say something because you don't wish to hurt the other person. Or, for whatever reason, you don't wish to say anything. If something needs saying, as a professional you need to say it. This is not an effective quadrant.
2. *Bottom Left:* Silent and emotionally disconnected – you actually don't care. I would challenge you to question why you are in the meeting if you have this attitude.
3. *Bottom Right:* You are emotionally disconnected and are direct. This is particularly risky because you could elicit a negative reaction from the other person.
4. *Top Right:* A combination of directness and empathy. This is the sweet spot. Whilst you are aware of the feelings of the other person, you are clear with your message so there are no misunderstandings.

Exercise:

Reflect on some conversations you have had with clients or colleagues. Using the Conversation Grid as a guide, consider which conversations went well and which were less effective.

Which quadrant did they take place in?

How effective were the conversations?

How could you have improved the conversations?

The PREPARE model (for before the conversation)

You will have noticed that Preparation is one of the steps in the SuperStar Communicator Methodology. This is a great way to remember to prepare with the PREPARE model.

P – Purpose

What is the reason or purpose of the conversation? What is the 'Why?'. Also consider what outcomes you want to achieve from the conversation. It could be anything as straightforward as a clear deadline to achieve, through to explaining clarity in a particular situation – which might not necessarily be what the client wishes to hear.

R – Risks

What could go wrong? Guess what – not all conversations run smoothly. However much you have prepared, your client might not agree with you; they might question your decisions; in the worst-case scenario they might ask to speak to someone more experienced. Of course, this is more likely to happen in difficult conversations.

E – Emotions

What might they feel? They, like you, will have prepared prior to the conversation. They may well have a list of questions to ask.

What might you feel? Of course, you might feel uncomfortable or nervous and it is important to be aware of this. Later I will look at ways in which you can manage your nerves so you become calmer. Being honest about how you feel is powerful – you can then prepare yourself for the conversation.

When I was a professional singer, part of my preparation was managing my nerves to ensure I performed to the best of my ability. Whilst I was in a performance – especially onstage in choral works as a soloist, so visible to the audience – I became acutely aware of being distracted by other elements, such as who was in the audience and my own nerves associated with that. By focusing exclusively on the music and following my score in "the moment" helped me deal with this. For you, it could be actively focusing on the other people in the room, or even maintaining the clear structure of the meeting.

P – Perspective

What matters to them? So often we focus on what we need to say, but the other person will have a different perspective on a conversation. They potentially have a different approach to a challenge or even a completely different outcome they wish to achieve. Finding out what their values are and particularly what matters to them is crucial. They, like you, could have the intention of resolving a particular issue; they might on the other hand be wanting to 'win' at all costs even if this involves breaking the law. If you are speaking to a colleague, they might believe their work is up to standard, when the reality is quite different. Possibly you and your colleagues have given the false impression that their work is satisfactory but haven't addressed it before. That is their reality of the situation. Being aware of this will aid you in leading the conversation.

One tip could be to ask what they want to achieve at the beginning of the meeting. This will help you both have a focused outcome. If it is a conversation with a colleague or team member, a "How's this project going?" type of opening could be very useful in assessing how much awareness the other person has of the situation. Their perspective could be completely different to yours. Alternatively, they might already be aware there is a problem.

A – Approach

How will you open the conversation? You are setting the scene and the mood of the conversation. I hope you intend to lead the conversation professionally. Framing this with a powerful start, with the intentions and possible outcomes from the conversation will make it clearer. Not only does it establish you as the conversation "lead" it provides a structure to the meeting. I will go into this in more detail later.

R – Response planning

How will you handle pushback? As mentioned before, conversations rarely remain on script. If it is a difficult conversation, it is likely that the other person will disagree with you. After all, this is a two-way conversation and they have every right to challenge you. You might anticipate responses from the other person. You could list these down and prepare responses. Collecting evidence will support you if the other person disagrees. For example, if a client is disputing the value of a property or company, you could provide assessments of other valuations. If the meeting is more disciplinary, data such as not completing tasks on time, specific client feedback, or regularly being late for client meetings could be shared as evidence.

The Power of Three rule

This is a powerful way to communicate information or to provide different options with impact. As human beings, our brains love patterns to retain information and three is the smallest number to create this. Many communicators create three points – in sales, offering three price points is used universally. You can adopt this too. You could:

- Share three reasons why a particular choice should be taken.
- Recommend three steps for progressing with a challenging situation with your client.

- Offer three options as part of a negotiation:
- A high-stakes option.
- A perfectly reasonable offer (it is likely to be the one they select).
- A basic option.
- If having a difficult conversation with a colleague or someone you manage, setting three targets for improvement will create clarity for the other person.

The next time you have a conversation with a friend, practice applying the Power of Three. Give three options or share three steps.

E – Environment

Where/how will this happen? Anyone who has had to have a conversation with a teenager will know that conversations when driving or when walking side by side are very effective. Why? Because you are not looking at each other; you don't have eye contact. You don't feel threatened. Likewise, we have all experienced the 'walk of shame' in the office where the manager says 'Can I have a word with you' in front of colleagues. Of course, we respond by being nervous and defensive – which isn't a good start to the conversation.

If it's possible, change the environment – go to a neutral location or, if it is a less formal meeting, go for a walk. If you are having a difficult conversation with a client, ensure they are welcomed positively and create a professional, friendly atmosphere. You could prepare other members of support staff to make the client feel welcome if they are attending the office and also warn them if there is any likelihood of this individual being stressed. A big smile from the receptionist to welcome a client goes a long way!

The OPEN model

We need to prepare our first sentence to be powerful. After all, it could define an effective or ineffective meeting. I call this creating a framework around the meeting, so that it is clear to everyone attending what the purpose is, as well as the outcome you would like to achieve.

O – Outcome first

"I'd like to talk through the next steps following..." or "We are here to discuss... By the end of the meeting we hope to achieve..." It sets the scene for the conversation very clearly. If you have already sent an agenda (formal or informal) the other person or people will be prepared.

P – Plain language

This is not time to be a smart Alec. Particularly if we are nervous, we can resort to bigging ourselves up by using complicated, overly professional language that excludes other people. No one likes the person who keeps reminding others how smart he or she is. Use clear language that everyone in the room understands. If you have to use specific legal terms, make sure you explain what they are in clear language.

E – Empathy

Consider the other person is important – this highlights that you are viewing the conversation from their perspective as well as yours. "I appreciate this may be frustrating..." However, do be mindful that you still need to maintain focus on the situation and outcome. There have been many situations where individuals have become over-empathetic and the core message and outcomes from the difficult conversations have been lost. This is also confusing for the recipient.

N – Next step focus

Keep it forward-looking and keep the discussion moving along. You will help yourself as well as the other people in the meeting if you keep reminding them of the outcomes. I have been in meetings where individuals become bogged down with a specific, unrelated topic, and the momentum and the focus of the meeting is lost. This results in time being wasted, overlong meetings and, in many cases, confusion. Keep reminding yourself and others in the meeting what you wish to achieve.

Exercise:

The next time you have a conversation with someone, challenge yourself to use the OPEN framework. How did the conversation go? Did it make the conversation easier to manage?

The LISTEN model

Any conversation, whether simple or difficult, is two-way. This is not exclusively one person speaking. We have already considered content, structuring the conversation, and some ideas around preparation. If we are nervous, it can be very easy to fall into the trap of talking more; however, a key part of any communication is listening. The LISTEN model is particularly useful when hearing other people's perspectives.

L – Let them speak
It can be very tempting to interrupt. Please don't. Let them speak and whilst they are doing this, listen carefully. Avoid listening to respond – be in the moment. Actively listen.

I – Identify emotion
By listening you will be able to identify how they are feeling from the language they use; the content and even the tone of their voice. Name it if appropriate; for example, "I can hear you are frustrated by the delays".

S – Summarize
One way of clearly showing you are listening is to summarize what they have said. It adds trust and also the value proposition that they are being heard. "So what I'm hearing is..."

T – Test understanding
The next step is to check what you have heard correctly. Asking a question to clarify something you have heard correctly such as "Have I got that right?" is an effective way to do this. It also clarifies it in your mind.

E – Explore options
When you have confirmed points from the other person's perspective, you can move forward with the meeting to consider different options. The "Power of Three" is an effective way to provide options in this instance.

N – Navigate forward
You want to ensure that the other person or people know you have listened to them; however, it is important to move forward with the meeting. If necessary, remind people what you have heard whilst focusing on the outcome.

Exercise:
Choose a conversation you are going to conduct (not necessarily a business one) and spend time really listening to the other person. How did it make you feel?

The CALM technique (emotional regulation)

I mentioned earlier that preparing yourself is crucial in performing professionally and with credibility. As a former professional singer, I have had to manage my emotions so that my performance is positively impacted by being calm. This is how you can achieve this:

C: *Center (breath, posture)* taking deep breaths before the meeting helps you to remain calm.

A: *Acknowledge (internally: "this is pressure")*; however, I have prepared for this meeting; I have the credibility and experience to deliver.

L: *Lower pace:* it can be very easy to speak too fast when you are nervous. Consciously speak slower; take deep breaths to maintain calmness. It will influence the other people in the room too.

M: *Maintain tone:* When we are nervous, our vocal tone alters. Ensure you are relaxed and then your natural voice and persona will show.

Exercise:
Before the next conversation you have, use the 'CALM' technique to put yourself into a positive, calm state. Did this help you?

Real-world scenarios

We have considered ways you can prepare and approach difficult conversations. Below I will give three examples of difficult conversations. In each of the examples, I would like you to consider:

- What goes wrong;
- What to do instead; and
- Example phrasing.

1. Delivering bad news to a client

Not everything runs smoothly when working in law. Here are some of the many challenges you could encounter and have to relay to your clients:

- Case delay.
- Unfavorable outcome.
- The other 'side' is being very difficult, by delays or other disruptive tactics.

2. Challenging a senior colleague

Within the legal profession, seniority, position, and experience are (quite rightly) highly valued. Professionals are intelligent, talented, and have worked hard to achieve their positions. However, occasionally they might have missed a crucial point or not noticed something a client said. In this situation, you can:

- Respectfully disagree.
- Notice and correct an error.
- Manage hierarchy.

3. Giving feedback to a junior

We have all been there. Everybody needs to experience constructive ways to develop. This is an opportunity to create a better framework for giving feedback, in situations where, for example:

- The junior person is still making basic errors on work.
- They are consistently late for meetings.
- They don't appear to be making progress with their skill development.

Exercise:

For each of these conversations, consider:

- What could go wrong.
- What to do instead.
- Example phrasing that you could use to make things clearer.

Voice and presence

Did you know that your voice changes in different situations? This happens when you are tired, as you age, if you are frightened, stressed, or angry. It can also change depending on the specific person you are speaking to. Even if you believe you are calm and focused, your voice might alter. The other person is going to pick up on this, especially if it doesn't match what you are saying.

- *Lower pitch.* Significant research shows that if you have a lower pitched voice, you are perceived as having more authority. This could be a particular challenge for women who naturally have higher pitched voices. However, if you speak with your natural, authentic voice, being relaxed as you speak, other people will sense your authority. Avoid forcing your voice to be lower than your natural voice, but reducing the tension in your neck and shoulder areas will help your natural voice to come out.
- *Slower pace.* We associate a slower pace of speaking with control.

Naturally we all speak faster when we are nervous. Remember the CALM technique to prepare before the meeting and consciously speak slower, taking deep breaths between each sentence.

- *Pauses*. These are indicators of confidence. You don't need to fill silences with more words. In addition, pausing allows your words to land and to emphasise what you have said.

Exercise:
In your next meeting, start adopting these three skill sets when speaking. Ask for feedback from a trusted person. Reflect on whether this is having a positive impact when speaking to others.

Non-verbal communication

In any conversation, our non-verbal communication is essential. The other person will sense if we are nervous, unsure, or lacking in confidence. Our aim is to demonstrate our credibility to reassure the other person as well as build trust and rapport. I call this 'Credible Performance'. Here are four ways you can do this easily.

1. *Eye contact*. The easiest way to connect with others on a human level is to look at them. If we look away, we risk the other person questioning our trustworthiness. This is not about staring at the other person, but acknowledging them.
2. *Posture*. How you present yourself will determine how successful the meeting is. By this, I mean your body language. If your head is held high, shoulders down, and you are comfortable in the space, others are going to respond to you with confidence. By contrast, if you look nervous, your head is down, and you are taking up less space, it gives people the impression you don't want to be there. Ensure you are demonstrating confidence to reassure others.
3. *Facial expression*. Ensure you match what you say with your facial expression. There are going to be occasions where showing empathy and understanding on your face will assist you. Likewise, a very neutral facial expression – rather like a "Poker face" where no expression shows – can be a powerful way to conduct a more difficult conversation.
4. *Stillness*. How often have we had conversations with people who are fidgeting – perhaps they keep looking at their phone, their watch, or over your shoulder! It is offputting, as well as showing they are distracted by other things rather than the conversation. Avoid being

this person. Keep still and focus on the other person and what they are saying. It gives you more credibility and shows you are listening.

Remember: you are always communicating, even when you are not speaking. Ensure you are maintaining your professional "performance" when listening for credibility.

Exercise:
Start observing other people in meetings. Who is effective at showing confidence with their body language? How do senior colleagues use their facial expressions and eye contact when speaking to clients? Observe how stillness could increase presence and influence in these conversations.

The five-minute hack – a quick exercise before any difficult conversation

This is an exercise I use regularly, as well as recommend to professionals in different sectors. You will already have prepared information, reviewed the case, and discussed it with colleagues. This is an exercise to do just before you meet your client or colleague.

1. Define the purpose of the conversation.
2. Who are you speaking to (include specific information about the case).
3. What is the key message.
4. What is the evidence to back this (make sure you have this to hand).
5. What's next.

Exercise:
Think of a challenging conversation you are going to have with a client or colleague. Use the five-minute hack to prepare. After the conversation, reflect on what worked well. Did this quick exercise help you in having a more effective conversation?

Conclusion

Difficult conversations, whilst challenging at times, are an opportunity to develop your skills and to be perceived as a professional who manages clients and colleagues well. The most respected lawyers are not those who avoid difficult conversations, but those who handle them with clarity, composure, and purpose. Avoiding these conversations risks creating bigger problems in the long run, so having the courage to have these conversations early on is essential. Every time you step up and have an effective conversation, it builds your skill set and conversation, so view these conversations as opportunities, rather than risks. Part of your role as a lawyer is to create clarity from confusion.

Chapter 8:
Giving and receiving feedback

By Wayne Hassay, managing partner, Maguire Schneider Hassay, LLP

Lawyering is still too often practiced as a solitary craft – the lawyer, the lawyer's judgment, everything between the lawyer's ears. That mindset produces a predictable tendency to tune out external signals. Feedback can feel optional, even intrusive, and "service quality" can sound like a distraction from "real law".

At the same time, the profession's business structure is different from most modern service environments. Most legal services are delivered by small, fragmented practices. In that setting, there is rarely a real client experience loop – no clear owner for service delivery, no consistent measurement, and no disciplined way to convert client reactions into repeatable improvements. A good client experience may still be delivered, but it cannot compound without a system.

That is the point this chapter is pressing – a feedback loop strengthens the real practice of law. It is not a corporate trend or a marketing gimmick. It is a basic professional discipline for any practice that wants to improve at scale.

The full discipline has four movements:

1. Clients give feedback about how legal work is experienced.
2. The firm receives and interprets that client feedback through standards, ownership, measurement, and evidence rules.
3. The firm gives that feedback to its team as part of the broader evaluation process, alongside the measurements lawyers already know such as billable hours, collections, and business development.
4. Lawyers and staff receive the feedback as information that can be tested and acted upon.

Of course, law firms have counted billable hours, collections and business development for generations. This chapter argues for something more complete: feedback that moves from the client, through the firm, and back into the work, so managers, lawyers, and staff can give and receive it as part of an ongoing process rather than an after-the-fact judgment.

Objections to a constructive culture of feedback

A constructive culture of feedback in a law firm starts with three clarifications that should be obvious but rarely are.

First, this is not about competence, and it is not an accusation of incompetence. At the individual level – one lawyer, one client, one interaction – feedback can *feel* like a judgment on the lawyer rather than a comment on the experience. Lawyers hear "feedback" and assume someone is questioning their credibility, their professionalism, or their judgment. That is the wrong frame. The premise here is that the legal work is competent. The loop is not an audit of the lawyer. It is a method for strengthening the client-facing part of the attorney–client relationship.

A second objection appears when feedback shifts from the individual to the system. Because every matter is bespoke, the assumption is the client experience must be bespoke. The legal issues will always be fact-specific. That is not in dispute. What can be consistent is the delivery system. Standardizing those mechanics is not "cookie-cutter law". It is professionalizing the parts of the representation that should not fluctuate.

Third, lawyers will object to the measurement itself. The professional reflex is to treat any quantified feedback, beyond money collected, as a claim that must be tested and, if possible, defeated – the question is poorly framed, the sample is biased, the respondent is unreasonable, the context is missing, the rating is unfair. The point is not that any measure is perfect. It is that the loop becomes credible in volume.

All of this resistance is hard to justify in a profession where outcomes are often uncertain and sometimes wildly unpredictable. That is precisely why the profession should overcome these objections and be disciplined about what can be controlled: communication, clarity, expectations, and follow-through.

The practical irony is that the loop is designed to reduce the very thing lawyers fear – clients recasting ordinary service friction as incompetence or an ethical problem. While a service gap is not a legal error, it is the easiest way for an otherwise reasonable representation to be interpreted as a problem of some sort. Professional liability carriers say this for a reason – many claims and complaints do not begin with a clear mistake in the law. They begin with a client who feels surprised, ignored, or uninformed about what was happening, why decisions were made, or what to expect next. When a firm standardizes service mechanics and improves them in the aggregate, the result is fewer disconnects and grievances.

Build the operating standard

Once those objections are overcome, the next work is building a shared standard that can be used in daily practice. This requires shared language. Different organizations use different labels for this – values, attributes, service standards, operating principles, or commitments. The label does not matter. What matters is whether the words translate into delivery mechanics that the team can actually execute and clients can actually experience.

"Delivery mechanics" are the repeatable, client-facing operations around competent legal judgment – who communicates (and when and on what channel), what is promised or confirmed (especially scope and next steps), how options and recommendations are framed, how updates are handled during waiting periods, how responsibility is handed off, and how matters are closed with clarity. These are system behaviors that can be standardized without dictating outcomes or second-guessing legal judgment.

In most traditional practices, an operating standard like this is never built. Candid legal advice therefore often lands as "no" because lawyers are trained to spot risk and identify constraints. Lawyers are trying to help within those constraints, but the client does not always experience that intent. The result is confused, frustrated clients reacting to tone and friction rather than substance. That is why the firm needs an operating standard translated into delivery mechanics – so sound judgment is consistently experienced as support rather than dismissal, without changing the substance of the advice or trading judgment for concessions.

So, how do you build the operating standard?

Build 1: A Standard, not marketing

Lawyers often hear values, attributes, service standards, etc., and assume they are "marketing". They are right. This language belongs on the website, in recruiting colleagues, and in any serious effort to attract clients. The mistake is thinking that "marketing" means puffery – fluff untethered from the actual work. When the language is done well, it functions as marketing only because it is operational first – it describes the firm's actual service behavior.

That is why the work cannot start with copywriting from management. It has to start with the team, because the exercise is foremost about accountability. It is the deliberate act of naming who we think we are and then confronting whether that is who we actually are in the moments clients experience. The words must be selected together because shared language is only a standard when the team owns it and can see themselves in it.

But that is still not enough, because this is where firms let marketing lead the build. They assume they already know what clients want – more speed, more empathy, more clarity, more updates – and then turn those assumptions into "standards" and advertised differentiators. Most of those claims are easy to make and rarely tested, especially in a service environment as fluid as law. What firms assume clients want, what clients say they want, what clients actually respond to, and what they experience as professional service are not always the same. That is why proposed standards must be pressure-tested against real interactions in the delivery system, not drafted as aspirational copy. If the firm does not test them, the "standard" is just a sloppy self-portrait, and the marketing that follows is only a louder version of the same guess.

Build 2: Shared language with shared meaning

Keep the vocabulary small enough to control. Use one definition per term, not a cluster of synonyms. For each term, write (1) a one-sentence definition, (2) two or three observable behaviors that would let a reasonable person say, "Yes, those delivery mechanics happened," and (3) one clear "does not mean" boundary so the term cannot drift into personality judgments or substantive case outcomes. If the firm cannot describe, consistently and concretely, what the standard requires in day-to-day functions and client interactions, the standard is not a standard. It is a slogan.

The test of whether the shared language is an actual standard is to ask: "What does this look like in our work?"

Build 3: Boundaries and purpose

The loop must draw a hard boundary around professional judgment. It cannot relitigate outcomes, bargain over legal advice, or treat disagreement with counsel as a service failure. If that boundary is not explicit at the build stage, the loop will be read as a referendum on judgment and will fail for lack of legitimacy.

Build 4: A listening method

The firm must also decide how it will listen. For most firms, the simplest starting point is a short, consistent survey at a few predictable moments (after a consultation, after a document is delivered, or at matter close). Other firms with greater resources may add additional touch points but must be careful not to add too many. The method matters less than consistency, because consistency is what produces comparable data over time. Further, a good strategy is to start small and then expand. Without an initial stable method and cadence, the firm collects anecdotes and noise. With consistency, it can aggregate feedback in volume, identify repeatable friction in delivery mechanics, and turn patterns into operational improvements.

Build 5: Ownership

Someone has to run the loop day-to-day. That is very hard for small firms, but it is a must. In a large firm, that might be an operations lead. In a small firm, it might be an office manager, a senior paralegal, or anyone trusted to understand the culture and track signals.

Two non-negotiables follow. First, the owner must have protected time and defined authority to triage and request clarification. Second, the owner must have closure discipline – every item ends in a recorded disposition, with a reason, for example: resolved, coached delivery mechanics, converted into a workflow change, or discarded as noise.

Build 6: Measurement and reporting

The build-stage task is to design measurement, so it reliably identifies repeatable friction in delivery mechanics and then converts that friction into new workflow. The easiest way to corrupt the system is to treat measurement as a report card on "who is good" rather than a disciplined way to learn what to fix.

When measuring, do not blend unlike work. Results must be interpretable within comparable work. If you blend unlike work and results, you will hand skeptics the perfect target – they will dismiss the output as illegitimate and default to the objection reflex of treating quantified feedback as something to be defeated.

Next, build this evidence rule into the measurement itself. One-off feedback is not a verdict. The system relies on aggregation – patterns over anecdotes, volume over isolated impressions, and repeatable friction over one-off frustration.

Finally, decide how comparative visibility will be used. League tables are permissible and can provide situational awareness. They are never sufficient. Comparative scores must be paired with the improvement layer – the concrete levers tied to the work, and short examples of what "better" looks like.

Implementation risks

Once it is built, how might it fail? The test remains the same: "What does this look like in our work?" translated into workflows, examples, and repeatable habits. If it is not showing up in the work, it is failing.

Implementation risk 1: The operating standard is treated as marketing

The marketing problem is the fastest way to discredit the project. The success is operational proof – show the team that the words describe real behavior and real, repeatable improvement. That means naming and celebrating wins that reflect the delivery mechanics. When the language is visibly tied to successful work, it stops sounding like copywriting and starts functioning as an operating standard.

Implementation risk 2: Shared meaning collapses without infrastructure

The risk is that management treats the adjectives as self-executing. Leadership must earn credibility. Further complicating matters, not all attributes are supported in the same way, and leadership must build different supports for different types of attributes.

Some attributes are workflow-native. "Dependable", "consistent", and "straightforward" are examples. They succeed or fail based on the tools in place, the training behind them, and disciplined use. In practice, that means case management infrastructure ranging from basic record keeping and email discipline to text and video capability, to the day-to-day strategic use of artificial intelligence.

Other attributes are relationship-native, and the firm should not shy away from them – "engaging", "empathetic", and "compassionate" are examples. These are not optional in an attorney–client relationship. But they are also the fastest to degrade into subjectivity unless translated into repeatable conduct. A practical translation is a simple and provable consultation sequence – reflect the client's concern, give advice, state the next step with owners, and confirm understanding.

Implementation risk 3: Boundary and purpose collapse into a concession model

This is where a well-designed loop can loudly fail. In law, some one-off service recovery is necessary and appropriate when there is a lapse, for example regarding delayed communication or true personality conflict. The serious implementation risk is drift – service recovery expands into a "make me, the client, happy" channel, and dissatisfaction starts functioning as client leverage rather than information for management.

That drift is dangerous for two reasons. First, legal services are not an ordinary consumer product where an unreasonable customer can be appeased by a concession and the matter ends. You cannot comp the meal, send a coupon, or ship a replacement device overnight. Second, once the loop trains clients to treat dissatisfaction as leverage, it erodes the relationship and becomes self-defeating for the client. It reframes counsel as a vendor taking instructions rather than a professional owing candid advice and sound judgment, including advice the client may not want to hear.

Implementation risk 4: Listening degrades into noise or risk

If a firm uses any free-text field to listen, caution is necessary. The narratives will sprawl and create more noise than actionable data.

A narrative loop also invites clients, lawyers, staff, and other service representatives to repeat sensitive facts, strategy, or documents that do not need to be repeated for feedback purposes. Even inside the broader service system, that is risky, because every unnecessary retelling creates one more opportunity for confidential information to travel farther than it should. For that reason, the loop must stay tight as part of the firm's reasonable efforts to protect confidentiality – any free-text field should be narrow, used sparingly, preceded by a clear warning not to include sensitive detail, and handled in a way that avoids substantive narrative back-and-forth.

Implementation risk 5: Ownership becomes cynical or meaningless

Ownership fails in two predictable directions. In one direction, the role becomes a complaint desk. Hearing only problems all day, the owner starts treating individual complaints as verdicts, and the role becomes a source of cynicism rather than operational learning.

In the other direction, the role becomes a worthless archive. Feedback is collected, nothing is changed, and the system teaches everyone that the loop is performative.

Implementation risk 6: Measurement becomes "do better"

A core risk is that measurement turns into grading – a bell curve or league table treated as a verdict. When that happens, the program stops producing learning and starts producing distortion. People conform to the metric, not the work, and "do better" becomes the entire management message.

You can see this failure mode quickly. Scores are published without levers. Thin signals are treated as truth. Outliers and low response rates are elevated into conclusions. Reporting becomes performance theater on both sides – management manages to the dashboard, and lawyers manage to the score, checking boxes for compliance rather than improving delivery.

The ultimate implementation risk – a failed loop poisons morale

The ultimate implementation risk is morale. When a feedback loop is implemented poorly, it does not merely fail to improve service. It makes the workplace worse, because it converts ordinary friction into perceived surveillance and turns professional pride into defensiveness.

The predictable talent consequence is selection. Lawyers with confidence, portability, or economic independence to practice elsewhere will not stay under a system that feels like grading, second-guessing, or administrative theater. If the program is helping them practice law better, they will support it. If it is not, they will simply leave. The opposite group does not solve the problem either. Instead of using the loop to improve, many revert to the objection reflex, argue with management, and turn feedback into a fight about legitimacy rather than a tool for better work. That tension rarely stabilizes. It usually ends with management driving them out or asking them to leave for perceived poor performance.

A failed loop thus encourages internal finger-pointing for those who remain, because unresolved friction must land somewhere. It shifts attention from systems to individuals or departments, because, in the absence of clear boundary rules and aggregation discipline, people start telling stories instead of fixing processes.

Regaining control when the risks appear

Always return to the question: "What does this look like in our work?" If the firm cannot answer that in concrete terms, what tool, at what touchpoint, with what real evidence, and with what closure, then the loop has drifted into personal verdicts. Firms that can answer that question can diagnose where the drift occurred and restore credibility.

Managers giving – and the team receiving – all feedback

Once client feedback is included in the broader performance management process, an old problem remains: how will the firm use all these metrics? This is where managers giving, and lawyers and staff receiving, all types of feedback becomes a real skill.

Traditional law firm management has too often been built around blunt economic thresholds masquerading as performance management. Hit the hours. Make book. Originate work. Those numbers matter, but for too long they were treated as enough. If the hours were high enough, the fees were realized, and the right lawyers were making book, the firm could pretend it was managing lawyer performance. In truth, it was often just counting production. That may help the firm know whether bills are being paid, but it does little to show whether lawyers are improving, whether clients appreciate the work, whether matters are being delivered well, or whether the firm is building the next generation of clients and lawyers.

For too long, the rest of the story was pushed into "mentorship". Mentorship matters, but in many firms, it has meant little more than learning how the older lawyer did it. That can transmit judgment, professionalism, and good habits. It can also transmit blind spots, bad habits, outdated workflows, and yesterday's operating model. Law firms often lament the lack of partnership-quality talent, but then train younger lawyers through memory, personality, and imitation. If the younger lawyer is not a mirror of the old partner, good habits and bad habits included, the partnership track can go off the rails without anyone asking whether the model itself is part of the problem.

This is where managers must evolve. The job is to translate *all* feedback from blunt thresholds into something more. What does the number show? What does it not show? What is worth changing? If a lawyer is short on hours, the useful conversation is not simply "bill more and work as hard as your mentor". It is whether the lawyer needs better matter assignment, better delegation, better workflow, stronger business development support, or a different use of time so the number becomes a path to improvement rather than a finish line missed. If client feedback shows confusion, the useful conversation is not "communicate more". It is whether the next-step explanation, handoff, update cadence, or scope confirmation was clear enough to be repeated reliably.

Receiving feedback is also a professional skill, but firms should not pretend it is easy, especially for younger lawyers and staff. Traditional numbers can arrive with force – I did not hit the billable hour requirement, so I failed. But that is not always the right conclusion. The question should be whether the lawyer failed, whether the system failed, or whether the firm has not yet built the system needed to support the intended result. Client experience data can trigger the opposite reflex. The lawyer may reject it too quickly. But automatic dismissal is no better than automatic submission. In either direction, the point is the same – the information must be tested against the systems that led to the feedback.

These are hard conversations. But when metrics show up once a year, or maybe once a quarter, as finish-line judgments, it becomes an impossible conversation. Constantly and thoroughly evaluated feedback becomes an improvement tool. *Real improvement, not just raw production, is the point.* That is the shift – from performance judgment after the fact to management that helps the next version of the work get better and from stale review to constant improvement.

Conclusion – this is not a gimmick

The profession is now operating in a service economy with real competition. Well-capitalized, operationally sophisticated law firms are already measuring and managing the delivery mechanics described here. Non-lawyer platforms are expanding, and they are pairing modern tools with modern service operations to deliver faster, more consistent, and more measurable client experiences. Client expectations are moving faster than the traditional law firm delivery model.

A feedback loop is a hard operational discipline that turns client experience into something a firm can improve deliberately rather than by accident. Lawyers who build disciplined delivery systems will scale what works and tighten what does not. Lawyers who do not will be outpaced, and many small and solo practices will feel that pressure first. The choice is not whether the market will improve service quality. The question is which law firms will build systems that improve it on purpose.

Chapter 9:
Delegation and supervision – leading modern legal teams with confidence, clarity and humanity

By Pam Loch, solicitor and CEO, with contributions from Lauren McLaughlin, solicitor, and Kate Rigby, HR director, Loch

Most of us can recall a time when a piece of work went wrong – not because of a lack of effort or intelligence, but because expectations, supervision or ownership were unclear. Delegation and supervision are skills not often taught when qualifying as a solicitor, yet they sit at the heart of delivering quality legal services, professional development, and trust within teams.

In a workplace landscape that is more flexible, diverse, and dispersed than ever, despite the intentions of people trying their best, these disciplines can no longer be left to assumption or habit.

Delegation and supervision as core leadership capabilities

Delegation and supervision are at the core of the quality of services delivered, risk management, capability building, and retention. As firms evolve their working practices, particularly in response to hybrid working practices and increased use of digital tools, there is a greater requirement for clarity and consistency than in the past. How work is allocated and overseen reflects the firm's attitude to risk control, junior development, team resilience, and the ability to deliver without overreliance on a few senior individuals, while also influencing whether this is a workplace where people feel supported, trusted, and able to grow.

This has both practical and regulatory significance. From a practical perspective, the delivery of legal services depends on sound judgment, clear accountability, and appropriate supervision. From a regulatory perspective, the Solicitors Regulation Authority (SRA) expects firms to have an effective system in place for supervising client matters and expects those who supervise or manage others delivering legal services to be competent and to keep their professional knowledge, skills, and understanding of legal, ethical, and regulatory obligations up to date. Supervision therefore sits at the intersection of regulatory requirements, people management, and business performance. It also requires firms to be clear about who is supervising legal work, as supervision is a distinct regulatory function even where the supervisor is also the individual's line manager. Accountability is critical. The SRA's Code of Conduct[1] states that individuals who supervise or manage others providing legal services remain accountable for the work carried out through them.

Drawing on Loch's perspective across legal, people, and advisory services, with experts not only in employment, commercial, dispute resolution, and family law but also in supporting clients and law firms with their HR needs and people development, this chapter offers a practical examination of how managers can set clearer expectations and boundaries, delegate work effectively, supervise in a way that supports both quality and autonomy, and respond to common points of breakdown in ways that will strengthen individual capability, team effectiveness, and confidence in day-to-day management.

Setting expectations and boundaries with modern teams

Teams in law firms are now more diverse than ever before, in working styles, motivations, and needs. This diversity shows up in different ways – apprentices and graduates are entering through different routes, career changers join with experience of other fields, with varying levels of confidence and maturity, and there is a broader range of communication preferences and support needs. One practical consequence is that assumptions about accountability, ownership, and feedback are less likely to be shared consistently across a team. Effective supervision has to recognize that from the outset.

This does not mean constant adaptation to every preference. Instead, it means that firms need a clearly defined framework – supervision works best where there is a baseline structure, but that structure is flexed for individual success.

In practice, that means making the fundamentals explicit.

- What good work looks like.
- When questions should be raised.
- What needs immediate escalation.
- What degree of autonomy is expected at each and every stage.
- What deadlines are fixed and which can be discussed.

Without this level of clarity, both junior staff and supervisors are left to fill in the gaps themselves. It also helps reduce inconsistency in how competence is judged, particularly across teams or departments where supervision expectations may otherwise vary more than firms realize.

Hybrid and flexible working make that need more acute. Flexibility works best where organizations are clear about how it operates in practice, rather than leaving teams or individuals to improvise their own rules. The same applies to supervision. If a team is not physically together every day, managers cannot rely on ad hoc corridor conversations, visual cues or quick desk-side checks to identify confusion or slippage. Review points, contact patterns, and communication norms need to be established. Bridging differences in expectations across generations and working styles depends on adapting management approaches and ensuring open dialogue. The fact that some teams may feel less formally hierarchical does not remove the need for structure – if anything, it makes clear supervision arrangements more important.

With teams working remotely, regular communication is not merely about staying in touch. It is a way of ensuring people are engaged, on track, and clear about the direction of travel. This can be achieved through employee surveys, listening exercises, team check ins, and conversations about priorities and workload. Used well, those mechanisms give supervisors better sight of what is happening without turning supervision into surveillance.

Weekly or daily to-do lists help to make supervision visible and shared without becoming oppressive. A brief written list or morning check in can help align expectations, identify pressure points, and provide a record of what has been agreed. Written follow ups can also be important where oral feedback alone is too easy to lose, misunderstand, or dispute later.

Boundaries are an important part of supportive supervision because they reduce guesswork. Where junior lawyers are unclear about when to ask for help, how quickly a response is realistic, or what should be escalated immediately, they may either seek reassurance too often or delay raising issues for too long. Clear communication norms help them develop better judgment about priority, autonomy, and escalation, while also allowing supervisors to provide support more consistently and sustainably. It is useful to teach teams how to use communication tools well so that they know which issues belong on email rather than Teams, what merits an immediate interruption, and how to respect others' working patterns without letting problems drift.

Onboarding belongs here too, as supervision starts from induction. A structured induction does more than cover systems and logistics. It can explain how the team works, who supervises what, how work is managed and reviewed, and how their role fits into the firm. A strong people plan should connect recruitment, onboarding, performance management, and development, rather than treating them as separate exercises.

A well-structured approach to supervision should also be capable of managing neurodiversity and differing communication or working preferences. Neuroinclusive supervision should not depend on conformity, disclosure, or one preferred communication style. Some people work better with verbal discussion, whilst others need written follow-ups. Some will benefit from live check-ins, and others prefer clearer lists with more time to process. Reasonable adjustments will need to be built into how work is delegated and reviewed, especially where there is a legal obligation to do so under the Equality Act 2010. Supervision should be structured enough to provide consistency and flexible enough to support different ways of working or different employee needs.

Checklist: setting expectations early

- Clarify what good work looks like in the team.
- Be explicit about who supervises what.
- Set out when questions should be raised and what needs immediate escalation.
- Agree communication norms, including channels, availability, and response expectations.
- Explain how reviews will work in practice.
- Use induction and early check-ins to reinforce expectations.

Managing people for quality, efficiency, and development

Delegation is often viewed through the lens of getting work off a senior lawyer's desk. Used well, delegation supports three connected outcomes – quality, efficiency, and professional development. These outcomes are closely linked in practice. A delegation decision that ignores one of them usually weakens the other two.

- *Quality of output is defined by the quality of the brief.* The supervisor needs to define the task, its purpose, the expected output, the deadline, the client or matter context, and any obvious risks or sensitivities. The review process then needs to be calibrated to the risks involved, the nature of the work, the experience and competence of the person carrying it out, and the support available around them. The SRA's guidance is useful here because it supports a risk-based approach to supervision arrangements rather than one standard model for every matter. High risk or unfamiliar work may require close review; lower risk or more routine work may justify lighter touch oversight. It is also helpful for firms to be clearer internally about the standards against which work will be assessed, so that competence is not left overly dependent on individual manager interpretation.

- *Efficiency depends on resource allocation.* Delegation is part of using the right resource at the appropriate level, including paralegals and junior solicitors, so that senior time is reserved for the work that genuinely requires it. Delegation makes better use of senior time for the success of the organization. However, efficiency is not created merely by passing work downwards. If the brief is unclear, the review disproportionate, or the work pitched at the wrong level, the result is reworking and frustration rather than efficiency. Ultimately, time spent on ineffective delegation may need to be written off, causing a commercial loss to the firm, not to mention the loss of confidence of those involved.
- *Development is the third outcome, and often the one that gets squeezed when a team is busy.* Yet it is essential. Delegated work should help build capability, confidence, and judgment rather than simply shifting pressure. Delegation can be used as a means for identifying areas for development, building confidence on both sides, and gradually expanding comfort zones over time. This progression does matter for development of staff. When supervisors keep every significant decision for themselves, junior team members do not learn how to assess risk, exercise judgment, or take ownership. When they are pushed too far too quickly, quality suffers and confidence can drop. Measured stretch must be the goal so that the opportunity to add value for years to come is maximized.

As capability develops, the level of correction of more junior lawyers should reduce, and they can become trusted with more ownership and less reworking. There is a difference between correcting a substantive error and rewriting work until it resembles the supervisor's own style. The former is part of development; too much of the latter can hold it back.

Commercial viability sits within this section rather than outside it.

Supervision takes time and so does development. Supervisors are often trying to balance billable work, client responsiveness, and resourcing pressure. The answer, however, is not to minimize supervision. Instead, the focus should be to make delegation more effective, so that reviewing is proportionate, support is focused, and the development of junior talent contributes to the commercial strength of the team over time.

There is a retention dimension as well. Learning and development remain powerful reasons for people to stay at an organization. Progression, mentoring, and visible investment in development are key to keeping people engaged. In a team, that means delegated work should evolve as capability evolves. Responsibility, client exposure, and visible contribution should widen in step with competence. If people see no route from support tasks to meaningful ownership, development then stalls and a failure to retain staff often follows. Development also needs to include a gradual transfer of client contact and relationship responsibility, rather than limiting junior solicitors to back office support while senior solicitors retain all external visibility. Part of good leadership is being willing to share visibility and success, rather than holding on to client-facing opportunities that could otherwise help others grow.

Checklist: before delegating work

- What is the purpose of the task?
- What outcome or output is needed?
- What is the deadline, and how fixed is it?
- What risks or sensitivities should the person be aware of?
- What level of autonomy is appropriate?
- When and how will the work be reviewed?
- Is this task pitched at the right level for both delivery and development?

Supervising without micromanaging

Effective supervision supports quality and regulatory compliance while still allowing autonomy, judgment, and confidence to develop. Getting this balance right is at the heart of modern management. The SRA expects effective systems of supervision, but that does not translate into a requirement for constant intervention. Proper supervision is more than checking that matters are progressing. It requires a risk-based approach that takes account of workload, competence, the nature of the work, and the systems and culture needed for people to raise concerns in good time. It also requires more than supervision arrangements on paper – firms need to take proactive steps to make sure those arrangements are working effectively in practice.

Good supervision tends to include a small number of consistent habits – regular check ins, visibility of live work, timely feedback, clear escalation routes, and open discussion about time and billing. These habits reduce the need for frantic rescue work later. They also help supervisors distinguish between someone who needs clarification, someone who needs coaching, and someone who may be struggling with capacity. This approach can also help distinguish between issues that relate to supervision of legal work and those that sit more naturally within broader line management, such as longer-term development, wellbeing, or overall performance.

Micromanagement enters when oversight stops being proportionate. A useful test is whether the supervisor is responding appropriately to real legal or client risk, or simply to a difference in style, which does not present that risk.

Over-supervision is not always driven by the demands of the work itself. In some cases, it reflects the supervisor's own anxiety, perfectionism, or uncertainty about what effective supervision requires. Where that happens, the result can be unnecessary control, slower development, and avoidable dependency. This is where management skills matter. Not every senior solicitor has been taught how to supervise well. Being more experienced or more senior does not automatically make someone a good manager. Many senior solicitors who are supervisors were trained in an environment where they were simply expected to "get on with it", and that experience does not provide a model for effective supervision of the more varied and remote working teams now. Firms should therefore be careful not to assume that progression into senior roles automatically equips people to supervise others effectively. Supervisory capability needs to be developed explicitly.

Checklist: signs that supervision may be drifting into micromanagement

- Work is being rewritten rather than reviewed.
- Updates are requested more often than the risk justifies.
- The supervisor is correcting style rather than substance.
- The junior solicitor is becoming more dependent rather than more confident.
- Oversight is being driven by anxiety rather than the demands of the task.

Psychological safety and supportive challenge

Psychological safety is important as it affects whether or not someone will say they are struggling with priorities, flag that a deadline is slipping, or ask a question before a problem escalates. Psychological safety not only reduces risk, it creates space for learning, new ideas, and stretch. A junior solicitor is more likely to take thoughtful responsibility where they believe raising an issue will lead to support and problem solving rather than frustration or blame. Effective supervision also contributes to wellbeing, because people are less likely to feel isolated or to carry hidden pressure where support and escalation are normalized. The SRA's guidance underpins this theme. It sets out its expectations that firms have necessary systems and culture in place to enable staff to raise concerns and be supported if they are experiencing problems.

Support also needs to take account of individual needs. Some people will prefer live check-ins, while others will work better from written lists or more structured follow-up. Neuroinclusion and reasonable adjustment sit naturally within this. Adapting the approach taken avoids falling into the trap that one method of supervision will produce good results for everyone.

Mentoring and buddying can help to create this safe working environment. A mentor or buddy, inside or outside the formal reporting line, can offer another route for questions, reflection, and support. This can be particularly useful where a supervisee is hesitant to raise early concerns directly with the person reviewing their work. It does not replace supervision, but it can support and improve it. More broadly, strong supervision is often supported by a wider culture of teamwork and knowledge sharing, rather than resting entirely on one formal supervision relationship.

Delegation as a leadership skill, not a liability

Delegation is often treated cautiously in law for understandable reasons. The work carries risk, client relationships matter, and supervision accountability remains with the senior solicitor. However, these concerns make structured delegation more important, not less. Delegation should be understood as a leadership capability – a means of creating clearer accountabilities, building confidence, and developing future capability without losing sight of standards.

The SRA position supports that view. Delegation does not remove accountability for supervision. Firms and regulated individuals remain responsible for ensuring that legal services are competently delivered and appropriately supervised. Therefore, this means the question is not whether to delegate, but how to do so with clear oversight, defined responsibility, and review levels matched to risk and experience.

This is where judgment becomes especially important. Effective delegation depends not only on sound structures and appropriate review, but also on the supervisor's ability to communicate clearly, calibrate support, and adapt their approach to the individual and the task. Managers may need to adapt their style in response to changing work environments and evolving expectations around autonomy, support, and clarity. Some newer entrants to the legal sector arrive with a strong self-belief and a desire for ownership – others need more support to build their confidence. Both can be managed well, but neither benefit from ambiguity. Clear responsibilities, defined accountabilities, and shared expectations produce better outcomes than assumptions about how a "good junior" ought to behave.

A good personality match between the supervisor and the person they are supervising can clearly help. However, firms also need to be careful not to over rely on a small number of "more likeable" or naturally adaptable individuals to do most of the supervision heavy lifting. Not only is that not fair, but it can create distorted expectations of who is "good with people". The better aim is for all managers to learn how to work well with a range of personalities and to get the best out of others to mutual benefit, while recognizing that some relationships will naturally be easier than others. Supervision skills should be monitored through performance reviews or built into internal promotion requirements within the firm.

Building resilient teams through delegation

Delegation also contributes to a growth culture and an environment in which people are trusted to develop, mistakes are managed proportionately, and supervisors see part of their role as creating future capability rather than simply allocating tasks. A resilient team is not built by concentrating all the judgment at the top. It is built by allowing people to grow into responsibility under proper supervision, so that sound judgment, ownership, and learning develop throughout the team rather than sitting only with the most senior solicitors.

Part of effective management is also teaching people how to be resilient at work. This means helping them to understand and be able to receive feedback without being derailed by it. They need to learn from mistakes, and learn how to move forward with greater confidence and better judgment.

Constructive feedback, clearer expectations, and proportionate stretch are part of how resilience is developed in practice.

Where those skills are less developed, firms should not assume they will emerge by themselves. Supervisors may need support to strengthen their supervision approach, whether through leadership development, management training, inclusion training, or more targeted support on communication, feedback, and people management.

Learning from delegation failures

Delegation failures are common, and they rarely arise from simple incapability alone. More often, the cause is a combination of unclear instructions, weak systems, poor timing, lack of appropriate review points, or communication breakdown. Problems are especially likely where ownership is vague, supervisory capacity is stretched, or the supervisee does not feel able to raise concerns.

The first priority when something goes wrong is how can it be resolved. After that comes diagnosis. What actually happened? Was the work badly scoped? Was the person given enough context? Was the deadline unrealistic? Was there a review point? Did the individual understand when to escalate? Only once those questions have been examined, in an environment of looking for improvement, not blame, does it make sense to decide whether the issue is one of capability, conduct, support, or process.

The distinction here matters because the response should differ. Capability and conduct are not the same. Capability relates to skills, experience, training, and capacity to perform the role. Conduct relates to behavior and choices. If a problem reflects weak systems or a lack of development, then coaching or training may be appropriate. If it reflects a refusal or failure to follow process or repeated disregard for expectations, a different route may be needed.

Early intervention is essential to ensure good habits are developed so concerns should be defined clearly, support identified where appropriate, and review points built in before the issue becomes entrenched. Improvement should then be measured in clear and practical terms, not only through technical markers such as accuracy, judgment, and quality of output, but also through personal skills such as ownership, responsiveness to feedback, confidence in raising concerns, and ability to learn and move on from mistakes. The earlier a concern is identified, the easier it is to correct without damaging confidence or client service.

Failure can also improve systems. Repeated issues may show that onboarding is too light, delegation briefs too vague, review processes inconsistent, or documentation weak. Record keeping is important – tracked changes, feedback notes, HR files, check-ins, quarterly reviews, and robust processes all help to identify and evidence concerns that need to be addressed. They support development, but they also matter where questions might later arise about insufficient supervision or inadequate support. Written evidence of feedback and supervision can also be important where recollections differ, where concerns later need to be escalated formally, or where the firm needs to demonstrate that support and oversight were in fact provided.

Checklist: when delegated work goes wrong

- Address the client or matter issue first.
- Identify what was unclear – task, timing, ownership, review point, or escalation route.
- Decide whether the issue is one of capability, conduct, support, or process.
- Identify what support, training, or clarification is needed.
- Record feedback and agreed next steps.
- Review whether the system or the supervision approach taken needs to change.

Clearer delegation, stronger supervision, better outcomes

Delegation and supervision shape how teams deliver work, manage risk, and develop capability. In a legal environment marked by hybrid working, broader routes into the profession and evolving expectations around communication and autonomy, delegation, and supervision demand more conscious management than firms may once have relied upon. It does not call for more control for its own sake. It calls for greater clarity, stronger consistency, and better judgment in how work is allocated, reviewed and developed.

This is not always straightforward, for a number of reasons. Time pressures can make supervision feel secondary to delivery, even when it is central to it. Many new supervisors are also working without strong models of supervision from their own formative years. If they have only recently stepped into a senior role themselves, the pressure to appear confident and capable can make it harder to ask for support or to recognize that supervision skills may need to be developed just as deliberately as legal knowledge. In that context, clear frameworks, well understood expectations, and effective support for supervisors are not administrative extras. They help reduce avoidable inconsistency and give managers something sound to work within as they grow into the role.

When those foundations are in place, the benefits are wide reaching. Clear expectations, proportionate oversight, and stronger management habits support better outcomes for clients, teams, and firms. They improve quality. They make better use of resource. They reduce the risk of problems being spotted too late. They allow junior solicitors to build confidence, refine their judgment, and increase their visible contribution over time, rather than remaining dependent on constant correction or being hesitant to take ownership. They also strengthen retention, because people are more likely to stay where development is real, support is meaningful, and progress is visible.

This is where the longer-term value of delegation and supervision truly sits. When expectations are clear and oversight is proportionate, quality improves, risks are identified earlier, and teams make better use of their collective capability. Junior solicitors are able to build judgment, confidence, and visible contribution over time, rather than remaining dependent on constant correction or hesitant to take ownership. Good delegation and sound supervision do more than keep work moving in the short-term. They build capability across teams and help develop solicitors who are not only technically strong, but commercially aware, accountable, and able to work well with others, with habits that endure as they move into positions of authority.

For supervisors, then, the challenge is not to find a single ideal model of supervision or delegation, but to create conditions in which good work can be done consistently, questions are raised early, responsibility expands safely, and accountability remains clear. Sustained attention to that is worth it because it does more than reduce risk – it maximizes retention, improves delivery today, and determines the caliber of leaders the profession produces next.

Reference

1 www.sra.org.uk/solicitors/standards-regulations/code-conduct-solicitors/

Chapter 10:
Negotiation as communication

By Jonathan Middleburgh, principal, Edge International

Negotiation as a core communication skill

To what extent is negotiation a core and necessary skill in the lawyer's toolkit? And to what extent is negotiation a separate skill from communication? This chapter argues that negotiation is indeed a core and indispensable skill for every lawyer and a core component of much communication. Indeed, negotiation is a key type of communication, especially for lawyers, and every interaction a lawyer has is potentially a negotiation.

One definition describes negotiation as "an interactive communication process that may take place whenever we want something from someone else or another person wants something from us". Viewed through this lens, many day-to-day client and colleague interactions can be thought of as negotiations, and when approached as negotiations the outcome might be a better one. For CILEX readers specifically it is worth noting that negotiation appears explicitly in the CILEX competency framework, and commercial awareness and negotiating skills when dealing with clients and other parties are listed as core competencies expected of a chartered legal executive. This chapter is therefore directly relevant to professional development and to CPD obligations.

Negotiation as communication process

Negotiation and communication cannot be separated. Every negotiation is a communication process – whether it is a face-to-face, phone, email, or video communication.

Miscommunication can derail even well-structured deals. Legal training historically has prioritized black letter legal training over communication skills and most law firms provide little or no negotiation training, perhaps because good negotiation – like good writing – is quite hard to teach.

Lawyers often confuse negotiation with adversarial communication and assume that negotiation is best achieved through adopting adversarial positions and driving that way towards an end goal through an adversarial process or battle. Or they default to assuming that they will achieve an optimal outcome by deploying a series of "points" or "good arguments" to argue against the other side's position.

When coaching senior lawyers or giving them feedback gathered as part of a structured 360 feedback process, I am often met with a series of forensic points, aimed at demonstrating to me that the points I have made are "wrong" or aimed at undermining or "contextualizing" the feedback that I have given them. Quite often, a coachee will explain to me how they have handled a communication with a colleague or a client. What they describe is how they deployed a series of knock-out points or arguments against their colleague or client and their subsequent puzzlement at their failure to achieve the result they want. This default process can be particularly acute with litigators, who engage in adversarial process for a living and often default to this approach, regardless of context.

The bottom line is that this type of forensic or adversarial approach generally does not achieve the best results with colleagues or clients. There are other, better, ways to negotiate and to communicate more generally. In this chapter I endeavor to suggest some alternative, better, approaches, in order to achieve optimal desired outcomes or better outcomes.

Two philosophies – positional vs interest-based negotiation

There is well-established literature on negotiation, with Fisher and Ury's *Getting to Yes*[1] the canonical text. The two approaches to negotiation outlined by Fisher and Ury provide a good analytical framework or model when thinking of how best to conduct a negotiation.

One key approach to negotiation is the so-called *positional* approach. In positional negotiation or bargaining, the parties are adversaries and the goal is victory – negotiation is a zero-sum game. One party's win is the other side's loss. So each side sets up positions and digs into them and applies pressure. This is a classic litigation or adversarial approach, where each side draws the battle lines and then deploys the full weight of forensic artillery and other weaponry to achieve the best result – ideally capitulation or surrender of the other side, or a win "in court". The result can be something like trench warfare, where there are huge costs and losses to both sides and the result is not necessarily optimal for either side. It can be an exhausting process and it can damage relationships, sometimes irreparably. Just as in trench warfare, the one side can advance their position fractionally at huge cost and then cede that ground, again at huge cost.

The other key approach to negotiation is the so-called *interest-based* approach. In interest-based negotiation or bargaining, the disputants approach the negotiation as joint-problem solvers, focusing on their respective interests rather than their respective positions, guided by objective criteria and reason.

One classic illustration of the two divergent approaches is a dispute involving a crop of oranges, where both sides lay claim to the crop. In the positional approach, either party A "wins" the crop or party B does, in which case party A's win is party B's loss (or vice-versa). In the interest-based approach, negotiation reveals that party A and party B have different interests – party A wants the crop for the juice of the oranges, party B wants the crop for the peel, and so the crop can be shared. Both parties end up securing their interests and both sides secure a "win".

One can think of many situations where both parties' interests can end up being met – or met to a greater extent than if one party seeks a complete "win" over the other side. One such example is given below.

Negotiation in practice – a family law scenario

Sarah and Mark are divorcing after 12 years of marriage. The central dispute is over the former matrimonial home. Sarah's solicitor's opening position is that the house should be sold and the proceeds divided equally. Mark's position is that he should be allowed to remain in the property.

In a positional negotiation, the lawyers go back and forth – countering, making small concessions, growing increasingly entrenched. The process takes months, costs are mounting, and both clients are exhausted and embittered.

An interest-based approach changes the conversation. When the lawyer takes time to understand Sarah's underlying interests, it emerges that she needs capital to rehouse herself and her children quickly – she is not attached to an equal split for its own sake. Mark's interest is not really the bricks and mortar either; it is continuity and stability for the children. He also fears the open housing market.

Once each party's interests are better understood, options emerge that positions had obscured. A deferred sale arrangement with a Mesher order may meet both needs – allowing Mark to remain while giving Sarah a secured entitlement to capital when the trigger event occurs. The "settlement" was always available; the communication had to reach it.

Key lesson: In family law, the emotional intensity of negotiations makes the temptation to argue positions particularly strong. The lawyer who can slow the process, listen actively, and identify the client's real needs – stability, security, recognition – will reach better outcomes than one who simply fires off offers.

The communication toolkit

The theoretical approach is all very well, but it only takes one so far. In many or most situations, parties do not adopt a purely "positional" approach or a purely "interest-based" approach. Often, the approach is a more blended one.

In this chapter, I am interested in helping readers to adopt a more nuanced approach or to think about what additional skills they need to incorporate into their communication toolkit, as well as the existing skills they need to strengthen, in order to achieve better results in negotiating with clients or colleagues.

Before I review some key skills in the negotiation / communication toolkit, please allow me one observation and one suggestion.

The observation is that it is often very helpful to think of colleagues as internal clients when communicating with them or negotiating with them. Very often, in my experience, lawyers divide their world into two distinct camps – clients (external) who they need to please and colleagues (internal) who they can treat as a lower priority to their external clients who pay the bills.

I would argue that this is a false and unhelpful dichotomy. Lawyers need to manage relationships internally with as much care and attention as they manage external relationships. Failure to do so will come back to bite. It is more helpful to think of colleagues – including those who are junior – as clients, whose interests also need to be accommodated as far as possible. Where there is an apparent disparity between your interests and their interests and you need to communicate (or negotiate), try to think about how you can best meet their interests while also meeting yours.

My suggestion? As you read through the list of skills that follow, conduct an honest self-appraisal or audit of how developed your skills are in each of the areas covered. Which skills do you lack? Which skills do you need to strengthen? How are you going to go about acquiring or strengthening the skill or skills in question?

Active listening

Lawyers often say that they are good listeners. This reminds me of the statistic that 75 percent of drivers rate themselves as above average. It simply can't be the case that most lawyers are above average listeners. Active listening means focusing intently on what the other person is saying, asking clarifying questions, paraphrasing, and mirroring back to ensure correct understanding. It means attending to both what is said and what is unsaid. It means attending to body language as well as what's spoken. It means tuning into the emotional content of what's being said as well as the "intellectual" content. It means demonstrating empathy and actively listening to concerns to foster an environment of openness and good communication. It is less likely that you will get to understand the other party's true interests if you are not able to foster such an environment of openness. The problem with adversarial communication is that it shuts down open communication rather than enabling it.

Clarity and accessible communication

The most effective negotiators are those who can communicate their points clearly and concisely, using language that is accessible to all parties. This is particularly relevant in client-facing negotiations where legal jargon tends to alienate rather than to enable or to persuade. Use plain language where possible and cut the jargon.

Non-verbal communication

Lawyers often discount the importance of non-verbal communication or think that talking about body language is psychobabble. The truth is that body language and non-verbal communication is incredibly important. The majority of communication is non-verbal and personal chemistry can achieve results and overcome hurdles to negotiation. Posture, eye contact, and the use of silence all play a role. Non-verbal cues play an important part in negotiations. There is indeed a lot of cod psychology when it comes to writing about non-verbal communication but it is worth spending time learning how to "read" non-verbal communication, taking some of the cod psychology with a liberal pinch of salt.

Emotional intelligence

It is well-established that there are various types of intelligence. Lawyers tend to excel (as one would expect) in the domain of linguistic intelligence. Precision in reading, writing, and oral argument is at the heart of a lawyer's professional skills. Lawyers are often great wordsmiths. Emotional intelligence is an entirely different domain of intelligence, consisting of the ability to read, understand, and manage one's own feelings as well as those of clients and adversaries, as well as knowing how to self-regulate emotionally. In my experience, many lawyers are very high on IQ and low or very low on EQ, spending insufficient time working on developing their arsenal of emotional intelligence-based skills. How to do so is beyond the scope of this chapter but there are numerous books and other resources that can help you to develop your emotional intelligence skills. Work on developing your emotional intelligence as well as your core lawyering skills.

Psychological awareness

According to Fisher and Ury, "people problems" fall into three categories – perception, emotion, and communication. The ability to see the situation as the other side sees it is one of the most important skills a negotiator can possess. Step into the other person's shoes and try to see the landscape from their perspective. You will develop a clearer understanding of their interests and what they are trying to get out of the negotiation.

The aim of this brief survey of some key components of the communication toolkit has not been to provide a comprehensive overview, but to highlight a few key areas and to encourage the reader to self-reflect on how strong (or weak) they are in each area. The key takeaway is to work on developing these so-called soft skills. They are every bit as important as the so-called core lawyering skills.

Negotiation in practice – a conveyancing scenario

A buyer's lawyer receives the results of a structural survey on a Victorian terrace. The surveyor has identified evidence of movement in the rear extension and recommends specialist investigation. The buyer requests a £15,000 reduction in the agreed price.

The seller's solicitor takes the position that the price was agreed, and that the survey findings are speculative. The negotiation risks becoming a positional stand-off that risks derailing the transaction for both parties.

A communication-focused approach explores each party's underlying interests. The seller wants to complete at close to the agreed price and avoid the transaction collapsing – they are committed to a purchase further up the chain. The buyer wants to manage risk – their real concern is less around trying to exploit the survey to negotiate a better price, and more around avoiding buying an expensive problem.

An interest-based approach suggests a different conversation. Rather than debating the price reduction, explore whether the seller would be willing to commission an alternative specialist report and to share the report at their own cost. If the report is reassuring, the buyer can proceed at the original price. If the report confirms that there is a real expensive problem, both parties will have better information on which to negotiate. The approach moves the negotiation from a zero-sum argument about price to a shared problem-solving exercise.

Context and medium – where and how negotiation happens

Negotiation no longer happens only across a table. Negotiations today take place in a myriad of ways, including face-to-face, via email, by phone, and online (via video link). Each mode of communication can impact the relationship, level of trust, and outcome.

Digital communication can lower the "personal" stakes of the communication – the so-called "online disinhibition effect", causing people to communicate in ways that they would be less likely to do face-to-face, for example with less formality. Email can be particularly problematic as an email can be read in multiple ways such that it is important to be alive to possible ambiguity when using this mode of communication.

In practice it is important to read emails back carefully before sending them. Nowadays it is worth running the draft email through AI for a sense check, but even better to have it read by another human being to check that the tone is right and to check additionally for any potential ambiguity. Be aware that your email might land in an entirely different way than intended. Follow up with verbal communication wherever possible and appropriate.

Online (video) communication also carries its challenges. It is significantly harder to establish rapport in an online environment and harder to get a read on body language and the emotional content of the communication. My preference would always be to conduct an important negotiation face-to-face but this is often unrealistic nowadays, requiring the lawyer to listen even more intently and actively. Try to ensure that high-stakes negotiations take place face-to-face. The extra cost will often be outweighed by the result.

Negotiation with your own client

One dimension of negotiation that is often overlooked is the one that happens before any approach is made to the other side – the negotiation that takes place with your own client. Setting realistic expectations, explaining the difference between a legal position and a likely outcome, advising on risk – all of this involves persuasion, active listening, and careful communication. A client who has been told they have "a strong case" and is then advised to accept a settlement they regard as inadequate will feel let down, regardless of the legal merit of the advice. Managing the gap between expectation and reality is itself a negotiation, and it requires the same skills as any other.

CILEX members, whose qualification route emphasizes practical client-facing competence alongside legal knowledge, are often well placed to develop this dimension of negotiation skill. The discipline of the CILEX competency framework – which requires demonstrable performance in real-world client interactions – is a genuine advantage in this regard.

Communication as a core skill

This chapter has argued that negotiation and communication are not merely related – negotiation is a communication process and every significant communication between a lawyer and another person is, in some sense, a negotiation.

The practical implications are significant. Investment in developing communication skills – in listening, clarity, and emotional intelligence – is not a soft add-on to legal competence. It *is* legal competence. The lawyer who understands what the other party really needs, who can articulate their client's interests persuasively without distortion, who builds trust through consistent and candid communication, and who knows when to speak, when to listen, and when to sit in silence – that lawyer will achieve better outcomes, maintain better relationships, and build a more sustainable practice.

Whether you are guiding a first-time buyer through a fraught conveyancing transaction, or helping separating spouses reach a financial settlement that lets them both move forward, the law tells you what is possible. Communication is how you get there.

Reference

1 Roger Fisher and William Ury, *Getting to Yes: Negotiating an agreement without giving in*, Random House Business, 7 June 2012.

Chapter 11:
Agile and Lean – new ways of collaborating and organizing work

By Maria Govis, KPMG

Introduction

In a project kick-off meeting, the client mentions that their team works "in iterations", following a "sprint" cadence. An in-house counsel asks whether the external legal team can accommodate providing updates in a "kanban board". The head of legal operations wants to know whether the legal team can join a "retrospective" once the project wraps up.

These terms come from Agile and Lean – frameworks and working philosophies that organizations across industries have widely adopted over the past decades.[1]

This chapter offers a brief introduction to these methodologies – where they come from, what problems they were designed to solve, and why they matter to modern lawyers. It covers practical tools drawn from Agile and Lean that can help you run legal projects with more transparency, less rework, and better outcomes – and help you make sense of how your clients organize their work.

This chapter does not argue that law firms or in-house legal departments should reinvent themselves as agile organizations overnight – in fact, it will also address where Agile tends to run into friction in today's corporations.

By the end of this chapter, you will have a working vocabulary and a practical toolkit based on Lean and Agile principles, ready to apply in your own practice or in conversations with clients, along with an overview of technology tools shaping how legal work gets done.

Where Agile and Lean come from

Let's start with the historical background of Agile and Lean. Over the past century, both have shaped how manufacturing and knowledge work gets organized, and their origins offer some genuinely useful context for legal professionals today.

Lean – from Toyota's factory floor

The origins of Lean – before it was called Lean – lie in production, specifically car manufacturing. By the turn of the 20th century, mass manufacturing in the United States was developing, with Frederick Taylor pioneering the concept of "scientific management".[2] His research focused on speeding up factory production by, among other measures, breaking down assembly work into the smallest possible tasks, each of them standardized, timed, and optimized by management experts. Henry Ford's approach differed from Taylor's in some respects, but his booming factories were broadly aligned with Taylorist principles of mass production.[3]

The rigid manufacturing system in the US came with its structural costs, though. The system required enormous inventory buffers at every stage. Defects were caught late because stopping the assembly line was not possible. Workers had no authority to flag problems, and manufacturing companies often viewed them as inputs to be optimized. These were logical consequences of "scientific management"-based mass production philosophy.

This model was not how Japan's, particularly Toyota's, post-war factories operated. In mid-century Japan, raw materials and capital were scarce (hence, no large inventories), while domestic demand was unstable. Toyota could not survive by copying Ford's principles of mass production. Instead, Taiichi Ohno, who would become Toyota's chief of production, came up with what would eventually be called the Toyota Production System (TPS).[4]

Ohno's goal was not to produce as much as possible, but to have exactly what was needed to meet demand.[5] This became known as the first pillar of TPS' "just-in-time" (JIT) production.

The second pillar was "jidoka", often translated as "autonomation", i.e. automation with a human touch. Unlike in Ford factories, Toyota plant workers had the authority and tools to stop the line the moment a defect was detected, to avoid delays and costs associated with discovering the issue later in the process. This meant having workers who not only performed their part in production line, but also understood the overall process and could look out for any associated issues.

Another influential element of TPS is its categorization of process waste – the inefficiencies that cost time and resources in any production system – such as overproduction, waiting, unnecessary transport, over-processing, excess inventory, and defects. These categories translate well beyond manufacturing, as we will see later in this chapter.

TPS remained a concept known only in Japan between the 1950s and 1970s

– Western companies first started learning about it following the 1973 oil crisis, when Toyota's car production began outperforming American manufacturers.

The word "Lean" itself was coined not by Toyota, but by American researchers studying it from the outside.[6] MIT's International Motor Vehicle Program conducted large-scale research into car manufacturing, finding that Toyota's plants significantly outperformed the best plants in North America and Europe.[7] Lean production principles became all the rage with Western consulting firms who began spreading ideas of the Japanese "economic miracle" to American and European companies between the 1970s and the 1990s.

By the 2000s, Lean became so influential it migrated beyond manufacturing into other industries, such as healthcare[8] and software development.[9] Lean became the foundation of a broader "management science" ecosystem that includes frameworks such as Six Sigma,[10] TQM,[11] BPR,[12] and Kanban.[13]

Today, Lean is less a methodology than a mindset with its own set of values – limiting waste and eliminating everything that does not bring value. Enabling the flow of information and ideas without interruption. Adding value by focusing on what matters most. Nurturing continuous improvement and lifelong learning.

Agile – from software industry crisis to Manifesto

Agile originated in software development, and was a response to the crisis that had been building for decades before becoming acute in the 1980s and 1990s.[14] At the heart of it was a disconnect between software development teams and customers – in expectations, communication, and the quality of what got delivered. Projects were typically run using a waterfall[15] approach – requirements were gathered first, solutions designed, then implemented, then tested, and each phase fully closed before the next opened. Logical in theory, but consistently problematic in practice – the Standish Group's Chaos Report of 1994[16] analyzed over 8,000 software projects in 365 companies and claimed that just 16 percent were completed on time and on budget, and 31 percent of projects were cancelled before completion.

Some of the reasons for such a high number of issues had to do with a disconnect between the gated phases – requirements were supposed to be gathered upfront, but customers rarely knew what they wanted out of software, or their understanding changed after they saw what software can do. A customer may know what problem they are trying to solve, but not how to get there or how to translate it into system requirements. Additionally, when testing begins after implementation ends, it can lead to situations where, if the customer dislikes the result, it can be "too late" to change it without significant cost.

This development prompted a group of software developers to meet in Utah and draft what became known as the 2001 Agile Manifesto,[17] focused on these core values:

- *Individuals and interactions* over processes and tools.
- *Working software* over comprehensive documentation.
- *Customer collaboration* over contract negotiation.
- *Responding to change* over following a plan.

This listing does not mean that the items mentioned second are not important; rather, it is about placing the focus on the solutions (in italics), ensuring alignment around the actual purpose of building software.

The Manifesto's principles emphasized focus on delivering working software; welcoming changing requirements, even late in development; keeping processes and solutions as simple as possible; empowering self-organizing teams; and building with regular reflection and feedback loops.

The Agile approach divides a project into short iterations. The output of each iteration is reviewed, priorities are adjusted if needed, and the overall plan evolves accordingly. New features are implemented in the order of business value, and quality is kept as high as possible throughout.

The Agile Manifesto's influence on software development was enormous. By the 2020s, Agile had moved from a niche movement to the dominant operating model for modern IT.[18] Its growth and commercialization even prompted a backlash – the software craftsmanship movement that emerged in 2008 was a call to return to original emphasis on technical excellence.[19]

A wide variety of Agile frameworks have been developed over the past two decades. One worth mentioning – because it is referenced so commonly in corporate environments – is Scrum.[20] Scrum introduced practical tools to support Agile delivery – a product backlog for prioritizing upcoming features (covered in more detail later in this chapter), structured team events to facilitate collaboration, and the role of the Scrum Master, whose focus is on removing the obstacles or escalating them so that the team can continue productive work.

Today, the tension between "doing Agile" and "being Agile" is real.[21] In many large organizations, the original framework has arguably become a commercialized, ceremony-heavy apparatus, more focused on compliance and reporting to leadership than on the values that inspired Agile. Still, the philosophy and mindset of Agile – team autonomy, rapid feedback loops, genuine responsiveness to change, and willingness to listen to the customer and keep improving – remains worth preserving.

Influence of Lean and Agile

The influence of Lean and Agile transcended the industries they were developed for, becoming the foundation of an entirely new coaching and consulting industry. It is worth noting that some of the original signatories of the Agile Manifesto argued that Agile should apply to software development only – yet the frameworks spread far beyond that boundary regardless. Perhaps inevitably so, as software has embedded itself into virtually every sphere of our work and life in the recent decades.

Understanding where Lean and Agile come from, and what problems they were designed to solve, is the first step towards practical fluency and informed decisions on how to use these principles.

Agile and Lean for legal teams

As discussed, Agile and Lean were developed outside of the legal industry, based on principles such as iterative work, continuous feedback loops, empowered frontline workers, and tolerance for small failures. Not all these principles will translate directly to legal work. Legal advice or contract review does not naturally map onto sprint cycles. Process waste, as Lean defines it, looks very different when what you "produce" is judgment rather than a physical product.

It is also undeniable that the mindset internalized by most legal professionals clashes with some of Agile's core assumptions, such as the willingness to ship imperfect work, fail fast, and improve through rapid iteration. For very good reason, legal work is about risk aversion and delivering carefully considered, high-quality results.

There is also a workspace culture dimension. As explored above, Lean succeeded partly because Toyota empowered workers to stop the production line the moment a problem was detected. The hierarchies of traditional law firms rarely extend that kind of structural authority to all professionals within the firm.

None of this means that Agile and Lean have nothing to offer legal professionals; direct translation is not the goal here. Instead, this section will focus on tools and principles that any team performing knowledge work can benefit from.

At their core, the principles described below are aimed at making collaboration and teamwork more manageable, more efficient, and more enjoyable. How can we create the best possible results within defined timelines? How can we collaborate effectively and ensure we understand and support each other? How can we do good work at a sustainable pace?

I encourage you to read what follows with these questions in mind, reflecting on where these principles might apply, and where they might need adapting, in your own practice and context.

Making work visible – an introduction to Kanban

The first principle worth introducing is Kanban, a method for process improvement.[22] It is a natural starting point for applying the Lean mindset to the way we work – Kanban is built on the idea of understanding your *current* process first, then making small improvements from there. Start with what you do now, and agree to pursue incremental change.

Kanban is not a project management system but an Agile method for improving the way a team works. Built on Lean values, it consists of a set of tools and practices to help teams improve and evolve over time. The two Kanban practices most relevant to this section are visualizing the current process and limiting work in progress.

To visualize the workflow, teams use a Kanban board – typically a set of columns, each representing a step in the process, displayed on a whiteboard (physical or digital). The columns will vary from team to team – in a legal context, they might include generic stages such as "client query received", "analysis", "drafting", "review", "sign-off", and "delivered to client".

Each work item (in agile software development this would typically be called a user story) is written on an index card or sticky note and placed in the column that reflects its current stage. This creates a visual picture of how work is flowing through the system. How many new client queries have come in? How many are in progress, and who is working on them? Are we on track for our deadlines?

Visualizing work on a kanban board enables two things in particular:

1. *Uncovering hidden process steps.* On paper, a process may look straightforward – a query comes in, person A reviews it, person B signs off, and the deliverable goes to the client. In practice, however, many of those queries may also require approval from person C – who has limited availability and a growing pile of items on their desk. That bottleneck is invisible until it is named. Mapping the actual process on

a kanban board creates an honest, transparent picture of how work *really* gets done, and enables the team to rethink it.

2. *Constructive workload and capacity conversations.* Visual representation of work allows teams to move beyond a more abstract "I'm busy and I can't take anything else on" to the specific "I'm working on A, B, and C and supporting a colleague with D; for me to take on something new, one of these needs to move on first". That shift makes capacity conversations far more actionable.

An important element of Kanban is that process improvements are owned by the team itself. For this to work, the board needs to reflect reality – not a version of the process tidied up for leadership review.

To experiment with kanban board principles, teams do not need to invest significant time or resources. Simple, readily available tools, such as MS Planner for firms using M365 suite, are sufficient to start visualizing current ways of working, understand how many items are in progress at any given time, and open more productive conversations about capacity.

Reviewing processes and eliminating waste

We have looked into how to visualize processes in their current state. Lean principles allow us to go deeper – reviewing processes and productivity with the specific aim of eliminating constraints and waste, and reducing both the time and cost involved.

The first step is to map out the processes in your practice that would benefit from improvement. Various techniques exist for process mapping, including swim-lane diagrams, BPMN 2.0-based mapping, and value stream mapping. A value stream map captures not just the process flow but also key data – work in progress items, processing time per unit, error rates, idle time, and so on.[23] This enables teams to distinguish between steps that add value and those that do not. As with the kanban boards, the depiction needs to reflect reality, not an idealized version of how things should work.

The next step is to analyze where the process breaks down. In a typical legal workflow, this might include work piling up between stages (because a partner does not have time to review the associate's output); errors in a drafted motion discovered at a late stage; or a client who did not provide sufficient details from the beginning, leading to multiple rounds of clarification.

This brings us to the framework of eight wastes – a structured way to uncover process inefficiencies.[24] The acronym DOWNTIME is often used to map the wastes:

- *Defects.* Flaws that result in rejection or rework. In legal context, these might include typos or inaccuracies in a drafted motion. Defects are a particularly costly form of waste – they carry reputational and financial risks, and consume additional resources to correct.
- *Overproduction.* Producing more than is needed without corresponding demand. This type of waste is less directly applicable for legal work – in a service context, it might look like a restaurant preparing more meals than ordered for a given service.
- *Waiting.* Time lost waiting for the next step in a process. An associate waiting for a partner's review, a legal professional waiting for approval from the authorities, or inefficient scheduling – all are forms of waiting waste.
- *Non-utilized talent.* Underusing people's skills, knowledge, or experience. An example would be assigning a professional to work they are significantly overqualified for, or overstaffing a task, engaging two people for work one could handle.
- *Transportation.* Unnecessary movement of materials or information. In an office context, this can manifest as too many disconnected tools in a single workflow, requiring the same document to be moved, reformatted, or re-entered across multiple systems.
- *Inventory.* Excess materials or work items not being actively processed. This waste ties to an organization's resources and increases the risk that accumulated materials will become obsolete before they are used (e.g., outdated templates or superseded draft versions).
- *Motion.* Unnecessary movement by people. This can be as straightforward as an inefficient office layout that adds unnecessary steps to routine tasks. It can also manifest as time spent searching for misplaced documents or navigating poorly organized shared drives.
- *Extra processing.* Doing more work, or producing higher quality output, than the client actually needs. This is particularly relevant for legal professionals who are trained to deliver the most thorough results possible. Does the client need a lengthy memo analyzing every possible scenario, or would a concise note in plain language, focusing specifically on their question, serve them better? Extra processing also appears in overly complex forms and approval workflows that request far more information than the decision actually requires.

Reviewing your current processes through the lens of these eight wastes can offer a fresh perspective on where to simplify, where common problems originate, and how to make the team's work more sustainable.

Delivering early and often – iterative work in practice

One of the original signatories of the 2001 Agile Manifesto[25] writes about the concept of the Iron Cross in project management – the idea that only three out of four constraints can be satisfied at once: good, fast, cheap, or done.

You can have fast, cheap, and done – but it will not be good. You can have good, fast, and done – but it will not be cheap.

This constraint applies to knowledge work of all kinds, including legal work.

Agile's response is to make early and continuous delivery of value the highest priority. Rather than delivering a complete piece of work at the deadline, agile teams are encouraged to deliver frequently, in the shortest iterations possible. In software development, these iterations are called sprints – time-boxed periods at the end of which the team is expected to deliver a defined set of completed work, sometimes referred to as minimum viable increments.

This approach allows teams to gather feedback and test ideas early, making adjustments along the way rather than discovering problems at the end. It also connects to the idea of psychological safety and creating an environment where it is acceptable to make mistakes early and correct them.

In the context of legal work, this does not mean delivering unfinished drafts to clients. Rather, these principles can be adopted for a more collaborative approach on complex matters. It is rarely in the client's interests to be surprised by a final product that does not reflect what they needed.

A practical way to apply this principle is to build regular check-ins with the client where feasible – running ideas by them, confirming that their input is being heard and reflected throughout the process. This reduces the risk of rework and frustration for legal teams, and helps achieve higher customer satisfaction that supports long-term client relationships.

Making priorities visible – the backlog

Another concept closely tied to workflow visualization and iterative delivery is the product backlog. The backlog is a tool from Scrum – it is a "to do" list of all the tasks the team needs to work on at some point. In agile software development, the backlog typically contains a list of features to be built, and each sprint draws its work items from the top of that list. Think of it as a prioritized queue – the most important items sit at the top and are addressed first.

In a legal context, the backlog can be a useful tool for capturing upcoming tasks – particularly recurring or foreseeable ones. If the team has seasonal or quarterly reporting obligations, or if a larger project is known to be arriving in a few months' time and will require effort from multiple team members, it can be added to a shared backlog.

This approach gives the whole team visibility into upcoming and outstanding work, ensures everyone understands what constitutes a business priority, and creates the conditions for constructive conversations about workload and resourcing.

Strengthening collaboration – team ceremonies

One of the core values from the 2001 Agile Manifesto is "individuals and interactions over processes and tools".[26] It is not enough to follow best practices or run efficient processes. First and foremost, we come together in our workspaces to perform work as a group of people. Mutual understanding among team members, and a healthy, psychologically safe work environment, are paramount to achieving good results.

There are many agile practices designed to support individuals and interactions between them – often called events or "ceremonies" in Scrum – ensuring teams have structured space for collaboration and reflection. Here are some of them:

- *Regular standup meetings.* The purpose of these is to have brief, focused check-ins as a team – typically 15 minutes – where everyone shares what they worked on yesterday, what they are focusing on today, and whether they have any blockers their colleagues might help with. These meetings can be daily or at any other frequency the team prefers. Crucially, they should not be treated as status reports for management, but as genuine moments of connection and mutual support. (In a tech start-up I worked in during the 2010s, these were literal standups – the team would gather in the office hallway, standing, to share their updates.)
- *Retrospectives.* Scrum also encourages regular sessions in which the team reflects on how a project or sprint went – what worked well, what did not, and what can be improved next time. A well-run retrospective is a genuine opportunity to exchange perspectives, give praise to

colleagues, and collectively improve ways of working. Needless to say, for a retrospective to be meaningful rather than ceremonial, it needs to take place in an environment where people feel safe to speak honestly.

A note on adoption

Agile and Lean are not remedies for every challenge in corporate life. In fact, there is often significant tension between adopting these principles in the rigid, hierarchical organizations that many legal professionals work in. Both Agile and Lean are meant to empower decentralized decision making – which may be a challenge in corporate environments that primarily operate through top-to-bottom instructions.

In such environments, these methodologies may gain some adoption on the surface while the underlying bureaucratic structures will remain intact. Ceremonies like standups or retrospectives risk becoming mere formalities when they are added as mandatory meetings to people's schedules – imposed from above, without shared understanding of what they are meant to achieve. In corporate environments already saturated with meetings, this can defeat the purpose entirely and be perceived as a burden.

Understanding this pattern – commonly referred to as "ceremonial adoption" – is important for legal professionals looking to introduce Agile or Lean principles to their organizations. Knowing that this dynamic exists makes it possible to navigate it more thoughtfully, and to focus on genuine culture change rather than process compliance.

In recent years, there has been growing momentum around legal project management and legal process improvement – disciplines that draw on Agile and Lean principles.[27] Even a basic understanding of the principles covered in this chapter can make a meaningful difference to how legal teams organize and experience their work. Kanban boards bring visibility to the team's focus and capacity. Iterative, collaborative work reduces rework and builds stronger client relationships. A shared backlog makes high-priority upcoming work visible and allows the team to plan accordingly. And regular team activities – when genuinely embraced rather than merely performed – build the kind of connection and psychological safety that good work depends on.

Speaking your clients' language

By now, the majority of corporations, technology companies, and professional services firms have adopted Agile or Lean practices in one form or the other. In-house legal teams sit inside organizations that run on these frameworks. General counsel report to CEOs who "speak" Agile fluently, and the same is true for legal operations functions. Agile and Lean have become the ordinary language of work for many clients, irrespective of whether these methodologies are implemented fully or in part.

The concepts explored above (not an exhaustive list) offer an initial idea and a better understanding of clients' operating models that are iterative, transparent, and continuously improving. Work is broken into small units and delivered frequently. Processes are reviewed regularly and adjusted when inefficiencies are identified. Priorities are explicit and understood by all.

Working smarter – technology tools for modern legal practice

Organizational frameworks have evolved significantly in the past few decades, and so has the legal market. With available technology, legal expertise has become ever more commoditized.[28] Clients can access competent legal advice from traditional or alternative legal service providers, in more formats and at a lower cost than at any point before.

In this environment, a lawyer combining sound legal judgment with basic operational and technological proficiency holds a stronger competitive position. A clear differentiating factor is understanding how work flows in a modern organization, and how that flow can be visualized, prioritized, optimized, and, where appropriate, automated, for better use of the legal team's time and expertise.

The final section of this chapter offers an overview of tools and capabilities that, even at a basic level of proficiency, can provide a competitive advantage for individual lawyers, legal teams, and firms. Technology tools are described in general terms only – the legal technology market is evolving rapidly, and specific products will continue to change.

Standardized intake forms

The intake process, i.e. how a new legal matter or request reaches the legal team, is often where inefficiency begins. In many traditional legal practices, intake is informal – an email, a phone call, a message from a business partner. The result is instructions that are incomplete, ambiguous, or inconsistently recorded, requiring follow-up before any substantive work can begin.

A standardized intake form, even a simple one, can help change this dynamic. Tools as accessible as Microsoft Forms allow legal teams to define exactly what information they need to process a request efficiently. In keeping with the "Extra processing" waste type discussed above, the form should ask for essential information.

Centralized knowledge libraries

One of the most persistent sources of inefficiencies in legal practice is reinvention of work that has already been done. A negotiation position carefully developed and approved on a transaction two years ago sits in the email archive of a lawyer who has since left the firm. Critical document templates live only in individual local drives. A standard clause that has been tested and refined over time is rewritten from scratch each time because no one can find the approved version.

A centralized knowledge library – i.e. a structured, searchable repository of templates, playbooks, approved positions, and institutional guidance – directly addresses this problem. Any basic document management tool can serve this function – SharePoint, Notion, Confluence, NetDocuments and others are all viable options.

The importance of shared repositories and their disciplined use only grows with the spread of AI tools. Even today, a simple query via a tool like Copilot can help a lawyer locate a template or precedent within seconds (provided this document has been stored in an accessible shared space). These capabilities will only improve in the years to come.

Matter and project tracking tools

A range of simple tools offering digital kanban boards for work visualization are readily available – MS Planner within Microsoft S365, Trello, and many others. The core functionality of these tools is broadly consistent – teams can view all tasks and matters on a visual board, with their current state, assigned owner, and due date at a glance.

Generative AI – responsible use in legal practice

Generative AI tools have entered legal practices faster than almost any previous technology. GenAI-powered tools now support document drafting, legal research, automatic redlining based on legal teams' negotiation positions, document summarization, and data extraction.

The lawyers who will be the most effective in using these tools are the ones who understand what this technology can do well, where it falls short, and how to deploy it in compliance with professional and ethical standards.

Generative AI offerings in the legal market continue to evolve rapidly. In the coming years, we will see capabilities moving beyond document work and toward an AI-powered work orchestration, reshaping not just individual tasks but how legal work is organized at scale.

Conclusion

The central takeaway from this chapter is a shift in perspective inspired by Agile and Lean principles. Legal work can be understood as a process, with steps, constraints, and opportunities for improvement. When viewed this way, technology can be applied responsibly to reduce friction, eliminate waste, and make work more transparent and more sustainable for everyone involved.

This chapter intentionally presents Agile and Lean as incremental practices rather than a call for radical transformation. Work with what you already have, see it clearly, and improve gradually. What matters most is the underlying mindset – oriented toward the client, committed to continuous improvement, and honest about how work is actually done.

In this spirit, modern lawyers are those who combine strong legal judgment with operational clarity, i.e. an understanding of how today's organizations work, the challenges they face, and how tools such as the language of Agile and Lean help them address those challenges. My hope is that this chapter sparks curiosity and encourages further exploration of Agile, Lean, and organizational design in the age of AI.

References

1 Mankins, M., "Lean Strategy Making", *Harvard Business Review*, May-June 2025. https://hbr.org/2025/05/lean-strategy-making

2 McKenna, C.D., *The World's Newest Profession: Management Consulting in the Twentieth Century*, Cambridge: Cambridge University Press, 2006.

3 Hounshell, D.A., "The Same Old Principles in the New Manufacturing", *Harvard Business Review*, November 1988.

4 Stellman, A., Greene, J., *Learning Agile*, Sebastopol: O'Reilly Media, 2015.

5 Shih, W.C., "What Really Makes Toyota's Production System Resilient", *Harvard Business Review*, November 2022.

6 Lean Education, "John Krafcik and the Birth of the Term Lean", January 2022. https://gb.creativesafetysupply.com/articles/john-krafcik-and-the-birth-of-the-term-lean/

7 Womack, James P., Jones, Daniel T., Roos, D., *The Machine That Changed the World: The Story of Lean Production*, Simon and Schuster, 2007.

8 Radnor, Z., Williams, Sharon J., *Lean as a Healthcare Improvement Approach*, Cambridge: Cambridge University Press, 2025.

9 Poppendieck, M., Poppendieck, T., *Lean Software Development: An Agile Toolkit*, Addison-Wesley Professional, 2003.

10 Six Sigma. www.sixsigma.co.uk/

11 Total Quality Management methodology. https://skillogic.com/blog/comparing-total-quality-management-six-sigma-and-lean-methodologies/

12 Business Process Reengineering methodology. www.6sigma.us/process-improvement/business-process-reengineering-bpr/

13 Kanban methodology. https://instituteprojectmanagement.com/blog/what-is-lean-kanban/

14 Martin, R.C., *Clean Agile: Back to Basics*, Pearson Education, Inc, 2020.

15 Waterfall is a term used in project management denominating a linear, sequential de-livery model, where each phase must be completed before the next begins. It is still used in many projects and industries where appropriate, i.e. construction.

16 The Standish Group, CHAOS Report, 1994. https://simpleisbetterthancomplex.com/media/2016/10/chaos-report.pdf

17 Agile Manifesto, 2001. www.agilemanifesto.org

18 Gitnux, Agile Statistics Report, 2026. https://gitnux.org/agile-statistics/

19 Martin, R.C., *Clean Agile: Back to Basics*, Pearson Education, Inc, 2020.

20 Schwaber, K., and Sutherland, J., *The Scrum Guide*, November 2020. https://scrumguides.org/docs/scrumguide/v2020/2020-Scrum-Guide-US.pdf

21 Horlach, B., Drechsler, A., "It's Not Easy Being Agile: Unpacking Paradoxes in Agile Environments", Nature Publishing Group, August 2020. https://pmc.ncbi.nlm.nih.gov/articles/PMC7510790/

22 Kanban board technique is also used in other frameworks, such as Scrum, where it serves as a project management tool providing a single source of truth overview of all tasks in a given sprint or project.

23 George, M.L., Rowlands, D., Price, M., and Maxey, J., *The Lean Six Sigma Pocket Toolbook: A Quick Reference Guide to Nearly 100 Tools for Improving Process Quality, Speed, and Complexity*, New York: McGraw-Hill, 2005.

24 GoLean Six Sigma, "8 Wastes". https://goleansixsigma.com/8-wastes

25 Martin, R.C., *Clean Agile: Back to Basics*, Pearson Education, Inc, 2020.

26 *Ibid.*

27 Fuesgen, I., *Next Stage Legal Project Management: Future-proof Your Matter Management*, Globe Law and Business, 2021

28 Susskind, R., *Tomorrow's Lawyers: An Introduction to Your Future*, Oxford: Oxford University Press, 2013.

Chapter 12: Networking with purpose

By Rebecca Overend, business development manager and associate, Irwin Mitchell

Why networking matters more than ever

According to *Oxford Languages*, the definition of networking is "the action or process of interacting with others to exchange information and develop professional or social contacts".

This definition feels especially relevant in today's legal market. The profession has shifted from being purely technical to being driven by relationships. Technical brilliance still matters, but it is no longer enough on its own. Legal services now operate in a landscape where commercial awareness, human connection, and long-term trust often determine who wins work, and who keeps it. As a result, law firms increasingly behave like most other professional services organizations – outward-looking, client-focused, and reliant on the strength of their relationships. In a competitive, transparent market, well-networked lawyers consistently stand out.

Networking is no longer optional – it is a core professional capability. It is the mechanism through which technical excellence becomes visible, trusted, and commercially relevant. Crucially, networking is not a responsibility reserved for senior lawyers, it is a discipline that develops over an entire career. The most successful lawyers understand that their networks, built gradually, authentically, and with intention, are one of their greatest assets. Client loyalty is no longer guaranteed. Increasingly, buyers rely on personal recommendations and trusted professional relationships when choosing who to work with, especially when switching advisers carries risk, cost, and disruption. Because selling legal services is rarely fast or straightforward, clients need compelling reasons to make a change. More than anything, they need confidence in a lawyer's judgment, reliability, and credibility. In a world full of technically excellent lawyers, trust is the differentiator. And networking is how that trust is created.

Debunking myths and reframing networking for lawyers – why networking is a skill, not a personality

Networking is often misunderstood as extroverted behavior or as a form of selling. Neither assumption is accurate, and both can make the idea of networking feel uncomfortable or even inauthentic for lawyers. Effective networking is not about being the loudest voice in the room or the most visible attendee at an event. It is rooted in curiosity, consistency, and authenticity. Many of the strongest networkers are quiet observers who build relationships steadily over time, often forging deeper and more durable connections as a result. Purposeful networking is not about lifestyle or personality. It is a deliberate professional skill that supports career longevity, business growth, and reputation.

Similarly, a common misconception is that networking is transactional or synonymous with selling. Approached in that way, interactions can feel forced or false. In reality, effective networking is about relationship building – understanding others, exchanging value, and allowing trust to develop organically over time. While formal events and dinners can play a role, networking happens everywhere – in internal meetings, coffee chats, shared interest groups, online communities, through colleagues, and through everyday conversations where genuine dialogue emerges. The challenge is not location, but mindset.

Another frequent concern is that networking detracts from fee-earning activity. While it does require commitment, the most effective approaches are deliberate, proportionate, and consistent. Even short, purposeful touchpoints such as a thoughtful message, a brief catch-up, or meaningful introduction can significantly strengthen a professional network over time. Consistency matters far more than intensity.

Professional relationship-building is a mindset, not just an activity

Professional relationship-building is not a task on a to-do list. It is rooted in genuine value exchange rather than self-promotion or transactional thinking.

A clear understanding of one's professional "brand" – the impression left after every interaction, is fundamental. It shapes how value is perceived and how confidently it can be articulated. Asking simple questions such as, Why am I networking? What is my purpose? What do I hope to gain and offer through this relationship? creates clarity and intention. Knowing what strengths, insights, or support can be brought to a connection is the foundation of meaningful engagement. Business development professionals often embody this instinctively. Even without providing legal advice, they recognize how to add value by connecting people, spotting complementary interests, and enabling opportunities others may miss. In networking, reputation is everything. A mindset grounded in reciprocity positions an individual as knowledgeable, dependable, and generous within their professional community. Sharing expertise, offering support, and becoming a trusted resource strengthens credibility and creates the conditions for collaboration, mentorship, and long-term career progression.

Ethical considerations unique to the legal profession

Networking is vital in legal practice, but lawyers face ethical limits unique to the profession. The principles of the Solicitors Regulation Authority (SRA) framework require integrity, independence, acting in clients' best interests, and maintaining public confidence. In practice, this can be interpreted as:

- Protecting client confidentiality, including the avoidance of "war stories" or casual comments that could reveal identifiable information or strategy.
- Ensuring referral relationships do not create conflicts or compromise independent judgment.
- Avoiding approaches to vulnerable individuals, the pressure to instruct, or unsolicited legal advice.
- Steering clear of relationships with third parties who might influence legal strategy or undermine duty to the client.
- Avoiding any appearance of impropriety.
- Never promising outcomes or misleading potential clients.

Online platforms such as LinkedIn, forums, and webinars bring their own challenges, for example where lawyers need to be particularly aware of accidentally giving legal advice, having comments interpreted as endorsements, connecting with judges that can present the appearance of bias, or sharing content that violates confidentiality or the duty of candor.

Building genuine professional relationships

The foundations of authentic professional relationships are curiosity, active listening, and empathy. This means taking the time to truly hear what others are saying, showing sincere interest in their work, and offering support or expertise where it is genuinely useful. Small, thoughtful gestures such as remembered details, timely introductions, or relevant insights compound over time. At the core of effective networking sits a simple truth – the more someone gives, the more they grow.

Reciprocity

The principle of reciprocity highlights the natural human tendency to return acts of generosity. Applied with intention, it creates a powerful ripple effect. Support, guidance, or introductions given freely often return value in unexpected ways. Reciprocity extends beyond immediate benefit. Consistently helping others contributes to a culture of generosity and collaboration across a network. Over time, this builds credibility and trust, strengthening the likelihood of support when it matters most.

Identifying who to build relationships with

Understanding a stakeholder ecosystem is the first step in deciding where to focus relationship-building efforts. This network may include clients, prospects and targets, colleagues and peers, opposing counsel, experts, referrers/intermediaries, and wider industry or community partners.

In the context of this chapter, referrers and intermediaries are third party professional contacts who introduce clients, cases, or commercial opportunities to a firm. They are strategically important because they:

- Generate a steady pipeline of high quality work.
- Extend reach into new sectors or markets.
- Support mutually beneficial, reciprocal relationships.
- Strengthen the firm's position within the wider professional ecosystem.

Common referrer groups include accountants, banks and financial advisers, insurers and brokers, charities, other law firms, and professional services firms. Prioritizing relationships in line with personal objectives, business goals, and practice strengths provides clarity and shapes a realistic action plan.

Mapping existing connections is a useful starting point. Visualizing current networks, as in Figure 1, helps identify where influence already exists and where deeper or new relationships would add value. A lawyer's primary stakeholders such as clients, prospects, and colleagues directly influence revenue, reputation, and career progression. Secondary stakeholders shape referrals, visibility, and market perception. Effective relationship-building recognizes the strategic flow of value between legal professionals and both primary and secondary stakeholders.

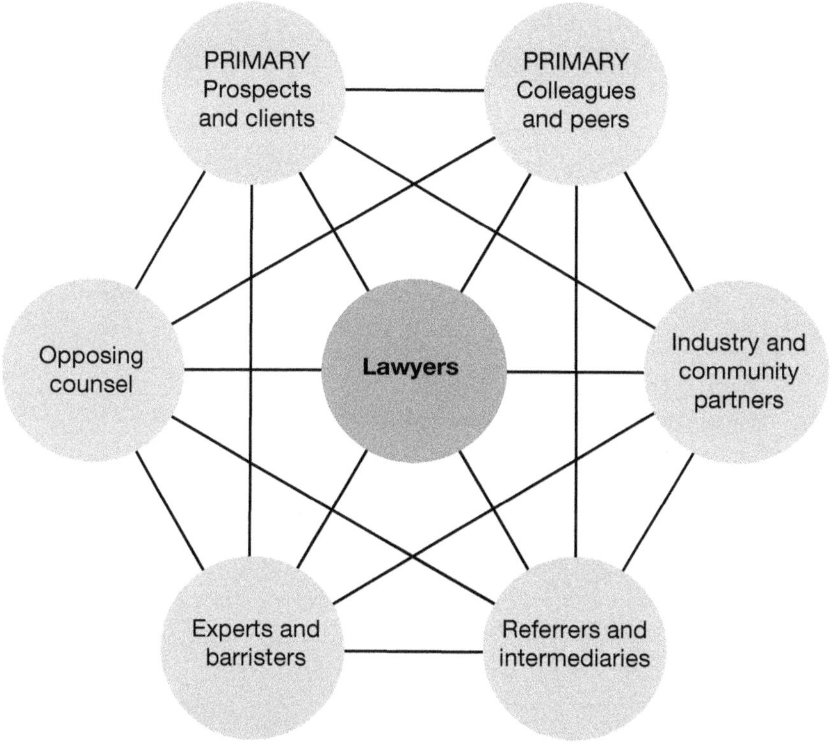

Figure 1: Relationship links between networks.

Practical skills and techniques

Building strong professional relationships is not about collecting contacts – it is about cultivating meaningful connections that strengthen both a practice and the wider firm. Successful lawyers often take a broad view of networking, remaining curious about expertise beyond their own discipline and alive to collaborative opportunity.

Starting conversations

For some, the idea of starting a conversation can feel uncomfortable. With a little preparation, the process becomes far easier. A small set of open questions prepared in advance often provides more confidence than a lengthy list and creates moments of shared insight, revealing opportunities that wouldn't surface in more transactional exchanges. See the box overleaf for some example questions.

Networking conversation examples

There are many ways to start, build, and end a conversation. Here are a few examples:

Introductions:

- *"Hi, I'm Rebecca Overend from Irwin Mitchell, what brings you here?"*
- *"Hello, I'm Rebecca. Would you mind if I joined you?"*

Conversation openers:

- *"How do you all know each other?"*
- *"How did you hear about this event?"*
- *"What attracted you to attend?*
- *"Have you been to this event before?"*
- *"Have you met any interesting people here so far?"*
- *"Is there a speaker/topic tonight you're looking forward to?"*
- *"What kind of work do you do?"*
- *"How did you get into your current field?"*
- *"What skills have you found most valuable in your career?"*
- *"What's the best piece of career advice you've received?"*
- *"Is there something you've learnt recently that surprised you?"*

Building deeper conversation:

- *"What challenges are you currently thinking about or navigating in your work?"*
- *"What's one professional goal you're focusing on this year?"*
- *"If you could collaborate with anyone on a project, who would it be and why?"*
- *"That's interesting, can you tell me more about it?"*
- *"What's the next step for you with that?"*

Simple exit questions:

- *"Before I circulate, is there anyone you think I should meet here?"*
- *"It's been great having this conversation, shall we connect on LinkedIn?"*
- *"If we don't get the chance to speak again this evening, let's connect on email and continue our discussion."*

Preparation
Light preparation improves effectiveness. Where possible, reviewing delegate lists in advance allows for more focused introductions and purposeful engagement.

Networking in person
When networking feels awkward or unfamiliar, or when there is a desire to make the most of limited time, the following strategies can help lay the groundwork for future business development opportunities:

- *Arrive early.* Walking into a packed room can be intimidating. Arriving early provides the opportunity to connect with other early attendees before the crowd builds.
- *Find the refreshment table.* For those unsure where to start, positioning yourself near the refreshments can help. It is a natural gathering point and an easy way to initiate casual conversations.
- *Take the initiative.* Making a direct approach and introducing oneself is encouraged. Most delegates welcome the opportunity to chat. While it may feel daunting initially, with practice this becomes a valuable networking skill.
- *Be curious.* Asking questions and listening actively is key. Taking the time to learn about others' roles, organizations, and challenges helps build understanding. Personal connection points, such as shared sporting interests, hobbies, or work–life balance, often foster genuine rapport.
- *Connect on LinkedIn.* While business cards still have a place, connecting on LinkedIn is often more practical and helps ensure relationships are maintained after the event.

Follow up
What follows the first interaction is often more important than the interaction itself. A brief, human follow-up message can convert a conversation into a lasting professional relationship. This is how relationships deepen – small, thoughtful actions that build trust over time.

The assumption that if someone doesn't respond, they are not interested, is rarely accurate. People are busy. A polite follow-up is normal and often appreciated.

Networking in digital spaces

The value of digital networking is not found in volume, but in engagement. Growing a relevant audience matters less than maintaining connections and showing up consistently with intent. Digital networks prove their resilience during periods of restricted in-person contact. Relationships nurtured in advance continue to deliver value when circumstances change.

Lawyers benefit from clarity about what they want from online engagement, whether starting conversations, positioning within a niche, or contributing to wider sector dialogue. They should begin by figuring out what they want from online engagement. Is it starting conversations, positioning as a go-to professional within a niche sector, or influencing thinking within the space? Most lawyers can achieve a solid digital presence in ten to 15 minutes a day by posting their own content, commenting on someone else's post, and sharing others' content with their own thoughts. Easy content to share includes:

- Acknowledging events in the diary.
- Summarizing the value gained from attending.
- Commenting on public cases, legal developments, reports, research etc.
- Sharing an article of interest to a particular practice area.
- Drawing parallels between work and downtime such as comparing the changing weather forecast with the ups and downs of a legal case load.

Internal vs external networks

Internal client development is frequently underestimated, yet it is a powerful lever for business growth and career progression. Strong internal relationships drive visibility, trust and influence, enabling more effective collaboration and client outcomes. Adopting a structured approach, such as a 100-day internal networking plan (see below), provides a practical framework for building visibility, identifying gaps, and sustaining momentum.

Externally, the same intentionality applies. Selecting a small number of networks aligned with interests, values, and goals, and committing to them consistently is more effective than attending numerous one-off events. Thought leadership, speaking opportunities, and authored content further reinforce credibility and expand reach when aligned with clear strategic intent.

Strategies for effective internal networking

When joining a firm or moving into a new role, establishing early credibility and visibility with partners, fee earners, and key business services colleagues is essential. In a partnership environment, internal relationships underpin trust, collaboration, and effective cross-selling, directly influencing client retention, growth opportunities, and firm performance.

A structured 100-day plan offers a practical framework for building these connections. Approached as though entering a new firm and divided into four quarter stages (as illustrated in Figure 2), it creates focus while allowing time to understand the firm and its dynamics.

The first stage centers on mapping the internal landscape. This includes identifying partners, associates, business services teams, and operational leaders alongside in-house counsel contacts, priority clients, and specialist functions such as knowledge, learning and development, responsible business, HR, and governance. Relationships can then be categorized as established, developing, or largely unknown.

The second stage focuses on prioritization. In a law firm context, this involves understanding which practice areas and sectors are strategic priorities, where influence sits, and which partners align most closely with growth objectives. This highlights gaps, cross-practice opportunities, and areas where relationship investment is likely to deliver the greatest impact. Targeted outreach and initial discussions can then begin.

The third stage is centered on active engagement. Meetings with partners, informal conversations with associates, and regular interaction with business development colleagues and operational leads help embed relationships across the firm. This phase is key for demonstrating value, whether by supporting partner-led pitches, identifying client development opportunities, sharing market insight, or facilitating introductions between teams.

The final stage emphasizes consolidation and follow-up. Developing short, practical action plans for priority relationships helps maintain momentum and ensures activity translates into outcomes. Consistent follow-through reinforces reliability and positions the individual as someone who understands partner priorities and the firm's strategic direction.

Alongside structured planning, involvement in firm initiatives provides further opportunities to build internal connections. Participation in diversity and inclusion networks, pro bono and ESG committees, sector groups, trainee development programs, social or charitable initiatives, and firm-wide events facilitates engagement across practices and seniority levels. Aligning with initiatives that reflect genuine interests supports authenticity. Additional value can be gained through mentoring and sponsorship arrangements, as well as informal peer networks, particularly in firms where collaboration and succession planning are key priorities. Attendance at practice group meetings, training sessions, and partner-led client discussions also strengthens relationships and deepens understanding of client and firm needs.

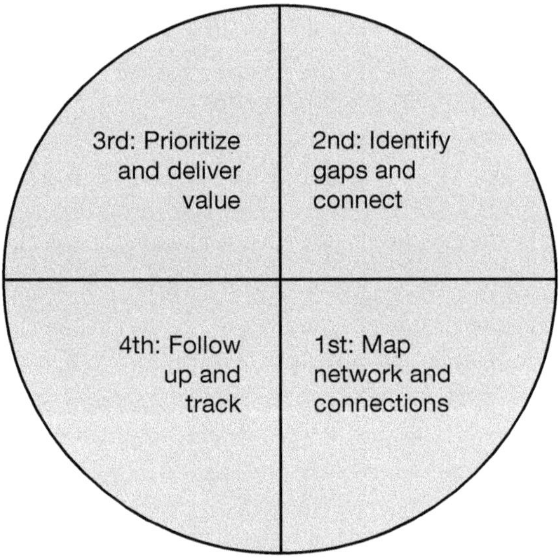

Figure 2: 100-day quarter plan.

Expanding influence externally

The market is saturated with industry events, legal associations, business networking groups, and sector-specific forums. The key is not to attend everything, but to be intentional. Select one or two networks that genuinely align with personal interests, career goals, values, or practice areas and commit to them consistently.

Registering for relevant forums, newsletters, memberships, external training networks, and selected sector insights or special interest groups is an effective way to stay informed about external developments. These resources should be reviewed regularly to assess their ongoing value and relevance. One opportunity may lead to another, opening possibilities such as All Party Parliamentary Groups (APPGs), steering committees, or panel and webinar speaking roles. Showing up repeatedly within the same series is more effective than scattering time across one-off events. Consistency builds visibility – as relationships deepen, familiarity with organizers and hosts can support positioning as a recognized contributor within that community.

From here, take initiative by proposing discussion topics, hosting sessions, clearly articulating what is gained from the network, and helping promote future events. Capture content for digital use, strengthen connections, and make a point of engaging with unfamiliar delegates. Thought leadership is an equally powerful networking channel. Speaking on panels, writing articles or blogs, contributing to wider publications, and participating in roundtables reinforces credibility and elevates profile. Workshops and training sessions, particularly for clients or key contacts, also provide strong platforms to demonstrate expertise while creating meaningful touchpoints. These activities do more than raise visibility – they create new conversations, attract relevant connections, and help establish a legal professional as a trusted voice in the market.

Adopting the 100-day quarter plan outlined above is as effective for managing external networks as it is for internal ones.

Choosing the right opportunities

When deciding where to invest time outside of fee-earning work, lawyers should prioritize networks based on strategic value, aligning the choice of network with practice area, industry focus, peer group interest, or long-term career goals. A useful benchmark is to ask: Would I pay to attend this event if there were a cost? If the answer is yes, it is likely worth the time.

Maintaining connections over time

Long-term relationship guardianship is a key success factor and keeping in touch matters more than the initial contact. Progress depends on the balance of human connection, combined with meaningful, value-led engagement.

Practical tools for staying connected

Remaining visible between in-person meetings does not have to be time-consuming. Small, consistent touchpoints often have the greatest impact. These might include sharing relevant content, sending a brief congratulatory message, or checking in to show continuing interest.

Practical approaches include:

- Adding contacts to relevant newsletters and event mailing lists;
- Engaging on LinkedIn through comments or appropriate tagging;
- Inviting contacts to firm-hosted events or webinars;
- Coordinating attendance at external events;
- Sharing content aligned to a contact's sector or interests; and
- Sending informal congratulations or brief check-ins at key moments.

Many firms support this through customer relationship management (CRM) systems. These tools are most effective when used consistently and kept up to date. Using a firm's chosen platform generally ensures that it meets GDPR requirements, integrates with practice management systems, is supported by training, and helps ensure data remains accurate and useful.

Deepening relationships gradually

Most professional relationships evolve over time. They move from polite acquaintance to trusted collaboration through a series of small, cumulative interactions. Early engagement may be exploratory or transactional, but trust develops through consistency, follow-through, and genuine curiosity. Shared experiences play an important role in this process. Working through challenges, navigating complex situations, and exchanging honest perspectives allows people to understand how each other thinks, responds under pressure, and aligns on values.

Effective relationship building balances personal connection with value-added interaction. Too much social contact without substance can stall progress, while purely transactional engagement can feel impersonal. Relationships that endure combine warmth with insight, conversation with contribution. Progress comes when social rapport creates space for honest, commercially relevant dialogue delivered in a thoughtful and tailored way.

Workload pressures fluctuate throughout a legal career, and relationship activity can slip during busy periods. This is when lighter touch contact is particularly valuable, helping maintain momentum until more meaningful in-person engagement is possible.

Dormant connections and reconnecting

Dormant relationships are a natural feature of networking. Regular reviews of your relationship plan may highlight connections that have faded. Some can be left aside, while others may be worth re-engaging where there was a genuine connection and mutual value. Reconnecting works best when it is honest and relevant. A simple, purposeful approach is often enough, for example: *"It's been a while since we last spoke. I recently wrote an article you may find interesting given your focus on X. It would be great to catch up over a coffee and hear how things are going."*

Networking for different career stages

For trainees and junior lawyers

Early in a legal career, work often flows down from senior fee earners, so networking may not feel urgent. But here's the problem: technically brilliant lawyers can miss out on partnership because they did not build a strong enough client base along the way. It is far harder to start at the top, where relationships are already established and difficult to dislodge. Building confidence in networking skills is key. Finding early mentors, official or unofficial, work well. This helps maximize internal exposure, which ultimately means more people to learn from.

Building a strong legal peer network early might not generate immediate instructions, but those peers will progress up the career ladder at the same rate. Today's associates are tomorrow's decision makers. When peers need advice or support, who will they turn to? Someone they know and trust. Someone authentic. Someone who has consistently delivered.

Mid-level lawyers

By career mid-point, most lawyers will typically have a clear sense of their core practice area and a growing idea of where they may want to specialize, whether that is a particular area of law or a sector they are increasingly drawn to. This is the phase where building subject matter presence really starts to matter. Even without full commitment to a sector or niche, lawyers should lay the groundwork now, by positioning within the sector of interest. That may involve authoring articles or thought pieces, sharing commentary on industry updates, or getting involved in sector-specific groups and initiatives. These activities not only deepen understanding but build networks and signal to colleagues, clients, and the wider market where interests and strengths lie.

As a lawyer grows, they should broaden their network beyond immediate team or practice group. Building relationships with colleagues across the firm, along with external peers and sector contacts, will provide a wider perspective, open doors to new opportunities, and ensure visibility in front of the people who can influence development and progression.

Senior associates and partners

Networking at this stage is less about broad exposure and more about intentional, high value strategic relationship building. Senior lawyers should focus on cultivating relationships aligned with their firm's strategic priorities, industry leaders, key referrers, influential intermediaries, and potential clients. The goal is not just visibility but credibility – being recognized as a trusted adviser with commercial awareness and a clear understanding of client needs. Senior legal professionals have the advantage of not requiring a large network, only a relevant, active one, where a revolving handful of strong, active relationships is far more valuable than hundreds of weak ones.

Client development and retention strategies
This is the phase where forward-looking client development becomes central. Senior lawyers need to model proactive relationship stewardship with regular touchpoints, meaningful engagement beyond active matters, and creating opportunities for clients to benefit from broader firm expertise. Strong client relationships are rarely transactional – they are built on consistency, value, and genuine investment in the client's long-term success.

Scaling and maintaining a high-quality network
As networks expand, maintaining their quality becomes both more challenging and more important. Senior lawyers must learn to prioritize relationships strategically and invest time where it will have the greatest impact. This may require adopting structured relationship management habits – tracking key contacts, planning touchpoints, and staying visible through thought leadership, speaking engagements, and sector involvement. At partner level, networks often become one of the most valuable professional assets, opening doors, enabling collaboration, and supporting long-term sustainability of the business.

Career transitions and networking
Career transitions can feel like hitting the reset button – sometimes daunting, but almost always a chance to sharpen focus and reintroduce with intent. Changing firms, for example, is the perfect moment to revamp your approach and roll out the 100-day quarter plan that reflects intention. Moving in-house or shifting practice areas often requires a rethink on how relationships are built, and which networks to lean into. But the toughest transition of all is coming back from a career break. It can feel like starting from scratch, yet it is also one of the richest opportunities to reassess career goals. A chance to reset, re-establish professional identity – a new 'style' or metaphorical new haircut. The key for a lawyer is making those first 100 days

count, and letting their network know exactly who they are now and where they are heading.

Practical frameworks

Effective networking is selective, intentional, and reviewed regularly. Beyond a 100-day plan, a simple four-step framework – monthly light touch, quarterly focus, biannual review, and annual reset – helps maintain alignment with commercial priorities. For example:

Step one: Monthly light touch

A monthly light touch could consist of:

- Reconnecting with a few contacts (clients, referrers, industry influencers).
- Sending a short, value-led touchpoint:
  - Insight on a legal/regulatory development.
  - Congratulatory note (promotion, deal, award).
  - Introduction to someone useful.
- Updating a CRM or contact list with:
  - Last interaction.
  - Emerging opportunities or risks.

Step two: Quarterly focus

A quarterly intentional objective is best structured around identifying 10-15 key relationships for focused attention. Activities may likely include:

- Arranging two or three coffees/lunches and attending one industry event or roundtable.
- Asking *'How is your business changing?'* and *'Where are you feeling pressure or growth?'*
- Sharing one specific capability or insight aligned to their issues (not a full pitch).

Step three: Biannual review

Reviewing contacts every half year should focus on curating a network by categorizing them as:

- *Advancing:* growing influence, mutual value, increasing relevance.
- *Stagnating:* static but potentially valuable.
- *Needs reigniting:* good history, lost momentum.
- *Ditching:* no relevance, no reciprocity, no realistic future value.

Step four: Annual reset

Finally, an annual strategic reset, aligning networking efforts with commercial priorities. For example:

- Clarifying three to five sectors, client types, or referrers/intermediaries requiring a closer relationship.
- Pressure test: does this network reflect practice ambitions in two to three years?
- Set clear networking goals (e.g. "five new referrer/intermediary relationships in the life sciences sector").

Keeping to this simple framework will help considerably in growing and maintaining a healthy and fruitful network aligned to strategic goals and aspirations. This can be applied to networking at any career level, for internal or external networks, or a combination of both.

Making networking a sustainable habit

Ultimately, effective networking is not defined by intermittent bursts of effort, but by steady, intentional investment over time. The key takeaway from this chapter is simple – relationships compound. A long-term mindset, underpinned by consistency and authenticity, will always outperform short-term, transactional behavior. Lawyers who approach networking with purpose, aligning it to their values, practice strengths, and career ambitions position themselves to create opportunity rather than chase it. By developing a personalized, realistic action plan and embedding relationship-building into everyday professional life, networking becomes sustainable rather than burdensome. Those who invest early build trust before they need it, strengthening both their personal credibility and their firm's commercial position. Purposeful networking is not about selling – it is a strategic form of career development, one that rewards patience, integrity, and genuine human connection.

Chapter 13:
Turning relationships into results – mastering business development in modern practice

By Yuliya I. LaRoe, JD, MBA, BD and leadership coach for lawyers and CEO at LeadWise Group, Inc

For much of the last century, the path to success in the legal profession followed a relatively predictable formula – develop strong legal expertise, work hard, serve clients well, and advancement would follow. Lawyers who consistently produced excellent legal work built reputations within their firms and with clients, and those reputations translated into thriving practices.

That model has changed. Today, as lawyers in private practice become more senior, their success is shaped not only by the quality of their legal work but also by their ability to generate, retain, and expand client relationships. In many firms, this expectation becomes explicit at the partnership level. Partners are no longer solely responsible for delivering legal services – they are expected to proactively contribute to the firm's growth.

The good news is that business development is not an innate talent reserved for a select group of charismatic rainmakers. It is, first and foremost, a professional skill that can be learned, refined, and integrated into the normal rhythm of legal practice.

To master this skill, you do not need more generic advice to "get out there" or "network more". What you need is a clear approach to understanding how business development actually works, where to focus your efforts, and how different activities fit together. This is where a proven business development framework, like the RainMasters™ Framework, becomes invaluable.

The RainMasters™ Framework – the foundations of sustainable rainmaking

Effective business development rarely happens by accident. While some lawyers naturally develop strong networks over time, relying on instinct or occasional effort is rarely enough to produce consistent results. Sustainable rainmaking requires alignment between how a lawyer naturally operates, how they think about business development, where they focus their efforts, and how they manage their professional relationships over time.

That's exactly why, almost 20 years ago, I began developing what would become the RainMasters™ Framework. I created it because I lived this struggle firsthand. After graduating from USC Law in 2003, I spent nearly a decade practicing international law at an AmLaw 100 firm in Los Angeles, advising Fortune 500 companies like Cisco, UnitedHealth, and Halliburton. But, like so many lawyers, I hit a wall when it came to business development.

I didn't have a background in sales or marketing, and I honestly didn't think I had the right personality for it. I wasn't a natural "schmoozer". I was focused on doing great work and keeping up with my caseload. Business development felt overwhelming.

So I started digging into what actually works. I studied, experimented, and refined for years. And I continued to refine the approach after I left the practice to open my law firm consulting and coaching firm – LeadWise Group – in 2012. Over the past decade and a half, as I earned my MBA, grew LeadWise, and coached and trained more than 5,000 lawyers, while also drawing on the ten years I had already spent in the legal industry, I built the business development framework I wish I'd had back when I was practicing.

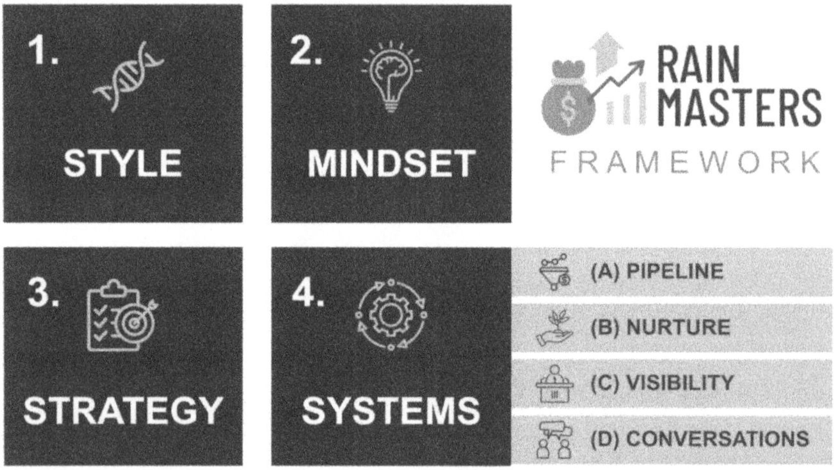

Figure 1: RainMasters™ Framework – BD for Lawyers (Copyright@ LeadWise Group, Inc)

The RainMasters™ Framework is a comprehensive approach that addresses both the *foundational elements* and *systematic processes* essential for sustainable business development success. It recognizes that effective business development isn't about random acts of BD or hoping that good work will magically generate referrals. Instead, this framework offers a pragmatic roadmap to unlock each lawyer's unique "rainmaster" potential.

The Framework identifies four foundational elements that must be in place before business development activities can produce meaningful results. These four elements are:

1. Discovering your natural rainmaking style.
2. Upgrading to a business development mindset.
3. Developing a winning strategy.
4. Designing and implementing business development systems.

The first three elements establish alignment. They help lawyers understand how to approach business development in a way that is authentic, psychologically sustainable, and strategically focused. Without this alignment, many business development efforts feel forced or inconsistent.

The fourth element introduces operational structure. It translates intention into action by organizing business development activities into systems that can be repeated and improved over time.

Understanding these elements is essential because many business development initiatives fail by focusing too heavily on tactics. The sections that follow explore each element of the framework in greater detail, beginning with the foundation that many lawyers overlook – discovering their natural rainmaking style.

Discovering your natural rainmaking style

"I hate those events."

When Nina said it, she laughed right after, the way people often do when they are trying to make a real confession sound lighter than it is.

"I mean, I *can* do them. That's the annoying part. I know how to do it. I can walk around, introduce myself, ask smart questions, and be perfectly pleasant. But by the time I get back to my hotel room, I feel like someone unplugged my internal battery and stomped on it."

I laughed. "So it's not that you can't do it. It's that it costs you."

"Exactly," she said. "And then I come back feeling like I'm somehow bad at business development because I'm not one of those people who seem to come alive in that environment."

Nina was a senior associate on the cusp of partnership at a national firm.

"So tell me," I said, "when do you feel most natural with people professionally?"

"Small groups," she said. "Or one-on-one. Definitely one-on-one," she said. "I slow down, I get more curious. I ask better questions. I listen better. I'm not trying to keep ten conversations alive at once."

"And how do people respond to you in those settings?"

She smiled. "Usually really well. They open up. They tell me what's *actually* going on. They stop giving me the polished version."

She laughed. "I know where you're going with this. You're about to tell me that maybe I'm not bad at business development. I just hate one particular version of it."

"That is exactly what I'm about to tell you!" I replied.

She shook her head. "It's just hard not to compare myself. I look around, and there are always these lawyers who can work a room like it's an Olympic event. They somehow know everybody, remember every spouse's name, make five people laugh in two minutes, and walk out with three lunches on the calendar."

"Let me ask you something," I said. "If you try to build your practice in a way that consistently drains you, how sustainable is that?"

She smiled. "Not very."

"That's the problem. A lot of lawyers confuse what is visible with what is effective. The highly extroverted rainmaker is easy to spot, so that becomes the model. But visible is not the same as optimal.

If you know that your real strength is building depth quickly in more focused conversations, then stop treating it like a consolation prize. That is a business development asset. A serious one."

She looked at me. "So you're saying my natural style might actually be an advantage."

"I'm saying it already is an advantage. You just haven't been fully claiming it yet. And once you get clear on your natural rainmaking style, we start to build from there. Not from who you think you should be. From where you are already strongest."

That is where discovering your natural rainmaking style begins. And not with the assumption that there is one, and only one, correct way to build a book of business.

The legal profession has carried around the same tired myth for years – that successful rainmakers all share a certain type of personality. Usually, the image comes to mind of some highly extroverted, relentlessly social, effortlessly confident lawyer who can move through a crowded room without ever seeming to hesitate or tire. For some lawyers, that description fits. For many others (if not most), it does not.

And that mismatch creates real damage. Because once you start believing that rainmaking has a personality requirement, one of two things usually happens. You either force yourself into someone else's style and burn out trying to sustain it, or you quietly assume that business development just is not for someone like you.

Both conclusions are wrong. The lawyers who build strong practices over time do not all share the same personality. What they share is something much more important – they learn how to use their natural strengths intentionally. They figure out where they connect best, how they build trust most naturally, what kinds of interactions energize rather than drain them, and how to turn those patterns into a business development approach they can actually sustain.

This is hugely important because, as my clients hear me say all the time, *business development is a marathon, not a sprint.* In other words, it only works if you can keep doing it. If your entire strategy depends on forcing yourself into environments that consistently exhaust you, overwhelm you, or make you feel inauthentic, this will be one very long and exhausting journey.

That does not mean you never need to stretch. You do. Every rainmaker has to grow. But growth works much better when it starts with building on your strengths rather than fixing your weaknesses.

Upgrading your business development mindset

Discovering your natural rainmaking style is important. But style is only part of the equation. You can have a business development approach that fits your personality beautifully and still avoid doing the work if your underlying beliefs about it are off.

That is where your BD mindset comes in. And yes, I know the word "mindset" is overused. It can even sound soft, vague, or suspiciously self-help-ish. But in this context, mindset is not fluff. The way I think about it is as the *operating system running quietly in the background, shaping what you do, what you avoid, what you tell yourself, and how quickly you retreat the moment business development starts to feel uncomfortable.*

For example, if part of you believes that good lawyers should not have to talk about business, you will hesitate. If you believe that raising your hand will make you look self-promotional, you will hold back. If you believe that rainmaking belongs to a certain kind of lawyer – smoother, louder, more senior, more polished, more naturally confident – you will unconsciously disqualify yourself before anyone else gets the chance.

The biggest challenge with mindset is that it does not just stay in your head. It shows up in your behavior. It determines whether you follow up, whether you ask the next question, whether you reconnect, whether you send that article, whether you let a good conversation turn into something more substantive, or whether you quietly back away and call it bad timing.

This is where I find neuroscience to be useful. A lot of lawyers treat their hesitation as a character flaw. It's not. More often, your brain is doing exactly what brains do when there is perceived social risk. Rejection and social exclusion activate many of the same neural regions involved in physical pain. Uncertainty also amplifies anxiety and avoidance. If even a part of you is not convinced you can do this well, you are far less likely to act consistently in the first place.

In plain English: if business development feels like exposure, your brain will try to protect you.

The most challenging thing about it is that this protection is holding you back while masquerading as something rational, even noble. You tell yourself you are focused on client service. You say you do not want to be transactional. You convince yourself you are being respectful, professional, or patient. Sometimes that is true. But sometimes, and this is the part worth being honest about, it is just self-protection in a nicer outfit.

I see this all the time with lawyers who are excellent relationship builders. In one of my early coaching meetings with Aisha, a newly elected litigation partner at a mid-sized firm, she said, "The whole idea of ranking people based on how 'lucrative' they could be rubs me the wrong way. I guess the way I naturally think about relationships is, do I actually like this person? Do we have a real connection? If we do, I'm happy to invest in that relationship. What feels off is looking at someone and thinking, okay, how useful could this person be to my book of business?"

"So it feels... calculating?"

"Yeah. Exactly. Calculating. And honestly, kind of gross. Like I'm taking something that could just be a genuine relationship and turning it into a business transaction."

"And that bothers you."

"A lot. Because then it feels disingenuous. Like, I'm not just being myself anymore. Like I'm angling for something."

"So in your mind, the minute you might benefit too, the interaction changes?"

"Yes. That's exactly it."

"Into what?"

"Into solicitation."

"So let me ask you something. Why does it have to be either/or? Why does it have to be either a genuine relationship or a relationship that could lead to business? Why are those two things mutually exclusive?"

She was quiet for a moment. "Because if I'm benefiting from it too, it starts to feel less pure."

"So giving feels clean, pure. Receiving does not?"

She looked at me and laughed again, this time a little more sharply. "Wow. Okay. That's uncomfortably accurate. Where I'm comfortable is, don't worry about me, let's focus on you. Tell me what's going on. Tell me how I can help. I'm very comfortable there. The minute there's even a hint that I might want something too, I tense up."

"Because?"

"Because then I'm exposed. Because now I'm not just being helpful. Now I'm asking to be seen as someone worth hiring. Worth choosing. Worth paying."

"So if they initiate, you're comfortable," I asked.

"Yes."

"But if you initiate?"

"Then I feel like I'm making it self-serving."

"Even if you can genuinely help."

"Even if I can genuinely help," Aisha said quietly.

"Okay, let me share with you what I see. You already know how to create value in conversations. You do it with current clients all the time. You ask smart questions. You help people think. You spot issues. You bring good judgment. The problem is not that you don't know how to do that. The problem is that when someone is not yet a client, you suddenly act as though there's a wall there."

"That's exactly what it feels like," she said. "Like there's some threshold I'm supposed to cross."

"There isn't."

"It feels like there is."

"It feels like there is because crossing it means being seen wanting something."

"Yes. That's it."

"And if you don't cross it?"

"Then I get to stay in the safe zone. I get to be generous. Helpful. Supportive. But I never really have to risk rejection."

"So here's the real question," I said. "Why not you? Why not you, the lawyer who is thoughtful, strategic, good with people, and fully capable of helping solve the problem? Why are you so willing to self-select out?"

"Because it protects me. And also keeps me small."

"Yes."

Developing a winning business development strategy

Now that we have explored the importance of uncovering and leveraging your natural rainmaking style and upgrading your business development mindset, the next step is strategy.

This is where I see a lot of lawyers get derailed. Not because they are doing nothing. Usually, because they are doing too many things without a real strategic filter. They attend events, reconnect with old contacts, go for coffee, join organizations, publish articles, say yes to panels, and so on. They put a lot of time and effort into it. And still, six months later, they don't see any results.

Why? Because they lack a winning strategy.

From an MBA perspective, strategy is not just an action plan. First and foremost, it's a set of choices – about where you will compete, where you will not, and how you will allocate limited resources to create the greatest return. In business development, those resources are not just money. They are your time (the most precious commodity for any lawyer!), your energy, your attention, your credibility, and your relationships.

Without a solid strategy, business development turns into a string of activities that sound good on paper but amount to little. If your activities are not connected to a clear strategic direction, you are not really building momentum. You are spinning your wheels.

David was a corporate partner at a large firm. Bright, hardworking, well-respected, and deeply committed to building his practice. He was not sitting around waiting for business to fall into his lap. If anything, he was doing too much.

When we met, he looked almost proud of the list. "I'm on the board of one non-profit, I just joined two industry groups, I've been going to alumni events, I'm writing more LinkedIn posts, I'm trying to reconnect with law school friends, and I said yes to speaking on a panel next month."

I said, "Wow, that's a lot of activity. Why those things?"

"Because they all seemed like good opportunities. For business development."

"Okay. Let's make that more specific. Good for what kind of business development?"

"I'm not sure I've really thought about it that way," he said.

"That's okay. When you say you want to grow your practice, who do you actually want more of?"

He frowned. "What do you mean?"

"I mean, not just more work. Not just more matters in the abstract. What kinds of clients are you especially well-positioned to attract and serve?"

"Probably privately held businesses," he said. "Founder-led companies. A lot of the work I've enjoyed most has been with owners who are growing, bringing in investors, or thinking about an exit."

"Why that group?"

"Because I understand them. The issues are rarely just legal. There are issues around their business strategy, family dynamics, growth pressure, control and management. I like that mix."

"So if that's where you're strongest, where do those clients and the people around them actually gather?"

He started thinking out loud. "Certain founder groups. Probably some accounting and wealth advisory relationships. Maybe lower middle market deal circles. Some regional business groups."

I said, "That sounds more targeted already."

He laughed. "Which is another way of saying I've been too broad."

"I think you've been understandably broad," I said. "You've been saying yes to things that seem worthwhile. The issue is that activity and strategic activity are not the same."

"Yeah," he said. "I can see that."

"What I want you to think about," I said, "is not just whether something is a good opportunity in general. I want you to ask whether it is a good opportunity for the practice you are actually trying to build. While being in action is critical to success, every action you choose costs you something," I said. "It costs time. It costs attention. It costs energy. Every activity creates obligations. Every yes takes up space that could have been used on something else."

"So what I really need," he said slowly, "is not more activity. I need a better filter."

"Exactly. Because at its core, strategy is about trade-offs. Which means it is not just about deciding what to do, but what deserves more of your time. It's also deciding what deserves less, and sometimes none."

He smiled. "That's the harder part."

"So what are your key takeaways from our conversation?"

David thought for a minute and then said, "Well, I've been thinking about business development as a visibility problem. I need to get out there more, do more, meet more people. But what I actually need is to get clear on the type of practice I want to build, the types of clients I really want to work with, and the types of activities that would actually help me achieve that."

"Yes," I said. "That's exactly it."

"Honestly, that feels so much better... almost like a relief."

That is what a good strategy does. It does not just make you more focused. It makes your choices easier.

The operating system of sustainable rainmaking

Once you understand your natural rainmaking style, develop a constructive mindset, and clarify your strategic focus, the next challenge becomes execution. This is another stage where many business development efforts begin to falter.

Even lawyers who genuinely want to grow their practices often struggle with consistency. They may attend an industry event one month, reconnect with a former colleague the next, and publish an article several months later. Each activity may be valuable on its own, but without a clear structure connecting these efforts, the overall process feels fragmented.

The problem is not effort. It is the absence of systems.

Business development can feel chaotic because it encompasses a wide range of activities – networking, relationship management, marketing, speaking, writing, pitching, and client conversations. When lawyers view these activities individually, it is easy to feel overwhelmed or uncertain about where to focus.

The RainMasters™ Framework addresses this challenge by organizing business development activities into four core systems. These execution systems translate strategy into repeatable actions that you can incorporate into your professional routines.

The four systems are:

1. The pipeline system.
2. The nurture system.
3. The visibility system.
4. The rainmaking conversations system.

Each system plays a distinct role in the overall rainmaking process. Together, they create a structured engine for sustainable business development.

When these four systems operate together, business development becomes significantly more predictable. Relationships are identified intentionally, nurtured consistently, reinforced through visible expertise, and ultimately deepened through meaningful conversations.

1. The pipeline system – identifying the right relationships

Every lawyer, including you, operates within a professional ecosystem of relationships. That ecosystem includes clients, prospective clients, referral sources, internal colleagues, industry contacts, and other people who move through the same business world you do.

Not all of those relationships matter equally. Some contacts will have a much more direct – and often disproportionate – impact on your ability to build a sustainable book of business. That is why an effective pipeline system is not just a contact list. It is a way of identifying which relationships are most strategically important and making sure they do not get lost in the noise.

At the core of your pipeline are four main categories of contacts:

1. *Prospective clients* – people or organizations that may one day hire you directly because their legal needs align with your expertise.
2. *Referral sources* – professionals who regularly encounter people with legal needs and are in a position to send work your way. Depending on your practice, these may include accountants, consultants, bankers, wealth advisors, other lawyers, or industry professionals with adjacent expertise.
3. *Connectors or centers of influence* – people with strong networks who may not hire you themselves or send you a business referral, but can open doors, make introductions, and create access to the right conversations.
4. *Internal collaborators* – colleagues inside your firm whose clients may need your expertise or whose practices naturally overlap with yours. Many lawyers overlook this category, even though some of the best opportunities are already sitting inside the firm.

Your job is not to build equally deep relationships with everyone in your universe. That is impossible. Most lawyers know too many people to do that well, and trying to stay meaningfully engaged with everyone usually leads to superficial contact with almost no one. The real work is prioritization. Which relationships sit closest to future opportunity? Which people are most relevant to the kind of practice you want to build? Which contacts are most likely to lead to direct work, referrals, introductions, or expanded opportunities over time? Those are the relationships that belong at the center of your pipeline.

2. The nurture system – strengthening relationships over time

Building a pipeline of meaningful relationships is only the first step. The next challenge is ensuring that those relationships continue to develop over time.

Let's say you meet someone at a conference, on a panel, at a client event, or through a mutual connection. The conversation is strong. There is real interest or connection. You both say some version of, "Let's stay in touch". You even follow up once or twice. But then nothing happens.

Not because the relationship lacked value. Usually, because there was no system behind it. And that's exactly what the nurture system is designed to solve.

At its core, relationship nurture means staying meaningfully connected over time in ways that reinforce trust, relevance, and goodwill. It is not about constant outreach. It is not about forced check-ins. And it is definitely not about popping up only when you need something.

It is about sending a consistent signal – this relationship matters. It's about being present, not persistent; relevant, not relentless. It's the difference between being a name in someone's inbox and being the person they think of when they need help.

Sometimes that looks small, and that is exactly the point. You share an article that is genuinely relevant to someone's business or industry. You congratulate them on a promotion, award, deal, or leadership move. You make an introduction that is useful to them. You follow up after a conversation with a thoughtful note. You check in when something in their world changes.

None of this is flashy. That is why many lawyers underestimate it. Relationships are rarely built through one dramatic gesture. They are built the way trust is usually built – through steady contact, repeated value, and enough consistency that you stay top of mind without becoming a nuisance.

Think of it like watering a plant. You do not dump a bucket on it once every six months and expect it to thrive. A little attention, applied consistently, works much better. And that is what effective nurture looks like.

3. The visibility system – strengthening your credibility by demonstrating expertise

While relationships are central to business development, visibility plays an important supporting role. Your visibility system encompasses the activities through which you can demonstrate your knowledge, experience, and perspective to the broader market. In essence, you are educating your key contacts about your professional value. That can happen through writing, speaking, teaching, participating in industry programs, leading discussions, hosting roundtables, sharing valuable content on LinkedIn, or showing up consistently in the professional communities that matter most to your practice. The goal of your visibility strategies is to ensure that when people in your network think about your practice area, they think of you.

And here is the most important caveat. The point of visibility is not to be everywhere. The point is to be strategically visible in the *right places*, in the *right way*, to the *right people*.

That is why visibility should always connect back to strategy. What you write about, speak about, teach on, or participate in should reinforce the kind of practice you are trying to build. If your strategy is focused on a particular client base, industry, or practice area, your visibility should reflect that focus. Otherwise, you may be active without becoming known for anything that actually matters to your future clients or referral sources.

Visibility also works best when it fits your natural rainmaking style. For some lawyers, writing is the strongest lane. For others, it is speaking, facilitating discussions, leading industry programs, or sharing insights in smaller, more interactive settings. The format matters less than consistency and relevance. You do not need to use someone else's model. You need a form of visibility you can sustain.

When your visibility is aligned with your strategy and your natural style, it stops feeling like self-promotion and starts feeling like professional leadership. You are not just trying to be seen. You are helping the right people see your value more clearly.

4. The rainmaking conversations system – turning relationships into opportunities

The final system focuses on the conversations that ultimately transform relationships into client engagements. This is another area where many lawyers get stuck.

You may be good at building relationships. You may be thoughtful, well-liked, and genuinely curious about other people. But when a conversation starts moving anywhere near actual business, many lawyers pull back. They worry about sounding too commercial. They do not want to seem pushy. Or they assume that if the relationship is strong enough, the opportunity will somehow surface on its own. Sometimes it does. But often it does not, or at least not without a more intentional conversation.

Part of the problem is that many lawyers are working from the wrong definition of a business development conversation. They assume the goal is to "make the ask" or to tell the other person what they do, explain how they can help, and somehow land the opportunity through a well-timed statement of value. And that is exactly why these conversations feel so uncomfortable. Basically, you are trying to talk about your capabilities without sounding self-promotional. It is a very narrow bridge to walk, and most lawyers can feel themselves wobbling on it.

The good news is that the best rainmaking conversations are about *asking thoughtful questions* that help the other person talk about what is actually happening in their business, their industry, or their world, which helps them and you uncover natural opportunities where you can help.

So, if there is one shift that I'd love to see you make after reading this chapter is that the strongest rainmaking conversations are not built on telling or selling. *They are built on curiosity*. Instead of trying to impress, you try to understand. Instead of leading with your services, you lead with questions. Instead of forcing your expertise into the conversation, you create the kind of dialogue where your expertise becomes relevant naturally.

The moment you stop thinking, "How do I explain my value?" and start thinking, "How do I better understand what this person is dealing with?" the conversation gets easier, more natural, and far more useful.

Here is an example. Let's say you are an employment lawyer. You could say something like:

"I help companies with employment issues, discrimination claims, and executive compensation. We work with a lot of businesses at your stage, and I'd be happy to tell you more about how we support clients in this area."

There is nothing wrong with that, exactly. But it puts the burden on you to make yourself sound relevant. A stronger version might sound like this:

"It sounds like you've grown quickly over the last year. How has that changed the people side of the business?"

The founder says, "Honestly, that's been one of the hardest parts. We've added layers of management, and now communication is messier."

You say, "That sounds like a lot. I'm curious, what do you think is causing these communication breakdowns?"

Now the conversation is alive. You are actually learning something real, something that matters to the person you are speaking to. As you continue to ask questions, listen carefully, and respond in ways that help them think more deeply and clearly about what is happening, you create a dynamic where trust deepens, value becomes visible, and opportunity can emerge naturally.

Bringing it all together

The legal profession may have changed, but this does not mean you have to become someone else to succeed in it. That is the point of this chapter. I hope that you now believe that to be successful in business development, you do not need to imitate the loudest rainmaker in the room or force yourself into a version that feels performative, unnatural, or exhausting. And you do not need to rely on scattered bursts of effort, hoping they somehow add up to a sustainable book of business.

What you do need is a clear structure – one that helps you understand the essential elements of effective business development and gives you a practical way to put them into motion. A framework that gives you a way to approach business development with more clarity, more confidence, and more intention. And with the RainMasters™ Framework, you now have one.

And the best news of all is that you do not have to have it all figured out today. You do not need to become instantly fearless, perfectly consistent, or naturally good at every part of this process. You simply need to begin approaching business development with the same seriousness, thoughtfulness, and professionalism you already bring to your legal work.

To help you put the ideas from this chapter into action, we created the LeadWise RainMasters™ Toolkit.[1] Inside, you will find practical tools to help you identify your natural rainmaking style, uncover limiting beliefs, clarify your BD strategy, build and track your pipeline, nurture key relationships, plan strategic visibility, and lead more effective prospective client conversations. These tools are designed to help you move from good intentions to consistent action – in a way that feels natural, focused, and sustainable.

The capacity to build strong relationships, create trust, and grow your practice is not reserved for a select few. It is something you can develop. And if you are willing to be intentional, stay in the process, and keep building from your strengths, you are far more capable of becoming a successful rainmaker than you may realize.

References

1 www.LeadWiseGroup.com/RainMasters-Toolkit

Chapter 14: Building your professional profile – taking control of your digital presence and winning more work

By Rebecca Harding, Saltwhistle

Why you cannot afford to ignore this

Every day, people receive information about professionals and what they can do for them. With so much information available it is essential to know what is out there about you and how you compare. People will not just accept a referral anymore and will look online to confirm your reputation and whether you seem like the type of person they want to work with.

Most lawyers are not actively managing their profile, so there is a clear opportunity for those that do. Building your professional profile can dramatically enhance your career, help you win work, and ensure you are presented with more opportunities.

Over recent years, opportunities for lunches, events and traditional networking have decreased significantly. The numbers of clients attending events had diminished even before COVID. Digital is now the main route for promoting yourself. As all traditional professionals know, people buy people. At the end of the day, we are expected to have the technical expertise as a baseline. Potential clients want to choose someone they have something in common with and feel they can work with. Building your profile and showing your individual characteristics allows you to attract people who will identify with you.

> *"Taking control of my profile was one of the best things I ever did professionally. It has opened up so many doors. At first it felt uncomfortable as I wasn't used to putting myself forward. Now I look for the opportunities without even thinking."*[1]

How clients actually choose you

Digital developments have completely overhauled the way clients look for information about a professional. They will research you independently and judge you on what they find. According to Forrester research,[2] potential clients look for information from at least three sources to confirm their decision. This is how they find out about you:

- 30 percent like to hear you speak.
- 20 percent read blogs and articles you have written.
- 17 percent have had some interaction with you on social media.
- 15 percent have read a book you have written.
- Eight percent think your website is impressive.
- Five percent look at online reviews.
- Five percent do an online search.

The fundamental question is whether those sources are presenting the right image of you. If not, it's time to take control. It's no good saying that you do not participate online as there are hundreds of professionals who do, and when a client does their own research, those are the people who will be found ahead of you. With the advantages of online working, people no longer need to restrict themselves geographically. Hiring a professional they have never actually met is becoming increasingly common.

"I needed to find a commercial lawyer and my contact sent me a choice of three. I researched them all and they had the right expertise. I made my decision based on what I found. One seemed modern in their approach and interesting, so I chose that one."

Defining who you are

Before you can build a profile, you need to be clear about what you are trying to achieve, who you are trying to reach, and what you want people to think. The clearer you are in your own mind about this, the easier every subsequent decision becomes.

Keep your objectives to five at most. Focus on one target audience if you can. The narrower your focus, the quicker you will see results. Trying to reach everyone is one of the most common mistakes in professional services and it means you reach nobody effectively. Two lawyers I knew set up a small online firm in the Midlands, targeted small retail outlets specifically, conducted all their meetings over digital platforms, appeared in retail trade materials, and spoke and wrote entirely about the common issues for small retailers. Their focus was the key to their success.

Think about your unique selling proposition. What is special about you that makes you stand out? Most lawyers find recognizing their own positive qualities the most difficult part. Talk to a trusted colleague about how you come across and what they see as your strengths. You may be surprised. Think about your tone too, which is the way you write and speak. Is it plain speaking or technical? Warm or formal? Practical or intellectual? Define it, and then be consistent with it across everything you produce. It will attract a certain type of client. The more like everyone else you are, the less interesting you become.

Your key messages are the points you want your audiences to take away. They do not need to be stated directly. You need to demonstrate them. If a post, article or opportunity does not fit your key messages, question whether it is worth your time. Be ruthless about it. With limited time available, focus is everything.

> *"Once I had it clear in my head what I wanted to say, writing posts and deciding what to do became so much easier. And gradually I noticed people starting to talk to me about those issues. The message was getting across because I just kept repeating it."*

The psychology that helps you win

Making people see you as a genuine person, a colleague, or even a friend is far more effective in building business relationships than anything else – whether you do it online or in person. Spend time on people. Be interested in them. Look for points of commonality and think about how you can support them. Make introductions. Share things they might find valuable. The best way to promote yourself is to take your time over others.

Nobel Prize winner Daniel Kahneman showed that roughly 90 percent of all decisions are made through fast, instinctive, and emotional thinking. Logic only accounts for about ten percent.[3] To open up opportunities you need to be tapping into that emotional side of how people make decisions, not just demonstrating your technical credentials. When people feel loyal to you, when they like you and trust you, they are more likely to involve you in projects and opportunities.

The concept of "Association" also works powerfully online. When you are seen alongside credible people, whether in a photograph, a joint article, or on a shared platform, some of that credibility transfers to you. Reciprocity works just as well. Make introductions for people, refer them for work or speaking opportunities, send them interesting articles. Ask nothing in return. The generosity comes back to you, usually with interest.

"I met a new business contact and soon realized that a lot of my network would be useful to her. I made a number of introductions and got her through doors she hadn't expected to ever get through. She was so grateful she gave me some of my biggest client jobs this year and has referred me to others."

Your digital presence

Your online profile

Your online profile, and particularly your LinkedIn profile, is one of the most important aspects of who you are to the outside world. People check it before they meet you and before they decide to instruct you. The photo matters. Does it match the image you want to portray? Does it reflect your tone and your key messages? Profiles without a photo are rarely read properly. You do not come across as a real person.

Most professionals are not good at writing their own profiles. Modesty gets in the way, or they simply find it difficult to see themselves objectively. Try writing in the third person. Using she or he, even though it is you, makes it easier to be authoritative and generous about yourself. It comes across as fact rather than self-promotion.

Include a strong testimonial right at the start of your 'About' section rather than leaving it to the formal recommendations section further down, which few people get to. A good sprinkling of testimonials throughout is better still. Third-person writing combined with external validation is a powerful combination. It is also worth getting someone else to write your profile for you if possible. They will be far more objective and more complimentary too.

"I couldn't believe the difference once I had worked on my profile. It was so much more interesting, attractive and professional. I could see how many more people were viewing it and asking to connect."

Social media – be where your clients are

A large number of people have no real idea why they use social media. They feel they need to be there, but are not sure what it is achieving for them. The trick with social media is to know who you are trying to reach and understand that it is a two-way channel. There is no reason to be on every platform if it is not relevant to your target audience. Know where your clients are and be there.

LinkedIn is probably the most powerful platform for business and most people are not using it anywhere near its full potential. The majority of people in business and professional services are present there. It is easy to search for different groups or specialisms and it makes suggestions for new contacts once it has worked out the type of people you are interested in connecting with. A good profile attracts attention. If you see that someone has looked at your profile, connect with them, spot the points of commonality and start a conversation.

"I met my biggest client on LinkedIn. I asked to connect and he suggested we meet. We had contacts in common and had worked in the same place in the past. He introduced me to others within his firm. As a result I ended up with three international jobs."

YouTube is a formidable search engine. Having a YouTube channel is a brilliant way to ensure any webinars or interviews you do will be found and watched again and again, long after the event. You can generate a link to use in a post on LinkedIn, which takes people directly to your channel.

Facebook can be useful for reaching certain groups. A family lawyer may find it valuable to look approachable and to access potential clients.

Build your following

The first hundred or two hundred connections are always the hardest. After that, there is a snowball effect. It is worth spending five minutes a day connecting with new people on LinkedIn. Look to see who has viewed your profile and offer to connect. When you reach out, make it personal. Look for a genuine point of connection rather than sending a generic request.

Liking and commenting on other people's posts is an underrated way to initiate contact. Professionals are always pleased when someone takes the time and it can start a real conversation. Keep the conversation going and suggest a call or a coffee. The worst they can say is no.

"There was a woman who kept liking my posts so I would always like hers back. Then we started commenting on each other's posts until finally, after six months, I suggested we should have a coffee. She thought it was a great idea."

Creating content that gets you noticed

Posts

The best posts are about the issues that others are facing and can identify with. The purpose is to get a message across. Ask yourself before you publish: why would someone else find this interesting? Is it about their needs or just what you want to say? Alternatively, can you film or interview someone? Business colleagues will share a post if they appear in it, which widens your audience considerably.

Keep it short. Most people write far too much. Make sure every word has a reason for being there. Is it too technical for the audience? Common mistakes professionals make are putting in far too much technical detail, making articles too long and unreadable, or giving it a title that is technical and not of interest to anyone else. The target audience either will not read it or will not understand it. People are in a hurry. Give them something they can read quickly and easily and take one strong point from it that grabs their attention.

Use photographs where you can. Include hashtags to help people who do not yet follow you to find your material. Think of hashtags as a way to connect your content to a specific topic or conversation and to attract an interested audience you have not previously reached. Look online to find out how to use hashtags if you haven't before. And always read your post back before you publish it, as if you were someone who does not know you and has no context for it.

"The most successful post I ever had was when I couldn't attend an award ceremony and sent my 14-year-old daughter instead. She was in all the photos receiving the award. The post I wrote was not about winning but about my daughter and how she got on in such an adult environment. This got more likes than anything else I have ever written. I became a human being. They could relate to me."

Articles

Articles are a good way of establishing recognition for your expertise. With the constant need for content across digital platforms, it is now possible to get your work published in many different places if you are prepared to do it for free. Many editors are keen to find willing contributors who can write on current topics in an engaging and original way. If you do a good job, they will come back to you.

Do not leap into densely technical pieces unless your audience is specifically technical and looking for that level of expertise. Make the headline count. Once you have written something, use it everywhere relevant – on your website, as an e-shot, on LinkedIn – and circulate it to other platforms. Maximize the value of everything you write.

If writing is not your strong point, consider a ghost writer. A good one will turn bullet points and a quick conversation into a polished article, often doing background research to add depth and fresh angles. That can be money very well spent. Alternatively, dictating your article on your phone can make your style more natural and improve the flow considerably. You can use AI to structure an article, but be wary of using it as the finished article. It can become very bland indeed and people can tell it was written by AI. This is discussed further below.

Thought leadership

How often do we actually see genuinely original thinking demonstrated in professional circles? Thought leadership means taking an opinion within your field that may be slightly different or alternative in its approach. The ideas you think are obvious are often not at all obvious to others. Keep a note of ideas as they occur to you. Read widely, attend webinars, talk to clients. If you look at what others are writing you will see the same basic points appearing over and over again. If you can find a different angle, you will stand out.

> *"I wrote a short article about inclusivity and laid out what I thought was holding firms back. I put it out on social media and email and had so many comments. It started conversations, brought in work and got me noticed internally. One of our senior partners contacted me about introducing some of my ideas into our workplace."*

The new digital landscape – what you also need to be doing

The foundations we have covered above remain essential, but the tools available have developed considerably over the last couple of years.

Use AI to create content faster

AI tools such as ChatGPT or Claude can draft a first version of a post or article from a few bullet points or a rough outline. Think of it as having a willing and very fast research assistant. You brief it, it produces a draft, and you then edit it into your own voice and style. For professionals who have always struggled with the blank page, this removes the single biggest barrier to producing content consistently. The key is that you do not publish the output as it arrives. You read it, improve it, cut what does not sound like you and make it yours. Used properly, it means you can produce more material in less time without sacrificing quality or authenticity. It can also help you research a topic quickly, suggest angles you had not considered, and help you draft social media posts in batches so you have material ready to go. But beware of putting it out without the edits as it will sound like AI and ultimately undermine its credibility.

Short video on LinkedIn

Short-form video now dramatically outperforms text posts in terms of reach on LinkedIn. Talking directly to camera for 60 to 90 seconds on a topical issue is highly effective and is still massively underused by lawyers. You do not need a studio or a production team. Your phone and a decent background is entirely sufficient. The authenticity of a short, direct-to-camera video is actually part of its appeal. People want to see that you are a real person with a genuine point of view. If the idea fills you with dread, record yourself privately a few times until you feel more comfortable. Like any skill, it gets considerably easier with practice and the results justify the initial discomfort. Even a short video commenting on a recent development in your sector, or answering a question you are commonly asked by clients, will outperform a text post of equivalent effort.

LinkedIn newsletters

LinkedIn now allows you to publish a regular newsletter directly on the platform. Subscribers receive it in their feed and via a notification, which means your material lands in front of them without competing with the algorithm in the same way a standard post does. If you are already writing articles, this is a relatively simple additional step to considerably extend your reach. Choose a theme that is relevant to your key messages and target audience and commit to publishing regularly, even if that is only once a month. Over time, a newsletter builds a subscribed audience who have specifically opted in to hear from you. This is a very different and much more valuable relationship than a passive follower who may or may not see your posts.

Build a subscriber list that you own

Social media platforms change their algorithms regularly, so the most valuable digital asset you can build is a direct email list of people who have actively chosen to hear from you. A simple, regular email newsletter sent through a basic email marketing tool allows you to do this without great expense or technical expertise. It does not need to be elaborate. A short, regular email with a useful point of view, a comment on a topical development, or a practical piece of advice for your target audience is sufficient. The people who subscribe are the most engaged part of your audience. They are the people most likely to instruct you, refer you, and share your material with others. Unlike a social media following, you own that list. Nobody can take it away from you.

Have your own personal website

A simple personal website, separate from your firm website, gives you a permanent home on the internet that you own entirely. It becomes the hub where everything lives – your articles, podcast appearances, videos, profile, and contact details. It does not need to be complicated or expensive. A clean, well-written one-page site with a strong "About" section, that links to your content, and gives people a way to contact you is enough to start with. The point is that you are not entirely dependent on your firm website, which may not present you in the way you want, or on social media platforms whose rules and reach can change at any time. Your profile has its own permanent address. It also gives you something concrete to point people towards whenever you publish something or appear somewhere new, particularly if you want to express your own opinions and not that of your firm.

AI search and how it affects your visibility

This is a newer development worth paying close attention to. Clients are increasingly using AI tools such as ChatGPT, Perplexity, or Google Gemini to ask for professional recommendations directly, in the same way they might previously have done a Google search. How your name and expertise appear in those results is a new and growing dimension of profile management. The good news is that the best way to improve your visibility in AI search results is the same as it has always been for traditional search – write clearly and consistently about what you do, publish regularly on the topics you want to be known for, and make sure your online presence is current and coherent. AI tools draw on what is publicly available and indexed online. Give them something strong to work with and they will present your name when it is relevant.

Online communities and sector forums

LinkedIn groups and other online forums are where many of your target clients are present. Contributing meaningfully to those discussions, answering questions, flagging useful resources, and sharing a genuine point of view puts you in front of the right people in a context where they are already engaged and receptive. It is a very different dynamic to broadcasting a post and waiting for reactions. You are entering an existing conversation as a genuine participant. The relationships it builds tend to be stronger and faster-forming than those created through one-way content alone.

Commission original research

One of the most powerful ways to establish genuine thought leadership is to commission or run a simple piece of original research among your target market and publish the results. An online survey does not need to be complex or expensive. Ask your target audience about the key challenges they are facing, how they approach a particular issue, or what they expect from their professional advisers. The findings give you something genuinely new to say that nobody else can say, because the data is yours. Original research is highly shareable, attracts press and media interest, and establishes authority in a way that commentary on other people's ideas simply cannot match. It also gives you a body of content to write about for months – the findings themselves, the implications, the trends, the questions it raises. It also gives you a platform to talk about the issues you want to raise and to demonstrate your own thoughts, solutions, and opinions.

Speaking, webinars, and podcasts

At the beginning of this chapter, we saw that one of the areas scoring highest for winning recognition with potential clients is speaking publicly. The prospect strikes terror into many people. However, it is something you can work on and it gets easier. As the world becomes more digital, webinars and podcasts make the whole process far more accessible and less daunting than it once was.

> *"I was asked to put forward one of the quietest people I have ever come across to be media spokesman for the press. I put him through media training and he realized that he could get better at it as it was a craft. He became a media star on the radio and in the newspapers. This was because he understood what was wanted by an audience. He abandoned his tech-*

nical skills and spoke as though he was talking to friends. He was easy to understand and got to the point quickly."

Being at the front of a room (or the main speaker on a webinar) has a distinct psychological effect. You often see a queue of people wanting to engage with the speaker at a conference. The speaker is seen as elevated. It is rather like being famous for five minutes, so make the most of it. Good speakers with engaging topics are in short supply and people will always be more eager to have you if you are prepared to do it for free!

Follow up with everyone who attended a webinar immediately afterwards, while they still feel warm towards you as the expert. That is the moment to capitalize on the effort you put in. Not two weeks later when the moment has completely gone, which is unfortunately what a lot of professionals try to do.

Making it happen

The biggest problem in professional services is a lack of implementation. Strategies are developed, ideas are noted, and at the end of the day everyone goes back to their client work. If you want this to work, you are going to have to commit to it. Even five minutes every day is enough to start with. It is far better to do one or two things regularly and well, than a great deal of activity every couple of years.

"As a professional services consultant I gave three different lawyers in the same marketplace an idea for a cutting-edge opportunity. They could all see how good it was and got very excited. None of them got round to implementing it. In the end I saw another firm had done a version of it and they made the money."

Some professionals lack confidence, fear failure, or suffer from imposter syndrome when they start building their profile. There is huge pressure on us to be perfect and perfectionism is something bred into professionals from an early age. The fact is, we are not perfect and we have to accept that and just have a go. You have nothing to lose. Something is always better than nothing.

The keys to success are regularity, consistency, and focus. Plan the time in your diary just as you would for an important meeting. If you leave a blank space in your diary, someone will fill it! Block it out and prioritize yourself.

Here is an approach that works well in practice. Block out:

- Five minutes in the morning with your coffee to connect with new people and drop messages to contacts.
- A couple of lunch hours each week to think about posts and read articles that inspire ideas.
- A regular slot, perhaps on a Friday, dedicated to writing articles or developing longer content.

Build it as a habit and the results will increase and gain momentum. Be consistent in posting online and building followers. What you cannot do is jump in and out and then expect results. Others are doing this consistently and getting better at it. Do not let them leave you behind.

"I had put off doing anything about my online presence because it seemed such a big task. When I realized it would be fine to do just five minutes a day I completely changed my approach. After a couple of months I started to see results. Starting to produce articles and posts was an easy next step."

In summary

Potential clients will look at multiple sources to confirm that you are the right person. Make sure your profile is present wherever they look or they will choose your competitors.

Treat yourself in the same way as you would your firm. Develop your own objectives, target market, key messages, and tone. Find your unique selling point and build your brand around it consistently.

Use all the digital channels available to you. If you write an article, put it everywhere relevant. The more often people see you, the more they know you and the more they trust you.

Use the new tools – AI to make content creation faster and easier, short video to increase your reach on LinkedIn, a newsletter to build an audience of your own, your own website as a complete representation of who you are, original research to say something nobody else can say. These are not complicated. They are just tools that most of your competitors are not yet using properly.

Whether you are speaking, writing, or commenting, always think: what is in it for them? Focus on solving the problems of others rather than just saying what you want to say. They will identify with it and they will remember you.

Be committed. Make a plan and stick to it on a regular basis. Implementation is what makes the real difference, and that is precisely where most people fall down and you can win.

References

1 The quotes used in this chapter have been documented following client meetings with lawyers or after discussions and brainstorming sessions. All contributions are gratefully acknowledged.

2 www.forrester.com/research/buyer-insights/

3 Daniel Kahneman, *Thinking, Fast and Slow*, Penguin (2012)

Chapter 15:
Change management for lawyers – the human architecture of change in legal

By Dr Andrea Miskolczi, MBA, managing director, InterAlia Consulting

Introduction

"We fully support the AI program. We announced it at the partners' meeting."
Managing partner, international law firm

When change initiatives fail to take root in legal organizations, the explanation is rarely the one that gets cited first. The strategy was not the problem. The technology was not the problem. The rollout plan was not the problem. The problem, consistently and across change types, is human. According to Prosci's research,[1] 38 percent of all implementation difficulties trace back to human and proficiency factors – the learning curve, the gap between training and practice, the absence of sustained support. Technical implementation issues account for only 16 percent of the same failures. This pattern holds whether the change in question is a new operating model, a process redesign, or – as is the defining challenge of this moment in legal – the adoption of artificial intelligence.

The implication is uncomfortable but important – most change programs in legal are not failing because the wrong approach was chosen. They are failing because the human architecture of change was not designed. The roles that every successful change requires were left unfilled, undefined, or misunderstood. AI adoption makes this visible more starkly than most changes because the gap between access and genuine use is so measurable – but the underlying dynamic is not new, and it is not unique to technology.

This chapter maps those roles. It describes what each one demands in practice – not as titles to be assigned on an organizational chart, but as functions that must be actively performed. Some individuals will hold more than one. Others will hold none, even when they might be expected to. Understanding the difference between what a role is called and what it actually requires is often the starting point for making change work.

The chapter covers seven roles – the sponsor, managers and partners, the change leader, the project manager, the power user, the change champion, and the sponsor alliance. Together, they form the cast of characters that every successful legal change story needs.

The sponsor – permission as leadership

The quote that opens this chapter captures the most common failure mode in legal change management – the managing partner who believes the announcement was the leadership. It is not a failure of intent. It is a failure of understanding what sponsorship, in the change management sense, actually requires.

A sponsor is not the person who signed off on the procurement budget. A sponsor is a senior leader who actively and visibly commits to a change – who demonstrates, through their own behavior and communication, that it matters. What managing partners and senior leaders provide – or fail to provide – in a change program is not primarily resource or budget, though both matter. It is *permission*. Not the formal permission of a policy or a mandate, but the subtler, more powerful signal that comes from visible personal engagement. When a managing partner uses an AI tool in their own work, references it in client conversations, or asks about adoption in practice group meetings, they communicate something that no training program can replicate – that this is real, that it matters, and that being part of it is professionally safe.

The problem is that most senior leaders in law firms believe they are already providing this. They have made the announcement. They have allocated the budget. They have appointed someone to lead the program. From where they sit, the sponsorship question has been answered. From where everyone else sits, it often has not. There is a consistent and striking gap between how leaders perceive their own involvement in change and how that involvement is experienced by the people they lead.[2] In legal, this gap is widened by structural factors particular to the profession. Partners are not accustomed to being led, and they are not accustomed to leading in the way that change requires – through sustained behavioral signal rather than positional authority.

Common failure modes are predictable. The most frequent is delegation – the sponsor transfers ownership of the change to a legal operations team, an IT function, or an external consultant, and then wonders why adoption is slow. Another is positional endorsement without personal engagement – the written foreword to the launch pack, followed by silence. Both signal to the organization that the change is, at some level, optional.

For the partner or legal operations professional who has been tasked with driving adoption, understanding this dynamic is the first practical step. The question is not how to find a better sponsor. It is how to help the sponsor understand that something different is needed from them – without framing that as a criticism of what they have done so far.

Managers and partners – the daily architects of culture

Legal has always been an apprenticeship profession. Associates and junior lawyers learn what it means to practice law not primarily from training programs or policy documents, but by watching senior colleagues work. They infer, from daily observation, what is valued, what is professionally acceptable, and what distinguishes good work from excellent work.

This dynamic makes managers and partners the most powerful change agents in any legal organization – and the most dangerous source of inertia if they are not engaged. When a partner integrates an AI tool into their working method and talks openly about how and why they use it, they communicate something that no policy mandate can replicate – that capable, serious practitioners do this. When the same partner delegates all technology decisions to associates or support staff, expressing quiet skepticism in the process, the signal is equally clear.

But the apprenticeship dynamic alone does not capture the full picture. Managers and partners carry a second, specific change responsibility – the personal *why* conversation. Research on change consistently shows that people do not move because of a business case. They move when they connect the change to something personally meaningful. What makes this conversation particularly delicate is that it needs to happen in both directions. Before a manager can help their team find their reasons to engage with AI, they need to have found their own – and the personal motivations that drive or block commitment at this level are just as real as those of any junior associate. They are simply less often asked about.

What lawyers at this level tend to resist is rarely the technology in the abstract. The concern is quieter and more personal – accountability for errors, loss of oversight, uncertainty about what their role becomes when AI handles the work that once defined their expertise. Managers who have not worked through these questions themselves will struggle to hold them for others.

Prosci's research[3] consistently identifies mid-level managers as the most resistant group in any organizational change – not because they are obstructionist, but because they carry the most conflicting pressures. Interventions designed specifically for this group – governance frameworks that position AI as supporting their oversight rather than bypassing it, clear accountability structures, and opportunities to voice hesitation without it becoming a matter of record – address the real concern rather than the one a training program assumes they have.

The change leader – bridging the gap between left and right

In many legal organizations, responsibility for AI implementation falls to one of two kinds of person – a partner who has been designated the task of rolling out a specific tool, or a former lawyer who has moved into an innovation, legal operations, or knowledge management role. Both bring genuine strengths. Neither typically arrives with formal change management training.

In my article "Lawyers and the Leap into (AI) Transformation: Embracing Change Management Techniques", I argue that this gap can be understood through the lens of what neuroscience loosely calls left- and right-brain thinking.[4] The legal profession develops and rewards a particular cognitive style – analytical, sequential, risk-attentive, precedent-oriented. These are the capacities that produce excellent legal work. They map broadly to what the left-brain metaphor describes – structured reasoning, logical argument, careful attention to what could go wrong.

Change leadership, however, depends on a different set of capacities – empathy, storytelling, comfort with ambiguity, the ability to read emotional dynamics and respond to what people are actually feeling rather than what they are stating. These map more naturally to right-brain modes of working. Lawyers are not incapable of them. But they are not the capacities that legal training systematically develops, and they are not the ones that professional recognition tends to reward.

The change leader who is also a lawyer therefore faces a genuine identity challenge. They must bring analytical rigor to program design and stakeholder mapping – their legal training serves them well here – while simultaneously developing the relationship skills and emotional intelligence that adoption work demands. The person who has built a professional identity around precision and risk control must become comfortable with a process that involves imperfect early attempts, resistance that does not respond to rational argument, and success metrics that are harder to pin down than a billable hour.

Beyond the identity dimension, change leaders in legal organizations frequently encounter a structural problem – they are expected to drive adoption without the mandate, resource, or organizational authority that the task requires. A partner-level change leader may have credibility but limited time. A legal operations professional may have the time but insufficient authority to compel senior engagement. Bridging this gap requires working closely with the sponsor and being explicit about what support is needed – including visible senior backing and the institutional cover to address resistance when it surfaces above the change leader's own level.

The project manager – when structure serves people

Lawyers and former lawyers frequently excel at project management. The disposition that makes a good lawyer – attention to process, careful planning, comfort with complexity – transfers naturally to the management of a structured program. This is a genuine organizational asset in an AI rollout.

The project management function in a change effort covers the architecture of implementation – stakeholder mapping and communication planning, milestone tracking, risk and dependency management, and the sequencing of activities that moves an organization from announcement to sustained adoption. Without this structure, change efforts tend to lose momentum between their initial energy and their intended destination.

The caution worth noting is that project management instincts, applied unreflectively to a change process, can produce a false sense of progress. A project can reach go-live on schedule while adoption remains shallow. Access credentials can be issued to an entire team while active use remains confined to a handful of enthusiasts. The project management lens measures delivery. The change management lens measures behavioral shift. Both are necessary; neither is sufficient on its own.

For legal organizations, this distinction matters particularly in how success is defined. An AI implementation project that reports 100 percent tool access across a practice group has delivered something real. An adoption program that reports measurable changes in how lawyers draft, research, and review – with sustained use three months after go-live – has delivered something different and considerably more valuable. The project manager who understands the difference will build adoption metrics into the program from the outset, rather than treating adoption as an output that follows naturally from delivery.

The power user – the most credible proof of concept

In any organization undergoing a technology change, there are individuals who engage early, experiment genuinely, and develop a level of working proficiency that others have not yet reached. In AI adoption, these are the power users. They are the most powerful existence proof available to the change program.

What distinguishes a power user is not enthusiasm for technology in the abstract. It is specific, practical competency in applying AI to real legal work. The power user has moved beyond exploratory prompts to a personal repertoire of reliable applications. They know which tasks AI handles well in their practice area, they have developed prompts that produce consistent and usable output, they keep pace with new tools and can identify how those tools might be developed further, and they have learned how to evaluate and verify AI-generated content rather than accepting it uncritically. This last capacity – knowing when to trust, when to check, and when to reject – is arguably the most important, particularly in a profession where the consequences of unchecked error are significant.

The power user's influence on colleagues is disproportionate to any formal role they hold. Research from McKinsey[5] identifies what it calls "superusers" as more effective change agents than top-down mandates, precisely because they offer something a mandate cannot – visible, credible evidence that the tool works, demonstrated by a colleague who does similar work and faces similar challenges. A skeptical senior lawyer who has not yet engaged with AI is unlikely to be persuaded by a vendor presentation or a leadership communication. The same lawyer is considerably more likely to be moved by a trusted peer who says: "Let me show you how I did that" – a very different register from "You should really try this". The first is an invitation. The second is a pressure. In a professional culture attuned to the difference, that distinction matters.

The power user's limitation is that their sphere of influence is, at this stage, primarily their own work. Their credibility is high; their reach is limited. For many power users, this is a natural resting point – they continue to deepen their own practice without extending their influence more broadly. Whether they remain there, or take a step further, depends on a choice – and on whether the organization creates the conditions that make that choice attractive. Identifying power users early, celebrating their results visibly, and offering them a path toward the champion role is one of the highest-return investments a change program can make.

The change champion – the bridge between vision and practice

The change champion is a power user who has made a deliberate choice to extend their impact beyond their own work. This shift in orientation – from "I use AI well" to "I help my team use AI well" – represents a genuine change of identity, not simply an additional task.

In practice, these are often two different people. The power user who has mastered the tools is not automatically the person with the instinct or the inclination to bring colleagues along. But combining both capacities in one individual has a real and underappreciated advantage – power usership creates credibility. A change champion who also knows the tools inside out is simply more convincing. Their technical fluency gives them access to the sceptic's real concern – "Will this actually work for work like mine?" – in a way that a colleague with influence but limited hands-on experience cannot. This is why equipping power users with at least the basics of change management thinking – rather than treating technical skill and change skill as entirely separate development tracks – is one of the more practical investments a firm can make.

What makes champions particularly powerful in legal organizations is their credibility advantage. They are peers – they carry the same professional responsibilities as the colleagues they are trying to support, they share the same concerns about accuracy and liability, and they understand the texture of the work from the inside. This gives them access to conversations that managers, IT teams, and innovation professionals cannot easily reach. A colleague who raises a concern about AI accuracy or confidentiality in the presence of a champion is not speaking to someone with an institutional interest in dismissing the concern. They are speaking to someone who had the same concern, worked through it, and can say what they found.

The competencies that effective legal AI champions need extend across three dimensions. The first is the technical foundation – prompt engineering for legal tasks, output evaluation, and a working understanding of where tools are strong and where they are not. The second is influence and communication – translating AI capability into colleague-relevant language, listening to resistance without dismissing it, coaching through imperfect early attempts. The third is organizational awareness – understanding where resistance is concentrated, knowing which colleagues are potential early adopters, and identifying when a concern needs to be escalated rather than handled peer-to-peer.

Champions do not need to convert everyone. The research[6] is consistent on this point – building a coalition of visible, active adopters creates the social conditions under which remaining colleagues begin to follow. A practice group in which five colleagues are visibly integrating AI into their daily work, sharing what they have learned, and talking about it naturally will change more profoundly and more durably than one in which a hundred colleagues have completed a mandatory training module.

What champions need in return is often underestimated. They need recognition, a community of practice with other champions, and senior air cover – the knowledge that if they encounter resistance above the level they can manage, the sponsor and change leader will support them. Champions who are left to champion without these conditions will burn out. The investment in building and sustaining them is not a luxury – it is the program.

The sponsor alliance – when one sponsor is not enough

Traditional change management has long operated on the assumption that a single, committed executive sponsor is the primary driver of change. For many organizational changes, this model works reasonably well. For AI adoption in legal organizations, Prosci's own updated research on AI-specific change dynamics identifies it as insufficient.[7]

AI is not a single initiative with a defined endpoint. It touches every practice area, every seniority level, every function of the organization simultaneously. It evolves continuously as the underlying models improve and new applications emerge. It raises questions – about ethics, data handling, professional responsibility, and quality standards – that sit across multiple domains of organizational authority. No single sponsor, however committed, has the credibility, the reach, or the domain authority to hold all these dimensions at once.

What AI adoption in legal requires instead is a sponsor alliance – a coalition of senior leaders who together cover the constituencies and concerns that the change addresses. In a law firm, this might include the managing partner (who holds the strategic narrative and models behavior for the partnership), a senior partner with deep practice credibility (who can speak to the professional dimension of AI adoption), the general counsel or chief risk officer (who can address governance and professional responsibility concerns with authority), and the technology or operations leader (who anchors the practical dimension of implementation). In an in-house legal department, an analogous coalition might span the CLO, senior business unit counsel, and the legal operations lead.

The sponsor alliance does not function by issuing joint communications. It functions by each member speaking to their own constituency, in their own voice, about the dimension of the change they are best placed to address. When the managing partner speaks about AI as a strategic priority, they are most credible with the partnership. When the risk partner speaks about governance frameworks that protect client confidentiality and professional standards, they are most credible with the lawyers who worry about those questions. The alliance's power is in its coverage, not its uniformity.

There is also a governance dimension to the alliance that is often overlooked. Senior leaders who are reluctant to commit visibly to a change are frequently, underneath that reluctance, concerned about what happens when something goes wrong and whether they will be left exposed. A clear, well-considered AI governance framework does not just protect the firm from risk. It protects the leader from the fear of risk – which is often the more immediate obstacle. When a senior partner can see that accountability is clear, that the firm has thought carefully about how AI output is reviewed and how client confidentiality is protected, the reputational calculus shifts. Endorsing something well-governed feels different from endorsing something uncertain. The substance may be similar. The perceived exposure is not.

Managing the alliance requires the change leader to invest in keeping its members aligned, informed, and active. Sponsors who are not regularly briefed on progress and emerging resistance tend to drift back to passive endorsement. The change leader's role includes making it easy for each sponsor to stay engaged – through regular briefings, specific asks, and connecting them to the parts of the program where their voice is most needed.

Conclusion

The organizations that succeed at AI adoption in legal are rarely those with the most sophisticated tools or the most generous training budgets. They are the ones in which the human architecture of change has been deliberately designed and activated.

Each role examined in this chapter is necessary. None is sufficient on its own. A committed sponsor without active managers will create energy at the top that dissipates before it reaches the front line. A network of change champions without sponsorship will generate enthusiasm among peers that stalls when it encounters institutional resistance. A technically excellent power user without the skills or inclination to influence others will demonstrate what is possible without helping others get there. The roles are interdependent – they work because they are connected, not because any single one of them is particularly powerful in isolation.

The reader of this chapter might usefully ask two questions. First, which of these roles exists in their organization's AI adoption effort, and which is missing or unfilled? Gaps in the cast are the most reliable predictor of adoption failures that are subsequently blamed on the technology or the strategy. Second, which role are they personally positioned to play – and are they playing it fully?

AI adoption is not a technical problem with a human dimension. It is a human problem that happens to involve technology. The change frameworks, roles, and relationships explored in this chapter are the response to that reality. Building them is not the softer part of an AI program. It is the part that determines whether the program succeeds.

References

1 Prosci, *AI Adoption Research* (2025). www.prosci.com/ai-change-management

2 *Ibid.*

3 *Ibid.*

4 Dr Andrea Miskolczi, "Lawyers and the Leap into (AI) Transformation: Embracing Change Management Techniques" Modern Lawyer, Globe Law and Business (2025). https://globelawonline.com/article/710/lawyers-and-the-leap-into-ai-transformation-embracing-change-management-techniques

5 McKinsey & Company, "Reconfiguring Work: Change Management in the Age of Gen AI" (2025). www.mckinsey.com/capabilities/quantumblack/our-insights/reconfiguring-work-change-management-in-the-age-of-gen-ai

6 Colorado Lawyer, "Managing Disruptive Change in the Age of AI" (2025). https://cl.cobar.org/departments/managing-disruptive-change-in-the-age-of-ai/

7 Prosci, "8 Ways AI-Driven Change is Different" (December 2025). www.prosci.com/blog/8-ways-ai-driven-change-is-different

Chapter 16:
The modern digital lawyer

By Daan Potjer, director, commercial and legal excellence, Loyens & Loeff N.V.

Introduction

For the first time in the long history of the legal profession, a true revolution is taking place. AI is changing not only how legal work is performed, but also impacting the value that lawyers create and reshaping the competitive legal landscape. Clients expect greater efficiency, transparency, and lower legal costs from their lawyers. They compare not only law firms, but also what AI technology itself can deliver. AI is therefore not just a tool – it is altering the economics of legal work and challenges traditional fee models, staffing structures, and the traditional division of work between juniors and senior professionals. These changes are structural and irreversible.

Digital skills and AI literacy are now core competencies at all levels of the legal profession, not just for junior associates. Even senior partners and general counsels (GCs) must recognize tech proficiency as a career-long asset for staying competitive and delivering client value. The role of a lawyer will not disappear, but AI will have a fundamental impact on what this role entails. If one does not adapt, it will be difficult to make a living as a lawyer, as per the oft-cited saying: "AI won't replace lawyers, but lawyers who use AI will replace those who don't".[1]

Being a "modern digital lawyer", however, is more than just being tech-savvy. It means strategically integrating technology into one's practice to work smarter, deliver better service to clients, and focus on high-value tasks.[2] Where the legal grunt work can be done by technological tools, the digital lawyer can concentrate on advising, creative solutions, client relationship management, and getting a better understanding of the client's needs.

To become a true digital lawyer, a broad range of additional skills is required. These include technological literacy, data competency, an innovative mindset, digital collaboration skills, and a commitment to continuous learning. In an AI-driven environment, lawyers will also need to be able to work in multi-disciplinary teams on the same matter for a client. Working on a matter with data managers, AI-experts, and other professionals is common in other professional services, yet new in the legal sector.

Examples of lawyers who have embraced the new way of working are starting to emerge, yet the traditional context in which much of the legal work is done today is an impediment to speedy adoption of AI and technology in general. Nonetheless, the speed of the AI revolution in the legal sector is accelerating, so making the shift to become a digital lawyer is now a necessity.

In this chapter, we examine the new skills lawyers need, how AI is changing daily work, ways to work smarter, the importance of firm culture, and how a lawyer's value proposition is evolving.

Future-proof skills and mindset for lawyers

Up to now, the training of lawyers mostly focused on creating and applying legal expertise. Of course, lawyers also learned to use tools like word processors, document management systems, client portals, Outlook and Teams, but were typically not trained in advanced technology or data management. More technical skills, and specifically a more innovative mindset, are now essential in legal practice.

First and foremost, lawyers need to have a high degree of technological literacy. That does not mean that they should be able to code themselves, but they do need to have a solid grasp of what technologies (like AI agents, document automation, e-discovery tools, etc.) can, cannot, and might – in the near future – be able to do. A modern digital lawyer must understand the power and the pitfalls of AI-generated output, be comfortable in trying out new tools and assessing their impact, and know how to balance technology versus human expertise. The goal is to have technology take over as much of the work that it can do better and faster than humans. A partner should, for instance, be at ease at using AI contract analysis tools, interpreting the results and deciding when further manual review is warranted.

AI tools are worthless without good data. Organizing data, adding correct and sufficient meta-data to documents, and assessing which data should be used in AI queries are already essential skills. This also includes having a good understanding of data privacy and ethics in combination with the use of AI, and the ability to collaborate with data specialists to ensure optimal data management when working on a matter. All of this highlights the requirement to work effectively in multidisciplinary teams. Litigation and M&A lawyers, for example, now use analytics on past cases or deals to inform strategy. That requires the ability to select and prepare the required data, and to be able to read and question data findings.

The shift from working in the office to working from home during COVID-19 accelerated the use of digital communication and collaboration tools. Proficiency with modern platforms (e.g. Teams/Zoom, document-sharing applications, electronic signatures) and the ability to communicate effectively through digital channels have become crucial. Even negotiations and client meetings are now often virtual, so skills such as running effective video conferences, managing remote teams, and maintaining client rapport online are essential. The emergence of digital co-working spaces on matters for clients and law firms in legal platforms like Harvey and Legora add a new dimension, going far beyond simple co-editing of a Word-document or sharing information via basic client portals.[3]

Technology is changing rapidly. Game-changing new AI tools are launched almost every week. This environment requires a willingness to experiment with these new tools and approaches, and adapt quickly to new technological possibilities. Lawyers usually have a "glass half empty" mentality and want to know all the facts before acting. This is simply not possible in an AI world. Adopting a more entrepreneurial mindset towards problem-solving, taking calculated risks in some areas while keeping clear boundaries in others, will help lawyers to keep up with developments. One should be open to redesigning processes or trying out new tools to see if they yield better results. The stance of "we have always done it this way" or "I only do what other law firms are also doing" must be left behind.

Since technology is changing so fast, mastering new tools is not a one-off task. Just as a lawyer has to keep up with new laws, case law, and opinions, they must also practice lifelong learning when it comes to technology. This means continuously updating one's knowledge of emerging tools, AI developments, and evolving processes and best practices. For managing partners and GCs, it also means fostering firm-wide training programs and personally staying informed (e.g. attending legal tech webinars or workshops).

How AI is transforming lawyer workloads

Through the use of AI and curated data, the daily work of a lawyer is changing. AI-driven tools can now handle many time-consuming, low-complexity tasks that used to fill the days (and nights) of junior lawyers. Document review is a prime example. AI can quickly scan and flag relevant clauses in thousands of documents, a job that once required an army of associates. Basic legal research queries can be answered by natural language AI assistants in seconds. Initial contract drafts can be generated by AI based on templates and past agreements. In due diligence, AI can identify anomalies or risks across contracts much faster than a manual review.

AI is, however, not the be-all-and-end-all for legal work. Human legal expertise and judgment remain indispensable. It should also be noted that an 80 percent-ready draft by an AI agent is not the same as an 80 percent-ready draft made by associates that have been trained by the seniors and partners to create such a draft. The review process is markedly different for both options. While AI does not replace human expertise, it does, however, certainly extend its reach.

Because AI takes over repetitive tasks, the workload balance is shifting. Lawyers can now handle a larger volume of matters, or devote more time to complex analysis, client counselling, and creative lawyering, instead of spending time on rote production. There's early evidence that this is changing law firm structures. For example, if one AI-driven tool can do the work of several junior associates, firms might hire fewer juniors only focusing on legal expertise. Instead, they may also invest in "hybrid" roles, i.e. lawyers who are adept at using AI, and in new specialists to support AI integration. The classic pyramid staffing model could thus also evolve to a diamond, pillar, or T-shape, with fewer entry-level tasks and a greater emphasis on senior expertise.[4]

Aside from pure legal work, AI tools like Copilot in Microsoft 365 are already impacting how lawyers are spending their time and are significantly increasing their efficiency. Adding other LLMs only amplifies this effect. When specialized platforms such as Harvey and Legora are added to the mix, the workload of lawyers shifts even more drastically. Effective use of AI requires "more than a click". It demands legal professionals who understand the tool's limitations and remain accountable for the outcomes.

Working smarter, not harder

With the availability of current technology, the question is how to make this technology really work for lawyers. Working smarter can be illustrated by the following example. Where one lawyer spends 12 hours grinding through a contract review manually, another uses an AI review tool and finishes in four hours, and then spends the extra time on preparing a complex negotiation strategy. The latter is working smarter by leveraging tech to handle routine work, so that their human expertise is applied where it adds the most value.

Modern tools can amplify productivity and quality, so lawyers should continually ask themselves, "Is there a technology or process improvement that could do this task more efficiently?"

Lawyers should be encouraged to regularly review their task list. Anything repetitive, standardized, or data-intensive is a candidate for automation or delegation to technology. By offloading such tasks, lawyers free up time for high-value activities, such as bespoke legal analysis, mentoring team members, or advising clients. This mindset shift to "What can I automate so I can concentrate on what truly requires me doing it myself?" is at the heart of working smarter.

Tech adoption isn't just about speed – it can also increase consistency and quality of the legal work. Automation reduces the risk of human error in routine tasks, for example, prevention of overlooked clauses or calculation mistakes in a complex spreadsheet. AI-driven proofreading or drafting assistants can enforce style guides and catch deviations. Similarly, automated alert systems can notify lawyers of new legal developments relevant to their practice, so no important information goes unnoticed.

Working smarter doesn't mean blindly trusting every new technology. It is prudent to pilot new tools on low-risk tasks, understand their failure modes, and establish best practices. Lawyers should develop a habit of verifying important AI-generated results, by for example double-checking key case citations provided by an AI tool, or cross-verifying an auto-generated contract against a checklist. For now, AI should always be supervised by humans.

Fostering an innovative culture in the firm

To make innovation and the use of AI tools work, it is key to create a culture in the firm that is conducive to incorporating new technologies. This starts at the top. Managing partners and general counsels must champion digital transformation.[5] They must actively encourage experimentation, celebrate efficiency gains, and use new tools themselves. If leaders are passive or skeptical about new technology, even the best tech initiatives will fizzle out. Leading by example is the crux here.

Just providing new tools is not enough to have people adopt new technology. This requires comprehensive training programs, ready access to experts who can answer questions, and ongoing promotion of use.[6] AI literacy has to be part of performance management and is required for all new hires. Only a general and complete upskilling of the organization will ensure that the tools are not just available, but also effectively used.

An innovative culture in a law firm is further strengthened when the silos between the lawyers and the tech specialists are broken down.[7] Creating hybrid roles or cross-functional teams can accelerate not only innovation projects, but also continuous improvements in client service through the use of technology. Cross-functional project teams of lawyers working side by side with tech experts, knowledge managers, or even external tech vendors have begun to emerge.[8] This approach brings diverse skills to the table and helps build solutions that truly fit lawyers' needs. It is a shift from the past when tech decisions were left to Innovation and IT alone. Lawyers themselves should now co-drive innovation efforts.

Innovation in law firms must strike a careful balance between creativity and responsibility. On the one hand, lawyers and staff should feel empowered to experiment. On the other, governance and risk management should be maintained. To foster innovation, lawyers must be able to experiment with minimal bureaucracy, provided this occurs within clear guidelines, like an AI usage policy (e.g., ensuring client confidentiality, and compliance with regulations like GDPR and the EU AI Act), so everyone understands the dos and don'ts of new tech.

Innovation and implementation of tech tools will not work when the incentives for lawyers are stacked against it. When a junior lawyer with an ambitious billable hour target has a choice to create a document themselves that allows them to bill three hours, or use AI and be done in 20 minutes, there is a conflict. However, if embracing technology can enhance their career progression or at least earn positive recognition, they are far more likely to embrace it. Turning senior partners into tech evangelists might sound fanciful, but nothing converts sceptics faster than seeing a colleague get praised or promoted for innovating a better way to do things. Switching pricing models from the billable hour model and fixed fee arrangements to value-based fees may make it simpler to bridge the gap between urging the use of AI and still being regarded as "profitable". A mix of intangible benefits (like kudos from your boss and management) and targeted changes to remuneration and promotion policies will help shift the culture so the firm embraces technology and innovation more quickly and effectively.

Rethinking the lawyer's value proposition in an AI era

In an AI era, law firms may become more like regular professional service firms, switching (at least partly) from the billable hour model (and its fixed fee derivative) to value-based pricing – charging what clients are willing to pay for a service. This would change how lawyer performance is judged, how profitability per matter has to be managed, and how the delivery of services is designed. More importantly, it will change the role of lawyers as well.

When much of the "grunt work" can be automated or delegated to tech, lawyers should focus on an expertise-driven, high value role. The value of a lawyer will increasingly lie in strategic thinking, judgment, creativity, and client advocacy, rather than being a walking legal encyclopedia or a human document scanner. In essence, lawyers are shifting from doers to advisors and from handling "context" work to focusing on "core" work. For example, historically, a client might have paid a firm for many hours of manual contract review. In the near future, the client will expect AI to handle such work quickly, and will instead pay the lawyer for analysis of results, risk judgment, and nuanced advice. This is a positive development for the profession, as it elevates those parts of the work that are intellectually stimulating and truly require human input.

Client demand is changing as well. In-house legal teams may no longer just be asking themselves which external law firm to use; now their first question might be whether to use an AI tool or outside counsel. The pressure to reduce legal costs is stronger than ever. When clients seek support from outside counsel, they will demand greater value for the fees they pay. Clients may even insist that lawyers use AI platforms like Harvey and Legora and that all documents and data be kept in those platforms so clients can continue to have access to them. The question for law firms is therefore, are we delivering something clients cannot get anywhere else? Being a true advisor, and being able to judge and explain AI outcomes, can certainly be such a role. Sharing law firm data with clients for a fee, so clients can use this data in their AI tools, may be another example. Such offerings can generate steady revenue streams and deepen the relationship of the client with the law firm.

Paradoxically, the more AI is incorporated in the delivery of legal services, the more certain it is that uniquely human skills will stand out. Qualities like emotional intelligence, persuasion, ethical judgment, creativity, and relationship-building will play an increasingly important role in getting client buy-in, ensuring that they value the services delivered and can be retained for repeat business. An AI tool might churn out a contract draft, but soft skills like empathy and understanding the client's real business concerns remain critical in negotiations and in being a valued advisor. As "commodity" tasks get a commoditized tech treatment, it matters how a lawyer connects with clients and solves their problems. To align to this new value proposition, lawyers should invest as much in these human-centric skills as they do in their technical skills.

Traditionally, lawyers were mostly trained in their legal expertise. While this can remain a track to follow, there will also be new types of career tracks such as that of a "tech lawyer" – someone who is both legally and AI/tech adept. Such roles should have a career path all the way from junior associate to partner. These roles create value by combining legal expertise with technical abilities to deliver faster, better, and more innovative legal services to clients. Their abilities include, for example, designing algorithms or configuring AI for legal analysis. The role of lawyers changes from providing legal memos or courtroom arguments to being problem solvers that leverage legal and technical tools to help clients.

As stated before, "AI won't replace lawyers, but lawyers who use AI will replace those who don't". Lawyers who embrace modern AI and other technical skills will likely thrive, and those who resist may find themselves left behind. It is key to adapt and empower oneself with technology to continue to be valuable to clients and successful in one's career. It's not just about avoiding obsolescence – it's about seizing the opportunity to elevate the profession. Lawyers who rise to this challenge are going to drive more value than ever, and enjoy more interesting work. That is a win for everyone – clients, lawyers, and firms alike.

Embrace and adopt new technology

The legal profession is at an inflection point where digital skills and AI fluency are becoming fundamental to being an effective lawyer. The modern digital lawyer blends traditional legal expertise with technological and AI-enabled legal solutions. By embracing these tools, lawyers can deliver better results faster, focus on what truly matters, and make their careers more future-proof (and arguably more interesting). The key skills and mindset outlined in this chapter – from being tech-curious and tech-literate to pursuing continuous learning and innovation – are not optional for lawyers. These capabilities are required to stay relevant as a lawyer in an AI-driven era.

Managing partners and GCs have to lead by example and drive the change towards a digital future in their organizations. That means they have to incentivize innovation, invest in tools, data management and training, update policies and guardrails, and be open to pilot new tools, new technologies, and new processes. Above all, they need to make clear that they truly believe that change is required. Firms that do this will likely gain a competitive edge in attracting talent and clients.

The modern legal sector belongs to those who embrace and adopt new technology and new ways of working. Lawyers should feel empowered through learning and innovation, and continuously evolve their skills and services to better serve clients. In this way, lawyers will not only stay relevant – they will be in the driving seat to shape the future of the legal sector.

References

1 See for example this article in Law.com: www.law.com/dailybusinessreview/2024/03/13/a-i-wont-replace-attorneys-but-tech-savvy-lawyers-might/

2 IDC report: What every company can learn from Frontier firms leading the AI revolution, Accelerating innovation with AI, p.41 https://marketingassets.microsoft.com/gdc/gdcvSFjHm/original

3 See https://help.harvey.ai/articles/shared-spaces and https://legora.com/product/portal

4 Rapoport, N.B. and Tiano, J.R., Fighting the hypothetical: why law firms should rethink the billable hour in the generative AI era, 20, *Washington Journal of Law, Technology & Arts*, 2025, p.57 https://digitalcommons.law.uw.edu/wjlta/vol20/iss2/2

5 Gartner: *Top Insights for Improving Legal Technology Adoption*, 12 September 2024, p.8 www.gartner.com/en/documents/5757015

6 Microsoft report: The roadmap for AI-strategies, the route to successful AI-implementation (in Dutch), 13 August 2025 p.26

7 Bucerius Law School: The AI-Conomics of Legal Services, How generative AI will transform the commercial model of law, 27 March 2025, p.14 https://mailchi.mp/5df71b4e027f/the-ai-conomics-of-legal-services

8 The Global Legal Post, Ben Edwards: Harnessing Gen AI in Law, Lessons from the front lines in Europe, May 2025, p.5 www.globallegalpost.com/lg/19_harnessing-gen-ai-in-law-lessons-from-the-front-lines-in-europe-1302501502

Chapter 17: Becoming a trusted advisor and beyond

By Stuart Maister, chief storyteller, Strategic Narrative

Ever since David Maister's *The Trusted Advisor* was written in 2002,[1] this phrase has been the declared ambition of most law firms in relation to their client relationship. But what does being a "trusted advisor" actually mean in practice? And is this the right target?

This chapter looks at this in detail and argues that this aspiration should now be updated to go even further – and become a trusted *partner* to clients. It discusses why this is important in a hypercompetitive world and looks at how to turn this into action at a practitioner and firm level.

First, be trusted

The number one focus should be to be trusted. That's an easy thing to say: "My clients must trust me, they call me for advice". However, clients use services they need and it may be a highly transactional decision rather than one based on high trust. A lawyer is expected to be able to deliver good technical services – this may not be evidence of trust beyond the commissioning of an approved supplier who appears to know what they are doing.

In this situation, the lawyer is trusted to deliver a service in the same way that a dentist is trusted to do a checkup. It is a transaction involving technical skills and can be switched to another supplier if cost or circumstance dictates. For some clients, this is an entirely appropriate commercial arrangement and for some firms this is the business model – for example, firms that have a high volume of routine legal transactions, or have unique characteristics such as its location or highly specialist service. The issue here is simply to be competent and professional. That is sufficient to be trusted in this context.

This chapter is aimed at those who are different – those who want or need to build deeper, bigger accounts with important clients that have ongoing requirements. These clients also have enormous choice, and the bigger they are, the more choice they have. Who will they choose? Those they trust the most.

Therefore, being trusted should be the primary focus of any client relationship of this type, and it begins from the first contact, through any assignments and beyond. It is not simply a tool to win business, but needs to be consciously, intentionally designed into client relationships by the firm and its people so that it becomes the question asked whenever any strategy is considered: will this build or destroy trust?

If they build a trusted relationship together, the client will retain the lawyer and come back when they have another issue that needs tackling. This is a critical point – even within major assignments, things will change. Over time they most certainly will. Therefore, positioning the lawyer as someone who can be trusted to be alongside the client when this happens should be a major part of the approach and will be more important than fees as a factor in the choice made.

Further, the evidence suggests that fear trumps greed when we make decisions.[2] We avoid loss more strongly than we seek gain. That means that the avoidance of risk is a primary motivator in our decision making.

Trust, therefore, is a crucial factor in who gets which piece of business and continues to be retained. There is increasing choice in a competitive market, but clients need to feel safe every time they make a move.

This is particularly true if the work is critical. Fees become less important than confidence in the individual and their team. When things can collapse if you make the wrong decision, do you find the least expensive advisor, or the one whose advice you trust?

What is trust?

This may seem obvious, and trust is a word used frequently, but often without real thought about what it means in practice. It's worth pausing to try to dig down on this in order to be clear and help lawyers be intentional about it.

The Trust Equation developed by David Maister et al is the best-known version of this in the context of professional services. It sets out what it means to be trustworthy.

$$\text{Trustworthiness} = \frac{\text{Credibility} + \text{Reliability} + \text{Intimacy}}{\text{Self-orientation}}$$

Figure 1. The Maister Trust Equation

Credibility and reliability are self-evident. Intimacy is a description of the nature of the relationship between the lawyer and their client, but the key is the divisor. In this equation, trustworthiness is reduced by the degree to which the professional is self-oriented rather than client- or relationship-oriented. However you seek to hide this, the principle of emotional leakage means it becomes clear if you are simply focused on your own interests. In other words, people just *know* it when they see it or feel it. If all you are doing is chasing the fees, it impacts their trust.

In our book, *Choose Trust*,[3] Kevin Vaughan-Smith and I developed a new model, which we call the Trust Triangle. The difference is that it focuses not on the lawyer's ability to be trustworthy – which in itself can be seen as self-oriented – but on the quality of the relationship itself. The big idea here is that trust is the characterization of a relationship between parties, with the question being "To what degree is this trusting or transactional?".

In our approach, the goal is to develop a high trust relationship, not simply sell more by being trustworthy. The ambition here is for both parties to be trusted so that they can do their very best work together. It recognizes that the greatest value is created between parties, not simply as the provision of a service by one side.

In the case of lawyers, this is self-evidently true, but not always explicit. As well as providing advice, a lawyer drafts contracts, negotiates with or on behalf of a client, advocates or litigates, helps make a decision about how to proceed, and often delivers practical outcomes such as claims processing. In all cases this involves execution, and the client has huge responsibilities in relation to the delivery of the work.

The idea that this is an external advisory service to be bought does not do justice to the relationship involved in a successful assignment. Any professional service provider is – together with the client – achieving an outcome.

The Trust Triangle recognizes that and has three dimensions. These can together be seen as a definition of what trust is in this context. If used proactively as the way to intentionally create a high trust relationship, they become the design guidelines.

When I work with clients on this, we dive into what each of these characteristics means in the context of their firm and its clients. In this chapter we can explore this more generically.

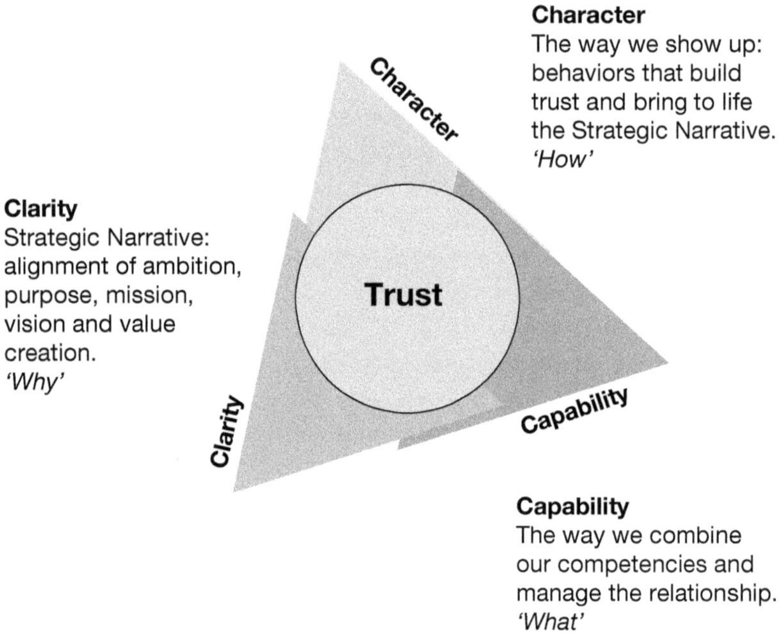

Figure 2. The Trust Triangle

Clarity

Clarity is the foundation of trust. It means everyone is exactly on the same page about the purpose of the relationship, and getting clear provides the basis for exploring greater ambitions together. It represents the "why" of this relationship.

So many lawyers and their clients just want to "get started" on projects without really setting out total clarity about what those involved can achieve together. Taking time to ensure there is clarity will pay dividends in terms of outcome – and the trust that is created through the process. Consistently focusing on clarity of outcome as the case or project develops will reinforce the sense that everyone is pointing in the same direction and avoid misunderstandings or misaligned expectations.

This is just as true in terms of the relationship with a client. With major accounts, it is essential to sit down and be really clear about what they want to achieve across their business, and develop an aligned approach to help them do this. Ask them what they most value and why. Really understand the impact your work has on their business and what they see as most important. This is the basis of a much deeper interaction and moves away from transacting as the deliverer of technical services.

At the start of every piece of work, ensure there is total clarity and mutual understanding of the ambition you have together and what this looks like in practice.

Character

Character is the way this translates into behaviors. It represents the "how" of this relationship.

The manner in which lawyers work with their clients is as important as the work itself in building and growing trust. It is a powerful exercise to spend time looking at the behaviors that are present in your biggest accounts and determine if they create or destroy trust. This work both ways – if you are not to be in a master–servant situation, it is also true that the way clients behave will impact the value you can provide for them and, if this is negative, should be addressed. I work with clients to decide how best to do this.

Behaviors are often simply assumed. It's a very powerful process to be proactive about this: articulate with a client the high trust behaviors they can expect from your team – and also those you would ask from them in order to do a great job together.

Many of these behaviors have been set out in earlier chapters of this book. Following these guidelines will be a key element in building trust.

I use five high trust behaviors as a template to define what this looks like in any relationship. They are a good starting point for an analysis.

They are:

1. *Consideration.* This about fairness and equity. Are both parties gaining value from the relationship? To what degree are they considering each other in decisions made?
2. *Courage.* Being proactive about trust sometimes takes courage. For example, raising the quality of the relationship as an important issue and addressing the challenges involved; not promising deliverables that will be unfair to colleagues and may not be achievable; turning down work that other firms or colleagues may be better suited to deliver. Having this courage usually pays off in terms of the trust that is built, but may involve short-term pain.
3. *Honesty.* This is much more than lack of corruption. It means being open, straightforward, telling truths (even when they are uncomfortable), behaving with high levels of integrity, being timely with information. All great, warm words, often assumed.
4. *Loyalty.* This is about loyalty to the relationship. So, for example, there

is a question of how you speak about the client (or a colleague) when they are not in the room. The principle here is to "Do unto others as they would do unto you" and be faithful to the trust you seek to build in this relationship.

5. *Ambition*. This is where the value of the relationship is fully realized – in focusing on how you create outcomes together, collaborating and sharing in order to make 1+1=3 or 33. If this behavior is fully present, then it is evidence of a higher degree of trust.

By defining what they mean in the context of this relationship you can flesh out potential challenges and considerations that may be relevant and ensure everyone knows "This is what we mean and how we will behave".

This can be a real point of difference for the firm, set out in bid documents and publicly. That's because it is as often *how* you deliver as much as *what* you do that leads to your people being chosen.

Capability

Capability is more than just what you can do. It is about the interdependence of the parties involved, and how they will work together to achieve greater value. It involves paying attention to the relationship together, alongside accountability for project delivery. It defines the capability of this relationship, and the greater the trust, the higher the ceiling. It answers the question: "what" kind of relationship are we in together?

Working on this involves key questions about those involved. Are they transacting or collaborating? Is this deliberate or simply how it is? How do they govern the relationship to make sure it remains healthy and high trust?

It is this dimension that takes us into the second part of the aspiration of most firms – to answer the capability question with "We are a 'trusted advisor'". Let's look at what this means in practice – and whether it is enough.

Be a trusted... what?

Assume you or your firm is trusted by the client. Now we need to dive deeper to understand how you are viewed.

When I work with clients on this, I set out three possible statuses:

1. Trusted supplier.
2. Trusted advisor.
3. Trusted partner.

A trusted supplier provides a service in a transactional way. They are trusted to do so. Those who want to move up the ladder aim to be trusted advisors.

What is a trusted advisor? They are essentially trusted suppliers who also have a deeper human relationship with the clients they serve. If you look at the Trust Equation in Figure 1, two of the three attributes – credibility and reliability – could equally be held by trusted suppliers. It is the third – intimacy – that elevates the status, and it describes the nature of the relationship of trust that exists. Furthermore, it is reduced by the degree to which there is self-orientation, and this again highlights that this is all about the human dimension to the business engagement. It implies that there are two people involved and the trusted advisor is a professional in a relationship with a client.

So, why aim higher? I advocate trusted partnership as something more. A trusted advisor is still essentially supporting the team, brought in when required, providing a service, even if with a high degree of professional intimacy. A trusted partner is on the team. Value creation is a team sport.

Being a Trusted Partner

A partner is a peer, not a supplicant. Those involved in partnership are working together to achieve an outcome. As I argue above, work delivered by a lawyer almost always needs to be done in a collaborative way and the professional and client are interdependent in the way they deliver this.

In the first instance, this is a mindset. It should create confidence in both the lawyer and client that they are working side by side and their interests and ambitions are aligned. This is already a step up from being advisory.

Mindset affects behaviors. If we see each other as on the same team, then this impacts every interaction, decision, and action. One of the key areas of trust is not to be self-serving or transactional. Being a partner states this clearly.

The question for the firm is then: what does it mean to be a trusted partner with my key clients? What value does it bring them – and my firm? What does it look and feel like in practice, and what changes as a result in the way we work together?

Use the Trust Triangle to answer these questions. One of its virtues is that it focuses less on the closeness of the relationship and more on the professional aspects of it. Are we clear together? Are we demonstrating and experiencing a set of behaviors that really build trust? Are we clear in the way we govern and manage the relationship to create more value together?

The question is not: Are we friends? It is: Are we aligned? Are we seen as on the same team?

It's fantastic if you are also friends with your client, but this is ultimately a question of professional trust.

This approach works well as an individual lawyer in relation to your clients. But it also provides a solid framework as a firm. A key point of vulnerability for firms is the personal relationship between individual lawyers and key clients. When a partner leaves, the relationship goes out of the door as well.

If the firm has a Trusted Partner strategy then it can intentionally design high trust relationships with important clients that are based on the team, not the individual lawyer, and so ensure a much deeper and wider relationship with a structured strategy.

Trusted partnership can bring firm-wide benefits

This is a leadership issue. From the top to the bottom it must be clear that the trusted partnership is the approach to be taken with clients. It starts internally. Having this mindset can be a way to build higher levels of collaboration between partners, tackling one of the biggest issues most firms face – the inability to cross-sell multiple practices.

If lawyers are trained and coached to focus on a trusted partnership, and then really approach their clients in this way, they should want to introduce colleagues who can bring more value and skills that they do not have. This is what a partner chooses to do – but it is not necessarily what an advisor (who focuses on their own specialist knowledge) or supplier does.

Furthermore, this approach can be embedded horizontally across the firm. Within the organization, being a Trusted Partner should be different from simply being a partner. At its heart is a willingness to collaborate, be open, and see the bigger picture. There should be a team spirit – a sense that we win or lose together. This is not always present in law firms, to say the least, and so the culture of trusted partnership can have wider benefits beyond direct client relationships.

A partnership mindset is the basis for sustained trust between the parties. This approach leads to mutual problem solving and greater ambition about what can be achieved. It's in everyone's interest.

When this is true, the whole firm can align their interests to that of their clients, and the client benefits from having a true partner focused on business outcomes and value creation, bringing all skills to the table.

Focus on the clients who are willing to build a partnership

This takes time and additional effort. Which clients should firms invest into in order to achieve Trusted Partner status? One possible answer is: those who are already important to them and have potential for growth.

Another is: the ones where that firm is at its very best, delights the clients, loves working with them, and knows they are the most profitable.

Once law firm leaders have identified the right clients to focus on, they should ask themselves and their teams: What is it about them and us that makes this such a great fit?

The point is to have a focus. This is like spear fishing, where you target the big fish you want, rather than net fishing, where you cast your net and see what you catch. It is critical to have a clear and well understood narrative that identifies who these big fish are, why the firm is the best choice for them, and the value it creates for them by leveraging its strengths. This allows the firm to develop tailored propositions around the client's needs, becoming much more relevant to their business.

This contrasts with firms that provide all variety of clients with a menu of separate services that they can choose. That leads to transactional buying, which is more typical in a trusted advisor relationship but less so in a Trusted Partner relationship.

Lawyers who are trusted partners can work with their best clients in an open way to see the world from their perspective. [1]For example, they can develop a proposition, workshop it with major clients on the basis that they are trying to develop services that fully meet their needs, and then refine it so that it achieves that ambition. In my experience, open discussion of this type with clients is rare in this sector, but it's a powerful way to explore what really works and demonstrates a real commitment to bespoke service – and partnering to create value.

The key is to then have a clear story of the value to be created – not the services being provided – that everyone knows and can articulate. The great thing is this: if it is true for these clients, it will also be true for others like them.

Be intentional about trust

It's a great ambition to be a trusted adviser. Those who say they are already there, well done. My advice is to check in with your clients – what does this actually mean in practice? When do they call on you, and why? What business value do you provide to them? How does their trust in you compare with their trust in other lawyers available to them? Get their perspective, and see what they think is important. These are powerful questions for a discussion, in an environment where you can have a relaxed and open exploration.

If you can move the discussion to becoming a trusted partner – and you know what you and your firm really mean by this – then you are one step toward a deeper relationship with that client. Be highly intentional about this effort with your most important clients. If you are a great fit for them, and them for you, then this is the formula to create much greater value together, with better outcomes for everyone involved.

References

1 *The Trusted Advisor* by D.H. Maister, C.H. Green and R.M. Galford (Simon & Schuster 2002). David is the author's cousin.

2 Daniel Kahneman and Amos Tversky (1979), "Prospect Theory: An Analysis of Decision under Risk", *Econometrica*, 47(2), 263–291.

3 *Choose Trust*, Stuart Maister and Kevin Vaughan Smith, Economist Books, 2024.

Chapter 18: The profoundly human law firm

By Jonathan Middleburgh, principal, Edge International

The majority of chapters in this book have focused on individual skills and argued that the acquisition of these skills is important to the lawyer of today. This chapter seeks to offer a somewhat different perspective – arguing that the stand-out law firm of tomorrow will be the firm that is profoundly human, with a focus on human interaction at its core; and that the stand-out lawyer will be equipped with, and expert in, a range of 'profoundly human' skills.

Legal practice is in the middle of a profound technological shift. AI tools already routinely draft complex contracts, review thousands of documents, analyse case law across multiple jurisdictions, and predict litigation outcomes with statistical confidence at a pace that is many times quicker than a lawyer ever could. The routine, the repetitive, and the research-heavy – tasks that have occupied much of a lawyer's working day for generations – are being automated at speed.

Much of this technology is new and evolving at breakneck pace. It is hard to keep up with the plethora of new AI tools. Our working hypothesis is that the cost of these technologies will decrease and that the technologies themselves will converge so that, over time, law firms will operate pretty much on an even playing field insofar as technology is concerned. It will not be the technologies that differentiate the standout law firms from the also rans – it will be the way in which their lawyers handle the human issues.

This chapter argues that the lawyer who will thrive in the AI era is not the one who understands the most technology or is most adept at using it. This is not to undermine the importance of embracing technology and using technology in as smart a way as possible. However, it is not the tech savvy lawyer who will flourish. It is the one who is most fully, most deliberately, and most skilfully human. We call this the Profoundly Human Lawyer – and we set out what it means, why it matters, and how to develop the relevant skills.

Learning from other shifts in technology

It is instructive to reflect on other shifts in technology, on the basis that past behaviour is generally the best predictor of future behaviour. One key observation is that technologies that are expensive generally drop in price significantly over time. Once initial costs have been amortised, the cost of the relevant technology tends to drop steeply. Examples are abundant – think, for example, of mobile phone technology or flat screen technology. When it comes to software, similarly costs often fall rapidly and much software becomes either open source or widely affordable.

The implications for AI technology are that what is now unaffordable will probably become accessible to most or all law firms over time. The largest law firms are making massive investments in customising AI so as to be reliable for legal applications. Once the applications have become reliable, it is likely that the relevant costs will be amortised by making the technologies available at affordable costs to the wide base of law firms.

A second observation is that, historically, it has not been the technology that has differentiated the higher value law firms from the lower value firms. Practical Law (Thomson Reuters) made available on a user-friendly technology platform best in class precedents to all law firms that could afford a subscription. Some of the largest law firms participated in (and continue to participate in) the creation of this content – which some might have thought was gifting their intellectual property and conferring significant value on lower value firms. To the contrary, having a PLC subscription did not magically transform a less skilful lawyer into a Magic Circle lawyer. The differentiation was not the tech subscription – it was all the other skills that make a Magic Circle lawyer a best-in-class lawyer. Those skills are partly technical skills, but more significantly they are what this chapter calls being a Profoundly Human Lawyer.

AI is already very reliable for some tasks (e.g. contract review). It is less reliable for other tasks and prone to hallucination. However, it is realistic to envisage that it will become reliable for a wide range of tasks within several years and that the cost of the technology will reach a point where it is affordable (in a reliable version) to the majority of firms.

The shifting landscape – what AI can and cannot do

AI is already competent – and in some cases superior to junior lawyers – at document review and due diligence, legal research, contract drafting and comparison, regulatory compliance checking, and the summarization of complex material. These tasks are not trivial, but they share a common characteristic – they can be reduced to pattern recognition applied to text.

What AI *cannot* do is more instructive. As Clio's analysts observed in their 2025 Legal Trends report,[1] AI cannot build the trust and empathy that client relationships require. It cannot read hesitation in a client's voice, gauge a judge's temperament, or know when a deal is about to fall apart because the other side's lead has just been embarrassed in front of their board. It cannot exercise moral courage, or make the judgment call that a technically lawful course of action is nonetheless the wrong advice.

The data – what clients are saying

The evidence from client research consistently points in the same direction. The Law Society's Legal Needs Survey 2023,[2] which canvassed over 17,000 people across England and Wales, found that among those who received professional help, 88 percent were satisfied with their adviser and 86 percent found it easy to communicate with them. Communication, not technical expertise, was the leading driver of satisfaction.

Research published by Thomson Reuters[3] found that the three most desired attributes among commercial clients were that their law firm should deeply understand their business (cited by 28 percent), adopt technology to enhance service (27 percent) and have business acumen / commerciality (also 27 percent). Understanding the business came first.

Accutrainee's 2024 Legal Leaders Survey[4] found that general counsels consistently identified commercial awareness and communication as the areas where junior lawyers most frequently fell short – not legal knowledge.

The message from clients is coherent and consistent – they expect technical competence as a baseline. What differentiates the lawyers they trust, recommend, and return to is human skill.

The Profoundly Human Lawyer – a model

My colleagues Joel Barolsky and Ray D'Cruz first articulated the concept of the Profoundly Human Law firm (PHLF), arguing that the PHLF, with highly developed and skilled lawyers at its core, will win out – every time. Table 1 captures the key characteristics of the PHLF (using the McKinsey 7S dimensions), as suggested by Barolsky and D'Cruz.

Table 1: Key characteristics of the Profoundly Human Law Firm. Adapted from Joel Barolsky and Ray D'Cruz, 2019.

Shared values	Love complexity | Love the law | Love collaboration
Strategy	Play in the world of complex client-defined problems | Win by predicting client needs and delivering transformational value | A human-centred Cx and Ex
Structure	Fluid networks within | Porous external boundaries | Democratic
Systems	Accelerated learning | Value capture | Algorithmic
Style	Purpose and values driven | Instinctively collaborative | Agile
Staff	Diverse in every sense | Flexible | Non-linear careers
Skills	Deep commerciality | Strategic critical thinking | IQ + EQ + DQ

For the PHLF to flourish it will need to be populated by Profoundly Human lawyers. Defining the skills of the Profoundly Human lawyer is a work in progress, but I would suggest that standout legal practice in the era of AI rests on five interconnected domains. These are not 'soft skills' in the dismissive sense that phrase is sometimes used – they are sophisticated, learnable capabilities that take years to develop and that no algorithm can replicate.

The five domains are:

1. *Trusted advisor.* The foundation of everything else. Clients do not hire lawyers – they hire people they trust with problems that matter. Trust is built through consistency, transparency, and the willingness to say uncomfortable things. A recent Thomson Reuters State of the Legal Market Report[5] noted that corporate clients increasingly view their law firms as vendors rather than trusted advisors – a shift that represents both a warning and an opportunity for those who invest in relationship over transaction.

2. *Emotional intelligence.* The capacity to understand and manage your own emotional responses, and to read and respond to those of others. In legal practice, this means recognising when a client is frightened rather than obstructive, knowing when to let silence do the work in a negotiation, and managing a difficult opposing counsel without losing your composure or your client's confidence. As the CEO of one of the world's largest law firms wrote in Fortune in 2025, "Emotional intelligence – the one thing AI still cannot fake – will become more valuable, not less".[6]
3. *Commercial acumen.* The ability to think like the client's business, not just their lawyer. This means understanding sector dynamics, competitive pressures, risk appetite, and what a "good outcome" actually looks like from the client's perspective rather than a purely legal one. Legal leaders surveyed in 2024 consistently flagged commercial awareness as a key gap in junior lawyers' skills.[7]
4. *Communication mastery.* Not simply the ability to write well, but the full range – active listening, plain language, the ability to adjust your register for a boardroom versus a distressed individual client, giving advice verbally with clarity and authority, and knowing when a phone call does what three emails cannot. Accutrainee's 2024 survey[8] identified a significant communication gap between senior and junior lawyers, with senior leaders often preferring direct, real-time communication while juniors defaulted to email – a disconnect that quietly erodes client confidence.
5. *Ethical judgment and moral courage.* The ability to maintain professional independence under commercial and client pressure, and to deliver advice the client needs rather than advice they want to hear. This is not merely a regulatory obligation – it is the quality that, paradoxically, makes clients most loyal. The lawyer who will tell a client they are wrong, clearly and without flinching, is the one they trust absolutely.

These five domains do not operate independently. The trusted advisor who lacks commercial acumen gives advice that is legally sound but practically useless. The emotionally intelligent communicator who cannot exercise ethical judgment becomes a people-pleaser rather than a professional. The model works as a whole – and development in one area tends to reinforce the others.

The skills matrix

The matrix in Table 2 sets out eight proposed core capabilities of the Profoundly Human Lawyer, the component skills within each, and what mastery looks like in everyday practice. It can be used as a self-assessment tool, a basis for supervision conversations, or a framework for CPD planning.

Table 2: The eight core capabilities of the Profoundly Human Lawyer.

Domain	Core capabilities	What this looks like in practice
Trusted advisor	Genuine rapport; proactive communication; transparency about risk and uncertainty; consistency over time	Clients who return, refer, and give more work without being asked
Emotional intelligence	Self-awareness; reading the room; managing your own reactions; handling difficult clients with composure	Keeping a deal on track when personalities clash; delivering bad news well
Commercial acumen	Understanding the client's business model, sector pressures and risk appetite; thinking like a businessperson first	Advice that solves the real problem, not just the legal one
Communication	Plain language; active listening; written clarity; tailoring message to audience; knowing when not to write	Clients who say, "You're the first lawyer who ever explained that clearly"

continued on next page

Domain	Core capabilities	What this looks like in practice
Negotiation and influence	Interest-based bargaining; knowing when to push and when to concede; managing the room and the relationship	Outcomes that hold – deals that don't unravel post-completion
Ethical judgment	Moral courage; independence of mind; ability to say difficult things to clients; professional integrity under commercial pressure	Advice that clients may not want but need to hear
Leadership and collaboration	Managing up and down; working across disciplines; building and motivating teams; mentoring others	Matters that run on time, on budget, without attrition
Resilience and wellbeing	Managing pressure; maintaining quality under stress; knowing your limits; sustainable practice	Longevity, consistency, and the capacity to do excellent work over a career

Developing human skills – practical approaches

Unlike legal knowledge, which can be acquired by reading, human skills are developed through practice, feedback, and deliberate reflection. Here are five approaches that legal executives at all career stages have found effective.

Seek feedback you would not normally get

Most lawyers receive feedback on the quality of their legal work. Far fewer receive honest feedback on how they come across to clients, how they perform in negotiations, or how their communication lands. Ask clients directly – not just whether they were satisfied, but what you could have done differently. Ask colleagues. Build in reflection time after significant matters.

Learn from disciplines outside law

The skills of the Profoundly Human Lawyer are well-studied in fields that lawyers rarely read – psychology, behavioural economics, negotiation theory, and management science. The literature on negotiation alone – from Fisher and Ury's foundational work[9] on interest-based bargaining to more recent research on the neuroscience of trust – offers insights that translate directly to legal practice. Reading widely is not a distraction from legal work – it is an investment in it.

Treat every client interaction as a learning opportunity

The lawyer who delivers advice and moves on is leaving information on the table. How did the client respond? Were they reassured or still anxious? Did they understand? Did the conversation go in an unexpected direction, and why? Developing the habit of reflection after client interactions – even briefly – builds the pattern recognition that underpins genuine emotional intelligence.

Invest in supervision and mentoring

The Life in the Law Survey 2025[10] found that investment in leadership training – particularly around empathy, feedback, and conflict resolution – was directly linked to the quality of a firm's culture and its client outcomes. The same applies at the individual level. Lawyers who have good supervisors and mentors develop faster. Lawyers who invest time in supervising others deepen their own skills in the process.

Embrace discomfort

Human skills atrophy without challenge. The negotiation you find uncomfortable, the client you find difficult, the conversation you have been putting off – these are precisely the situations in which the skills of the Profoundly Human Lawyer are built. Actively seeking out the harder interactions, rather than delegating or deferring them, is one of the most reliable paths to development.

A word on AI literacy

The Profoundly Human Lawyer is not a technophobe. Understanding what AI can and cannot do – and being able to use it effectively – is itself a professional skill. The lawyer who can leverage AI to free up time for relationship-building, strategic thinking, and complex judgment is better placed than the lawyer who either fears the tools or relies on them uncritically.

AI literacy and human skill are not opposites. They are complementary. What AI changes is not the value of human judgment – it increases it, by removing the tasks that obscure it. The lawyer who once spent two days reviewing a data room and three hours advising the client now spends 30 minutes on the review and three hours on the advice. That shift, if embraced, plays directly to the strengths of the Profoundly Human Lawyer.

The competitive advantage that cannot be automated

The legal profession has faced technological disruption before – from the printing press to word processing to the internet – and each wave has changed the nature of legal work without eliminating the need for lawyers. The AI wave is bigger, faster, and more transformative than anything that came before. But it shares one characteristic with every previous disruption – it cannot replicate what is distinctively human about excellent legal practice.

The research is consistent. Clients value technical competence as a given, but they choose, trust, and remain loyal to lawyers who understand them, communicate clearly, exercise independent judgment, and bring genuine commercial insight. These are not peripheral qualities. They are the core of what it means to be a truly excellent lawyer.

The Profoundly Human Lawyer is not a reaction to AI. It is a description of what outstanding lawyers have always been, made more visible – and more commercially decisive – by the fact that everything else can now be automated. The lawyers who invest in these skills now, deliberately and consistently, will be those who matter most to clients in the decade ahead.

The technology is accelerating. The question is whether you are changing and developing at a similar pace.

References

1 Clio, Legal Trends Report 2025: www.clio.com/uk/guides/legal-trends-report-2025/

2 The Law Society: www.lawsociety.org.uk/topics/research/find-out-what-your-clients-need-with-the-results-of-our-legal-needs-survey

3 Thomson Reuters *State of the UK Legal Market Report 2022*: www.thomsonreuters.com/en/reports/state-of-the-uk-legal-market-2022

4 Accutrainee, Legal Leaders Survey 2024: https://accutrainee.com/2024legal-survey-results/

5 Thomson Reuters, 2024 *Report on the State of the UK Legal Market*: www.thomsonreuters.com/en-us/posts/wp-content/uploads/sites/20/2024/04/State-of-UK-Legal-Market-2024.pdf

6 Kate Barton, "I'm leading the largest global law firm as AI transforms the legal profession. Lawyers must double down on this one skill", *Fortune*: https://fortune.com/2025/07/14/lawyers-artificial-intelligence/

7 Accutrainee's 2024 Legal Leaders Survey: https://accutrainee.com/2024legal-survey-results/

8 *Ibid.*

9 Roger Fisher and William Ury, *Getting to Yes: Negotiating an agreement without giving in*, Random House Business, 7 June 2012.

10 LawCare, *Life in the Law 2025*: https://lawcare.org.uk/wp-content/uploads/2025/09/Life-in-the-Law-2025.pdf

About Globe Law and Business

Globe Law and Business was established in 2005. From the very beginning, we set out to create legal books that are sufficiently high level to be of real use to the experienced professional, yet still accessible and easy to navigate. Most of our authors are drawn from Magic Circle and other top commercial firms, both in the United Kingdom and internationally. Our titles are carefully produced, with the utmost attention paid to editorial, design and production processes. We hope this results in high-quality publications that are easy to read and a pleasure to own.

In 2021, we were very pleased to announce the start of a new chapter for Globe Law and Business following the acquisition of law books under the imprint Ark Publishing. Our law firm management list is now significantly expanded with many well-known and loved Ark Publishing titles.

We are also pleased to announce the launch of our online content platform, Globe Law Online, which allows for easy access across firms. Details of all titles included can be found at www.globelawonline.com. Email glo@globelawandbusiness.com for further details and to arrange a free trial for you or your firm.

We'd very much like to hear from you with your thoughts and ideas for improving what we offer. Please do feel free to email me on sian@globelawandbusiness.com. Happy reading and thank you for your time.

Sian O'Neill
Managing director
Globe Law and Business
www.globelawandbusiness.com

www.ingramcontent.com/pod-product-compliance
Lightning Source LLC
LaVergne TN
LVHW050407040726
842462LV00007B/39
* 9 7 8 1 8 3 7 2 3 1 8 8 1 *